RETHINKING
COLLEGE
ADMISSIONS

RETHINKING COLLEGE ADMISSIONS

Research-Based Practice and Policy

EDITED BY

OiYan A. Poon and Michael N. Bastedo

HARVARD EDUCATION PRESS
Cambridge, MA

Paperback ISBN 978-1-68253-777-0

Library of Congress Cataloging-in-Publication Data is on file.

Published by Harvard Education Press,
an imprint of the Harvard Education Publishing Group

Harvard Education Press
8 Story Street
Cambridge, MA 02138

Cover Design: Wilcox Design
Cover Image: aimintang/iStock.com

The typefaces in this book are Joanna Nova and Adobe Garamond Pro.

CONTENTS

Part II. Considering Different Approaches to the Work in Admissions Offices

Part III. Considering New Models for Admissions Practice and Research

PREFACE

O1YAN A. POON AND MICHAEL N. BASTEDO

COLLEGE ADMISSIONS SYSTEMS, policies, and practices are perennial hot topics in public debate. It may be that they are just part of American culture, with college admissions narratives central to Hollywood movies and popular fiction, and passionately discussed in schools, parent groups, social media, and other community spaces. With the 2019 Operation Varsity Blues federal investigation, which has been featured in several documentaries, television shows, and popular podcasts, these debates even showed up in supermarket tabloids. As a result of its investigation, the federal government indicted dozens of university administrators and athletic coaches as well as wealthy and famous parents for conspiracy, fraud, bribery, and racketeering. Several high-profile parents were convicted of criminal activities. The scandal revealed how questions of equity and fairness in college admissions are not just of interest to policymakers and educational leaders, but also to the public.

Although there was public shock over how privileged parents manipulated the selective admissions systems and practices, some researchers and practitioners familiar with the norms and expectations of admissions work were not as surprised about "side doors" that relied on admissions practices for student-athletes.[1] They "were only surprised by the complete moral disregard"[2] exhibited by those engaged in criminal activity that leveraged norms of athletic admissions, which often operate on collegial trust between admissions professionals and campus athletic coaches and staff.[3] The differing responses to the Varsity Blues scandal suggest a disconnect between knowledge on admissions held by the public in comparison to admissions practitioners and researchers. Given the opacity of selective college admissions, this is not a surprise.

In the year after Varsity Blues, the COVID-19 pandemic became a much more central concern the world over. With the pandemic and public health crisis in 2020, many colleges and universities chose to (at least temporarily) put a stop to requiring applicant submissions of test scores. At some institutions, COVID-induced policy changes perhaps also expedited the national debate and movement for test-optional and test-free admissions. At the University of California, which represents a sizable market for College Board and ACT test products, administrative and governance leaders eliminated test score requirements in November 2021, perhaps motivated by a lawsuit.[4]

In the field of college admissions, Varsity Blues and the COVID pandemic have both created significant challenges in different ways. The Varsity Blues federal investigation forced leaders at selective institutions to contend with a crisis of public trust in their admissions systems and practices. With the pandemic, leaders across selective admissions systems have had to reconsider tools and data points they have used to make admissions decisions. At more open access institutions, such as community colleges, they have also had to confront declining enrollments and the budget challenges accompanying such decreases. As institutional and policy leaders seek new paths forward in response to these and other crises, research can play an important role to support evidence and data-informed leadership. Research can bring attention to the multifaceted ways in which selective admissions systems reproduce race, income, and gender inequalities, and offer critical analyses to motivate change for equity. More importantly, critical inquiries and analyses may also illuminate innovative possibilities for change.

BRINGING RESEARCH, POLICY, AND PRACTICE TOGETHER

Far too often, debates, discourses, and leadership decisions related to college admissions systems, policies, and practices are conducted in isolation from relevant research and analysis. Through our respective conversations and work with enrollment management and admissions leaders, we have both observed how admissions practitioners and leaders have taken up (or not) research and evidence to guide change initiatives intended to increase equity in college access. Different bridge-building efforts at research-practice partnerships have produced varying degrees of success. We have also observed the pitfalls of research conducted in ways that are siloed from practice. For example, limited connections and the lack of shared language between practice and research in admissions can create barriers to optimizing the impact of research for tangible systemic change.[5] Research that is disconnected from practice can also be irrelevant or miss important nuances that are crucial to making research relevant to professional practice. There is a need for more sustained discussion and collaborative dialogues about the implications of research for practice, and of practice for research.

Such bridge-building between research, policy, and practice can open up spaces and possibilities for both inquiry and transformative leadership for systemic change. It can facilitate connections and collaborations between researchers, who wish to make their scholarship matter, and admissions professionals hoping to effect change that centers equity in college access. Accordingly, we intend this book to be an inroad and example for developing and thoughtfully designing reciprocal relationships in research and practice for the future.

Since the 1990s, admissions research has expanded and proliferated in exciting ways that bear implications for policy, practice, and leadership. Leading up to and since the 2003 US Supreme Court rulings in *Grutter v. Bollinger* and *Gratz v. Bollinger* ("the Michigan cases") on the legalities of race-conscious admissions, scholars have completed myriad inquiries to understand multiple dimensions of the educational benefits of diversity. Since then, there have been great strides in research charting new ways to examine systems of postsecondary education access. In addition to addressing questions raised during litigation about campus diversity and educational benefits, research scholars have taken up questions about college aspirants' behaviors in navigating college pathways, recruitment, holistic review systems and practices, the use of tests (e.g., ACT, AP, SAT, etc.), innovative approaches to admissions processes (e.g., percent plans, lotteries, etc.), organizational routines in admissions practices, among a host of other topics. This revival and growth of research is necessary for robust analyses of systems that facilitate or prevent college access along race, class, gender, and other demographic lines. However, the vibrant proliferation of admissions research often remains siloed from communities of practice, policy, and public discourses more generally.

In response to the divide between research, policy, and practice, we have designed this edited volume especially for a wide array of audiences, from K–16 educators, counselors, and especially college admissions professionals and leaders, to policymakers, community-based and public interest advocacy groups, and research scholars and students. This edited volume is intended for anyone interested in gaining an evidence-based understanding of admissions that can inform one's leadership, engagement, or research on admissions structures that shape college access.

Through this book, we offer a model for bridging the gap between higher education research and higher education practice and leadership. In addition to our shared conviction that research can enrich organizational leadership for change, we also value how being in dialogue with the professionals leading and enacting admissions work can shape research for impact. As publicly engaged scholars whose own research agendas tackle questions of admissions systems through organizational studies in higher education, we have found ourselves concerned about a general disconnect between research and practice in higher education admissions. This problem is not unique to this area of research. As such, this book provides an example and tool for building bridges between research, practice, and policy.

BOOK OVERVIEW

The goal of this book is to present research to generate new ideas and considerations for practice and policy in admissions, which is a key function of gatekeeping in higher education. The contents of this book include some of the most current and boundary-pushing applied research bearing implications and raising questions for practitioners, policymakers, and anyone interested in gaining a better understanding of postsecondary admissions structures and possibilities for change.

We have organized the chapters in this volume into three parts. The contributions in the first part offer critical analyses of the current state of admissions in higher education. In chapter 1, Frank Fernandez and Liliana Garces provide an overview of state laws and federal case law related to race-conscious admissions. They focus on how admissions professionals and higher education administrators may be interpreting legal environments in ways that suppress legal equity-oriented practices, through the concept of repressive legalism. In chapter 2, Awilda Rodriguez, Katherine Lebioda, Joshua Skiles, and Bhavani Bindiganavile critically examine the role of high school student coursework in admissions decisions. They argue for the need to redress "racialized and classed inequalities in academic preparation," which "requires a reimagining of what equitable admissions entails, who admissions professionals believe is worthy of their institutions, and what they need to do to attract, evaluate, and admit historically marginalized students." Relatedly, in his chapter, Eddie Comeaux encourages admissions professionals and offices to conduct their work of review and decision-making through a community cultural wealth framework. Similarly in chapter 4, Sunny Nakae assesses and offers ideas for improving holistic admissions practices in medical school admissions that center equity. Finally in this section, Julie Park (chapter 5) synthesizes research and demonstrates that test prep is an ineffective solution for equity in admissions. Taken together, the five chapters in part I present important critiques of current practices.

Moving our attention from admissions work as it is currently done to considering new and different ways to do the work and potential areas for change, the chapters in the part II are intended to encourage readers to think more broadly about organizational practices in admissions. Julie Posselt and Steve Desir (chapter 6) provide readers with a framework for examining and intervening on racism in admissions, offering a starting point and lens to critically assess admissions work and norms. An area of practice needing further analysis is the use of criminal records in admissions decisions. In chapter 7, Robert Stewart offers insights into this problematic policy and practice. Relatedly, in chapter 8, Nathan Harris forwards conceptual and methodological perspectives to consider ethical hazards in college admissions work. Douglas Lee, Joanne Song Engler, Jessica Hurtado, Ali Raza, and OiYan Poon (chapter 9) close out the section with an examination of admissions office staffing. They point out the need to improve how professional staff learn to integrate diversity and equity values into their practices and organizational norms. Collectively, the chapters in part II remind readers that admissions decisions are made through practices, routines, and processes created and enacted by people with careers in the admissions field.

The third and final set of chapters considers, reviews, and proposes different models for admissions work and for bringing together research and admissions practice through partnership. In chapter 10, Dominique Baker, Michael Bastedo, and Amanda Addison provide an empirical analysis of the admissions lottery idea—an idea that is often discussed as a fair approach to equity. They present arguments for and against this idea through a synthesis of existing research and presentation of new research. Another approach that diverges from current holistic systems of selective admissions is the idea of direct admissions, such as in

Idaho, which Jennifer Delaney and Taylor Odle examine in chapter 11. In chapter 12, Kelly Slay and Kristen Glasener offer an analysis of another model of admissions practice; they study student experiences in an institutional promise program that recruited low-income students to the University of Michigan. Finally, we close this book with chapter 13, which is authored as a conversation between two admissions practitioners—Nikki Chun and Shawn Felton—and a researcher—OiYan Poon. In this closing chapter, the authors contemplate some key barriers to bringing together research and practice. They offer ideas for new ways to build bridges and long-term partnerships between administrative leaders and research scholars in the field of college admissions, to improve both research design and the impact of our work in the field.

CONCLUSION

Researchers have a responsibility and the potential to produce scholarship to both inform and influence leadership, practice, and change initiatives that can advance equity in higher education. Accordingly, scholarly leaders in the field of higher education have long advanced a call for research to be relevant and to seek public impact.[6] On the other side of the bridge between research and practice, practitioner-leaders in admissions need to be engaged in relevant research to be effective at their jobs in the academy, as Chun, Felton, and Poon explain in chapter 13. We present the chapters in this edited volume with the intention of building connections between innovative admissions research and communities of admissions practice, policymaking, and the public interest.

PART I

Questioning Current Practices

CHAPTER 1

The Influence of Repressive Legalism on Admissions

Frank Fernandez and Liliana M. Garces*

LEGAL DEVELOPMENTS AROUND race-conscious postsecondary admissions policies have substantially undermined racial equity on college campuses. A series of judicial opinions, for example, have changed the policy of affirmative action from its original goal of addressing racial discrimination to requiring a focus on diversity and so-called race-neutral approaches that can ignore the very real ways racism shapes educational opportunity and outcomes.[1] Bans on affirmative action in nine states, moreover, have led to declines in student body racial diversity across various educational sectors, including at selective undergraduate institutions, graduate fields of study, and professional fields of law and medicine.[2] These changes in the focus of race-conscious admissions and declines in racial diversity have had long-term negative consequences for students' educational experiences in higher education.[3]

A related and less well-known dynamic undermining racial equity on college campuses includes how administrators' perceptions of the legal environment and the law-based pressures that they face, such as the threat of lawsuits, shape their everyday actions to undermine racial equity. For example, even when permitted by federal and state law, universities have voluntarily chosen not to use race-conscious admissions to avoid the

---

*The authors contributed equally to this chapter and should be considered co-first authors.

threat of litigation.[4] At public institutions in states that have prohibited the consideration of race in postsecondary admissions, such as Michigan, the ban has silenced administrators' conversations around race, undermining their ability to support students of color.[5] These consequences manifest as color-evasive practices that ignore the ongoing need to address racialized social and educational inequities and confront racism.[6]

In this chapter, we draw attention to this broader and coercive influence of the legal environment on race-conscious admissions policies and other areas of campus life. Specifically, we apply the concept of *repressive legalism* to explain findings from empirical studies that examine how administrators respond to their surrounding legal context to make decisions about how to serve racially minoritized students.[7] We apply this concept to argue that the legal environment, as interpreted and implemented by administrators in their everyday work, has suppressed equity and inclusion-promoting practices beyond what is required by law. This coercive power of the law operates even when the actions that administrators would otherwise undertake would be lawful and would further other institutional values of racial diversity and inclusion. Understanding this repressive force of the law on diversity- and inclusion-focused efforts requires intentionally countering the repressive force of the law and empowering administrators to engage in practices that promote racial equity and inclusion.

Below, we first outline the concept of repressive legalism. We then describe the legal environment at the federal and state level that places limits on race-conscious admissions policies and practices and that serve as the backdrop to administrative action. After that, we apply the lens of repressive legalism to explain how administrators responded to these legal developments and illustrate how administrators' perceptions of the law unnecessarily repressed race-conscious policies in admissions and other areas of campus life. We conclude by offering some practical steps administrators can take to counter the repressive force of the law on race-conscious policy and practice.

REPRESSIVE LEGALISM

The concept of repressive legalism emerges from a cultural analysis of how the legal environment influences college and university operations.[8] Repressive legalism is defined as "the interpretation and application of legal norms and other facets of the legal environment in a manner that suppresses, or holds back, [inclusion-promoting policies] for students of color."[9] Drawing on sociology of law, Garces et al. coined the term to describe "how administrators' understanding of the legal environment, including taken-for-granted assumptions driven by legal precedent and institutional norms defined in reaction to coercive pressures, repressed [otherwise permissible] inclusion-focused responses."[10]

Specifically, their study documented how administrators at a public institution navigated real and perceived tensions between protecting freedom of expression and promoting institutional values of inclusion in the context of external law-based pressures, such as a conservative legislature and advocacy organizations that leverage the threat of litigation. Findings revealed how "administrators' interpretations of the legal environment shaped their understanding of hate speech–related incidents, and the permissible responses, in ways that make it nearly impossible to consider and implement inclusion-focused policies and practices."[11] For example, while higher education administrators cannot prohibit hate speech that is protected by the First Amendment, they may—and should—condemn it as going against the university's values and offer support to students who are targeted by hate speech.[12] Yet, administrators viewed such equity-promoting practices (e.g., denouncing hate speech, fostering dialogue about the negative impacts of hate speech on campus), as out of reach because of various pressures from the legal environment.

This dynamic—when administrators perceive practices as not possible because of the law or because of pressures from the legal environment, even though such practices are perfectly legal and would further other institutional objectives administrators themselves believe in, such as diversity and inclusion—represents repressive legalism. Stated differently, as a concept, repressive legalism serves "as a prism to help identify areas in policy or practice where the law compromises organizational actors' autonomy to advance other institutional espoused values."[13]

While the concept of repressive legalism emerged in a study on the topic of free speech and inclusion, it applies to many other areas of institutional policy and practice, including race-conscious admissions. In this chapter, we apply the concept in this new context, to help explain findings from studies documenting instances when the law restricted higher education administrators from engaging in an equity-promoting practice, even when that practice was not prevented by state or federal law and the practice was within their discretion. In other words, we do not use the concept to describe the actual limits set by laws or judicial opinions for considering race in admissions or other inclusion-related practices outside admissions. Rather, we use it to help illuminate a dynamic in which administrators' *perceptions* of the pressures of the legal environment (e.g., the threat of litigation) shape their actions and practice to *unnecessarily* repress attention to race, even when those actions or practices—over which they could exercise discretion—are legally permitted.

As we explain below, the perceived pressures from the legal environment not only inhibit policy or practice to support campus diversity, but they can also lead administrators to overcorrect so that they actively avoid advancing racial equity. Consider how administrators at public universities in Virginia responded to cases opposing race-conscious admissions. In Virginia, several universities had developed race-specific bridge programs under the state's Virginia Student Transition Program. The bridge programs were specifically meant to recruit African American high school students to state public institutions. As legal challenges to race-conscious admissions increased throughout the country, administrators bowed to pressures to be "race neutral." One bridge program now allocates half its seats to international and white students.[14]

In summary, repressive legalism illuminates how organizations, driven by pressures in the legal environment, halt or roll back progress toward equity. The concept helps us consider how the dynamics of complex organizations facilitate or inhibit the pursuit of equity in higher education.[15] As sociology scholars have demonstrated, organizations sometimes change as a response to coercive political influence.[16] In studies of race-conscious admissions, interviews with admissions personnel suggest that "the organizational culture of university administration in general, and specifically in the admissions profession, has become explicitly pro-affirmative action and pro-diversity."[17] Yet, repressive legalism allows us to consider how, even if administrators are in favor of race-conscious admissions, environmental pressures supersede their personal and professional beliefs and negatively impact equity policy and practice.

THE LEGAL ENVIRONMENT AROUND RACE-CONSCIOUS ADMISSIONS AND INSTITUTIONAL RESPONSES

In this section, we outline the legal environment around race-conscious admissions and explain findings from studies that have examined institutional responses to these legal developments at the federal and state level through the lens of repressive legalism. We first address legal developments at the federal level, which take place through US Supreme Court opinions that continue to uphold the consideration of race in selective admissions, even as they scrutinize and narrow the ways in which race is evaluated as one factor among many. We then address legal developments at the state level, which emerge through the legislative and executive branches or through changes to state constitutions by voter initiatives or referendums. These state-level developments have banned the consideration of race at public colleges and universities in nine states.

Judicial Developments and Institutional Responses

Despite a series of legal challenges, for over four decades, the US Supreme Court has upheld the constitutionality of race-conscious processes in postsecondary admissions. This has been the case even as the Court has placed increasingly strict limits on how admissions officers may consider race in response to ongoing challenges by advocacy organizations to restrict the practice. The Court's stance on the constitutionality of race-conscious admissions was first established in *Regents of the University of California v. Bakke*, a case that perpetually limited how future courts would debate the practice.[18] In terms of legal analysis, the Court applied a strict scrutiny test—the highest level of scrutiny—for determining whether it is constitutional to consider race. The decision established an overarching legal framework that considered "racial and ethnic classifications of any sort [as] inherently suspect" thus calling "for the most exacting judicial scrutiny."[19] Under this strict scrutiny review, the Court dismissed the need to address racial discrimination as a permissible rationale for the consideration of race, endorsing instead the goal of attaining the educational benefits of diversity. It also required a process for attaining these benefits where race could only be used as one of many decision factors and where ostensible "race-neutral" approaches would not suffice.

The challenge to the constitutionality of the policy nevertheless continued with two lawsuits against the University of Michigan that culminated in two US Supreme Court decisions in 2003: *Grutter v. Bollinger*, which centered on the process for admitting undergraduates, and *Gratz v. Bollinger*, which focused on the university's law school admissions process.[20] In both cases, the Court upheld the rationale underpinning the *Bakke* case, finding that universities may consider race during a selective admissions process to further a compelling governmental interest in achieving the broad set of benefits that result from admitting racially underrepresented students. The Court also held that the process must be narrowly tailored to that effect, meaning that admissions offices could consider race as part of a "holistic" and individualized review (*Grutter*), but not award additional points for race as part of a cumulative quantitative scoring of applicants (*Gratz*). Though the Court allowed a more limited use of the practice, the opinion included language outlining the hope that race-conscious admissions would be phased out within a generation (i.e., around 2023).

After the *Grutter* and *Gratz* cases, the challenge to race-conscious admissions returned to the Court a decade later, this time in a lawsuit filed against the University of Texas at Austin, which had reinstituted race-conscious admissions after *Grutter* overruled a prior court of appeals case (*Hopwood v. University of Texas*) that had prohibited its use since 1996. In 2013, the Court issued its first decision in the case, *Fisher v. University of Texas* (also known as *Fisher I*), sending the case back to the lower courts to examine more closely whether the university's consideration of race was indeed necessary—particularly because it worked alongside an ostensibly race-neutral program increasing diversity based on segregation of local school districts.[21] Following the remand, the court of appeals concluded that the university's race-conscious policy was constitutional. Thereafter, the Supreme Court agreed to hear the case again and in 2016 issued a second opinion (referred to as *Fisher II*) agreeing with the court of appeals' assessment.[22] The Court affirmed that society benefits when universities pursue diversity in admissions. However, in its opinion, the Court reminded institutions of the need to consider the workability of race-neutral policies before considering race-conscious policies to advance diversity and about the need to collect and analyze data to demonstrate an ongoing need to incorporate race in holistic review of applicants.

Although the Court continues to allow the practice, it does not directly implement its own rulings or assist colleges and universities in implementing admissions processes that are likely to survive potential legal challenges. Therefore, in states that do not ban race-conscious admissions, the practice can only continue if college and university attorneys interpret the Court's legal opinions in ways that support the practice and college or university professionals choose to implement race-conscious admissions policies.[23] In fact, despite the legality of the practice, some institutions have chosen not to adopt race-conscious admissions. For instance, the University of Georgia has voluntarily operated without a race-conscious admissions policy since 2001, even though it would be allowed to do so under state and federal law.[24] The University of Georgia lost cases at the lower and circuit court levels over its affirmative action policy—not because it was illegal for the university to consider race in admissions, but because its consideration of race was not narrowly tailored.[25] Rather than revise the admissions policy to differently consider race or to continue to appeal the court's decision, University of Georgia abandoned the practice altogether. Twenty years after University of Georgia backed away from race-conscious admissions, it remains unrepresentative of state demographics. While nearly one-third of the state's population is Black, less than 8 percent of undergraduates are Black.[26] More recently, schools like College of Charleston have voluntarily stopped considering race, even though College of Charleston had one of the lowest Black student enrollment rates in South Carolina.[27]

These institutional policy changes, we argue, can be explained through the lens of repressive legalism. The findings from a specific study of a related institutional policy change at Penn State University represents such an example.[28] In 1973, Penn State University was ordered to desegregate as part of the *Adams v. Richardson* case.[29] Over several decades, Penn State worked to improve racial diversity by creating administrative positions, chartering the Equal Opportunity Planning Committee, hiring a Vice Provost for Educational Equity, and adopting an institutional initiative known as the Framework to Foster Diversity. However, even after the *Grutter* and *Gratz* rulings—which permitted the consideration of race under limited circumstances—the university nevertheless changed its strategy to no longer consider race in its admissions policies. Some administrators described the university's change in policy as a "concerted effort to avoid litigation"[30] While they acknowledged that the university had "taken chances," they discussed how legal developments (e.g., legal decisions like *Bakke*) had supported a rationale and bolstered a political context where being race-conscious was equated with anti-white discrimination. They understood that whatever the university does "is probably going to come under a microscope" and therefore the university needed to be "challenge proof."[31] Administrators believed that the pressure to be "challenge proof" led the university to remove the consideration of race as one of many factors in admissions, even though case law permits it and administrators supported it.

This process of implementing policies and practices that are not required by law but are driven by overly cautious interpretations of legal developments and associated pressures, such as the threat of litigation, scrutiny by public officials, or in some cases retaliatory budget cuts,[32] represents repressive legalism. In the case of Penn State, the repressive force of the law extended outside admissions and into other areas, like financial aid, as administrators discussed instances in their everyday work where they had to prevent legal (mis)conceptions from being implemented. In one instance, for example, administrators had to advocate for keeping "diversity" as a criterion for awarding financial-aid scholarships after some faculty members wanted to eliminate it because it could be perceived as discriminatory against whites, a narrative that underlies the attack on race-conscious admissions. These dynamics illustrate the repressive force of the law on administrators' efforts to advance racial equity. In fact, as administrators fight just to keep diversity as a scholarship criterion, it becomes increasingly difficult to advance policy that accounts for race and racism in students' experiences.

Statewide Affirmative Action Bans and
Institutional Responses

Apart from battles in federal courts and the threat of litigation, universities have been hampered from using race-conscious admissions through state-level actions. Administrators' responses to these legal developments, such as bans on affirmative action, can also be explained through the concept of repressive legalism. Although the Supreme Court has ruled that universities may consider race in admissions, states may pass laws that prohibit the practice at public institutions.[33] State bans on affirmative action can take place via well-organized and systematic campaigns to end the practice state by state via referenda and other practices. For instance, with millions of dollars in funding from conservative foundations, groups like the American Civil Rights Institute and its spokesman, Ward Connerly, were successful in getting five states to ban the practice between 1997 and 2003.[34] California was the first state to ban race-conscious admissions by a statewide vote in 1996. After California, the states of Arizona, Michigan, Nebraska, Oklahoma, and Washington also banned affirmative action through ballot initiatives or referendums. In Florida, former governor Jeb Bush signed an executive order to ban the practice. State legislators adopted bans in New Hampshire and Idaho.[35]

Studies of the impacts of these affirmative action bans on the enrollment of racially marginalized student populations in postsecondary education show that these bans have led to overall declines in student body racial and ethnic diversity at public undergraduate institutions, graduate fields of study, and professional fields of business, medicine, and law.[36] Some of these declines are particularly large. For instance, banning affirmative action led to a 26 percent decline in the number of graduate students of color in engineering programs.[37] These declines occurred despite sustained outreach and recruitment efforts to increase racial diversity at colleges and universities in these states.[38] Unfortunately, several states that have race-conscious admissions bans are home to highly selective public universities, and there is evidence that the effects are particularly strong at state flagship universities.[39]

These declines in racial and ethnic student body diversity undermine equity- and inclusion-focused practices on campus because a less racially diverse student body is associated with a less welcoming campus climate for students of color and with perceptions of a lack of institutional commitment to diversity.[40] Students who have negative racial experiences on campus are likely to feel less of a sense of belonging during the first two years of college and are more likely to be dissatisfied with their overall college experience.[41] Moreover, a less racially diverse student body undermines an institution's ability to promote the educational benefits of diversity, including cross-racial interactions, and to bring about institutional change.[42]

In addition to declines in student body diversity, laws banning affirmative action have had a lesser known, but powerful influence in other areas of campus life, which is explained by repressive legalism. For example, in 2006, Michigan voters adopted Proposal 2 and amended the state constitution to bar public universities from using the practice after the Supreme Court upheld the University of Michigan's use of the practice in the 2003 Grutter v. Bollinger case. Prior to Proposal 2, the University of Michigan had implemented a visible, sustained campaign, known as the Michigan Mandate, to support racial diversity. In a legal sense, Proposal 2 was limited to admissions policy. However, after voters adopted Proposal 2, University of Michigan administrators throughout campus were reluctant to discuss issues related to race and racism on campus.[43] Race came to be seen as "controversial, politically charged . . . [and] crowded out" of conversations about how to deliver academic support and student affairs programs.[44] After Proposal 2, the university's efforts in support of racial diversity were muted to protect the university from criticism or lawsuits. The law, as perceived and enacted by administrators, ultimately had a more restrictive scope on inclusion-focused practice than written.

In sum, the lens of repressive legalism helps identify areas in policy or practice where organizational actors' interpretation of the law unnecessarily compromised administrators' autonomy to advance equity. Two state flagship universities (Penn State and University of Michigan) once had focused institutional plans for improving racial diversity. Then, in the early-2000s, either as a result of legal cases on race-conscious admissions or as a response to a ban on affirmative action both institutions took more limited approaches to diversity, equity, and inclusion than required by changes in the law. Administrators at both campuses shared that their institutions observed the increasingly anti–race-conscious conservative legal and political context. As they responded to these legal pressures and environment, they integrated these pressures in their practice with responses that prioritized concerns over avoiding the threat of litigation and public criticism rather than being race-conscious in their practice.

COUNTERING REPRESSIVE LEGALISM

Efforts to promote racial equity within and outside admissions requires intentional efforts that help counter the powerful and repressive cultural force of the law on administrators' actions. These efforts are particularly timely and critical as the legal environment is punctuated by ongoing, well-funded challenges to race-conscious admissions.[45] Even under a Biden Administration, the coercive pressures have continued and will likely intensify as more than a dozen states have sought to ban the teaching of critical race theory.[46] In fact, legal challenges to race-conscious admissions filed by organizations such as Students for Fair Admissions (SFFA) have continued, with lawsuits against Harvard, the University of North Carolina at Chapel Hill, the University of Texas at Austin, and Yale University.[47] Two of these cases, SFFA v. President and Fellows of Harvard College and SFFA v. University of North Carolina at Chapel Hill, are now being considered by a solidly majority conservative US Supreme Court.[48] SFFA's tactics of suing both public and private,

Ivy League and non–Ivy League universities reveal a larger strategy at creating legal pressure against administrators throughout higher education. The message in the current sociopolitical context is that as long as universities remain committed to pursuing racial equity through their admissions processes, they can expect to be dragged into high-profile, costly court battles.

We argue that in the face of these persistent coercive pressures, we need to reclaim race-consciousness in educational policy and practice, which requires, in part, engaging in practical strategies that counter a repressive legalistic approach from taking hold.[49] When the primary concern of administrators and general counsels is to avoid public scrutiny or the threat of litigation in the current sociopolitical context, they allow repressive legalism to flourish. The first step to resisting these external pressures is to cultivate a more expansive approach to interpreting and implementing law and policy—an approach that serves as a counterbalance to the sociopolitical pressures brought by courts, elected officials, and an organized conservative anti–affirmative action movement.[50]

In this chapter, we limit our recommendations to practical steps that institutional leaders and other administrators may take. Overall, institutional leaders should help empower high- and mid-level administrators to engage in a race- and racism- conscious approach in their everyday practice. Institutional leaders can empower administrators by allocating funding to support staff and faculty trainings, hiring, and promotion, and by issuing public messages that prioritize goals of racial equity and inclusion. These efforts should be grounded in a dual understanding of how legal developments have constrained racial equity- and inclusion-focused policy and practice and how leaders' and administrators' own actions and *perceptions* of the law may have allowed for repressive legalism to operate.

To understand and reveal whether repressive legalism may be at play in their everyday practice, institutional leaders and administrators might ask themselves: (1) *Is the impetus for a specific policy or practice to avoid the pressures of the current sociopolitical environment?* (2) *Does the policy or practice attend to the lived experiences of students of color and other marginalized communities on campus?* (3) *How do legal principles of equal access and opportunity in the context of racial inequality require us to act?*

Answers to the first question can help disentangle what the actual boundaries of the law are versus how actors are interpreting and implementing the law on the ground in relation to external pressures and sociopolitical forces that ultimately compromise administrators' professional judgment and the institution's educational mission. In answering this question, it is critical for those who work within admissions offices and other areas of campus life to partner with members from the legal community who are also versed in racial equity advocacy to help translate the intricacies of the law in a specific area of practice. Ideally, general counsel would be well versed in anti-racist policy and practice, though such an ideal may not be realistic at many colleges and universities for myriad reasons, including lack of professional training on these topics.

Answers to the second question can help illuminate whether a policy or practice can be considered "race neutral" in light of historical and contemporary manifestations of race at the structural, organizational, and individual level, or whether it exacerbates existing racial inequities. Fully capturing the experiences of student of color and other marginalized communities requires, and would promote, what legal scholar Lani Guinier termed "racial literacy"—that is, the understanding that race is "dynamic and in relationship with fluid identities and access to power" and that individual agency is "connected to larger environmental and institutional factors."[51] Racially literate admissions personnel understand that applicants of color may not have had desirable college-preparatory experiences—not because they did not want to go to college, but because they have traversed racialized education systems with limited access to programs and services that make them competitive applicants. Focusing on racial literacy is essential to prevent approaches to policy and practice that frame students as the problem, rather than the broader structural constraints they may have faced.

Related to this second question, admissions office personnel should work with colleagues in financial aid, registrar, and institutional research offices to analyze data on how applicants of color are affected at each stage of the admissions process. Institutions should complement this information with qualitative data that captures the experiences of marginalized students. They should also partner with student affairs professionals who can bring their professional judgment about how policies and practices may account (or fail to account) for lived experiences of students of color. Such systematic examinations can help reveal processes that reinforce barriers for applicants of color.

Administrators should answer the third question in ways that help them develop legal arguments that prioritize principles of equal access and opportunity in the context of a racially unequal society. Despite the constraints that legal cases on affirmative action have placed on admissions processes, the Court's opinions have consistently endorsed the right of institutions to advance their educational mission. A compelling interest in the educational benefits of diversity requires race- and racism-conscious approaches in admissions and other areas of campus life to help realize those educational benefits. These legal arguments continue to prevail in ongoing challenges to race-conscious admissions, with three court decisions—the lower court and court of appeals in the case against Harvard, and the lower court in the case against UNC–Chapel Hill—continuing to uphold the legality of race-conscious admissions.[52] It is critical to continue to advance these and related legal arguments grounded on concepts of academic freedom, equal opportunity, and an acknowledgment of racial inequality, to protect against ongoing legal challenges to race-conscious policies and practice in education.

CONCLUSION

The law has direct implications for higher education's capacity to admit and support historically marginalized students on campus. As we have shown, it can also have a coercive pressure on the actions of administrators that unnecessarily represses equity- and inclusion-promoting practices. This influence must be understood, revealed, and intentionally countered with practical steps that actively guard against these pressures and empower administrators to engage in equity-promoting policies and practices.

CHAPTER 2

The Role of Rigorous Coursework in Admissions and Enacting Equitable Practice*

AWILDA RODRIGUEZ, KATHERINE LEBIODA, JOSHUA SKILES, AND BHAVANI BINDIGANAVILE

COLLEGE ENROLLMENT AND ADMISSIONS at selective institutions is historically rooted in exclusionary practices. What we now consider selective institutions were originally created to educate primarily white, wealthy men to the exclusion of students who were not part of dominant social groups.[1] This privilege persists today, whereby selective colleges remain racially and socioeconomically segregated, continuing to serve whiter and wealthier students than the overall college population.[2] College applicants of means, the highly resourced high schools they attend, and selective institutions set the expectations and processes in admissions and recruitment—in the nature of college preparatory activities and the communication between families, school personnel, and admissions representatives—and reify their privileged positions.[3] In contrast, low-income and racially marginalized students face intentional and enduring deprivation of access to educational experiences valued by selective admissions offices.[4] In particular, rigorous course-taking opportunities like Advanced Placement (AP) were historically developed for and exclusively

*This study was funded by the William T. Grant Foundation.

found at elite high schools until recent decades.[5] Anchored in these histories, the use of course rigor as one of the most important components of the admissions process has served as an established way to exclude students with marginalized backgrounds from selective institutions by privileging and benchmarking against the course offerings of wealthy, white schools.[6]

The differential levels of access to rigorous coursework that low-income and racially marginalized students face has been well documented and, in many cases, normalized.[7] For example, while AP course-taking took off at high schools with few (less than 25 percent) students eligible for free- or reduced-price lunch (FRL) between 2000 and 2009, participation remained flat at schools that served many FRL students (greater than 50 percent)—resulting in a large widening of preexisting class-based gaps.[8] During this same time, the Black-white AP participation gap nearly doubled—from 8 to 15 percentage points. Despite decades of policies to improve access by increasing the availability of AP courses and teacher professional development, the gaps across high school resources have endured.[9] Today, high schools serving the largest share of low-income students are still less likely to offer AP courses than those that serve few (61 percent versus 80 percent, respectively) and on average only offer about half of the AP courses at schools with few low-income students (eight versus fifteen courses, respectively).[10]

In their current form, many holistic admissions practices aim to acknowledge these race- and class-based inequalities across educational contexts, including in rigorous course-taking, by accounting for the opportunities available to students in their environment.[11] Yet selective colleges cannot *meaningfully* reduce class- and race-based inequalities in enrollment unless their admissions officers engage in *meaningful* equity work. In essence, admissions representatives engaged in holistic admissions praxis are charged with alleviating centuries of racist practices and disparities by determining students' performance within their racialized and classed educational experiences. True equity work, however, transcends descriptive acknowledgments of disparities in resources and concomitant adjustments in the evaluation process and requires an intentional reallocation of resources and unlearning of taken-for-granted social hierarchies and stereotypes.

In this chapter, we rely on data from interviews with high school and admissions personnel as well as existing literature on rigorous coursework and admissions to highlight three aspects of admissions practices critical to advancing equity in selective institutions. We first discuss an overlooked aspect of school contexts—school-specific policies that dictate who can enroll in rigorous coursework and the extent that admissions representatives understand the complex inequalities students face in accessing advanced courses. Next, we examine how one of the cornerstones of recruitment and understanding context, high school visits, reinforces the privileges high-resourced schools enjoy. We then round out this chapter by probing the beliefs individual admissions professionals have about marginalized communities. We argue throughout that redressing racialized and classed inequalities in academic preparation requires a reimagining of what equitable admissions entails, who admissions professionals believe is worthy of their institutions, and what they need to do to attract, evaluate, and admit historically marginalized students.

OUR DATA

The data used in this chapter came from a larger project that examined how resource inequalities across high schools shaped AP participation. For this project, we conducted interviews with both high school and college admissions personnel. Part of our goal was to gather information on how school personnel understood the role of AP participation in college admissions and the policies and practices they deployed to provide AP course-taking opportunities. Between winter 2018 and spring 2019, we interviewed thirty-three school personnel (e.g., counselors, AP coordinators) at thirty-one schools in Michigan. We intentionally recruited participants from a range of schools that varied by resource level. The majority of school personnel in our sample identified as white (69.7 percent) and female (66.7 percent); and on average, our schools were mostly located in suburban areas (51.6 percent).

To compare the perspectives of high school personnel to those of admissions personnel on the role of AP in admissions, we also interviewed admissions representatives. We recruited a combination of colleges in the Midwest situated in the same college admissions market as our school counselors (Illinois, Indiana, Michigan, Ohio, and Wisconsin) as well as a national pool of "most competitive" colleges in Barron's Competitive Index. We interviewed twenty-three admissions representatives between February and April 2019 regarding the different approaches they deployed when interacting with low- versus high-resourced schools. We discussed both how they assessed AP in the admissions process and how they engaged with the schools regarding AP. Seventy percent of the admissions representatives self-identified as white and occupied high-level management positions. In this chapter, we focused on the most and highly selective institutions, because they were most discerning about AP in their admissions processes. Together, this unique combination of datasets spoke to the complexities of considering the school context in assessing course rigor in admissions.

THE LIMITATIONS OF UNDERSTANDING HIGH SCHOOL CONTEXT

When communicating with students, families, and schools, most admissions professionals at selective institutions highlight the importance of context in their holistic consideration of each applicant. Tacit in this practice is the acknowledgment that the same systems of power and privilege that established selective postsecondary education have also unequally distributed educational opportunities and resources along race and class lines (e.g., vast differences in facilities, teachers, materials, and funding across high schools). Considering context through holistic admissions policies, then, theoretically affords admissions personnel at selective institutions an opportunity to offer admission to students from communities that have been historically marginalized and may not have the profiles of privilege (e.g., in test scores, course work, and activities) that have become benchmarks. In short, the process of considering students within their unique context is ostensibly the principal vehicle to enact equitable admissions practices and reduce race- and class-based inequalities in enrollment.

While an important practice, admissions officers widely acknowledged challenges to understanding students' contexts. Our own data and previous research have shown school profiles—the formal document intended to provide context for students' academic preparation and performance—were not standardized. Due to the abundant resources (e.g., funding, personnel, and time) available in high-resourced schools, they generally produced extensive, detailed, and visually-appealing profiles, while resource constraints prohibited low-resourced schools from submitting equally elaborate or complete profiles.[12] Similarly, other documents generated by school personnel that could provide insight into students' participation and performance in rigorous coursework (e.g., letters of recommendation) could vary drastically across schools.[13] While some admissions offices trained personnel to reach out to obtain or clarify information, most had limited time to do so: many representatives indicated the average file review was allotted fifteen to twenty minutes. All of these limitations disproportionately inhibited the understanding of low-resourced school contexts. Thus, with such asymmetries in the information that admissions representatives rely upon to understand schools, current praxis meant to situate students within their own contexts falls short of meaningfully improving equity. Below, we highlight an important aspect of school contexts that emerged from our data collection that admissions officers should be aware of and consider: school policies and practices that shape AP participation.

High School Policies That Shape Rigorous Course-Taking

In describing how they assessed students' academic rigor, generally, and differences across schools, specifically, college admissions representatives regularly said they compared the courses students took to the set of offered courses. "*Did the student challenge themselves?*" was a common question posed by admissions officers in our conversations. This "challenge yourself" framework was undergirded by the assumption that all students had the autonomy to shape their coursework. Yet one important aspect of understanding context was the school- or district-level policies that governed how many and which courses students could take relative to the courses offered in their schools, especially in the case of rigorous courses like AP. From our interviews with school counselors and administrators, we know that some of these policies were formally codified and applied to all students within a school—such as caps on the number of courses students could take, restrictions on students from lower grade-levels, or only offering certain AP courses in alternating years.

However, in addition to these formal policies, ample research illustrated how schools enacted *informal* policies and practices underpinned by race- and class-based bias that discouraged or disqualified marginalized students from rigorous courses—even in schools that reported open-access enrollment policies.[14] In our own data, schools with "open-enrollment" policies still commonly used teacher recommendation forms or application processes to control student enrollment in AP courses. Yet, we know that these practices are biased against students of color in math and low-income students in English (and concomitantly favor white students), whereby they are less likely to receive teacher recommendations for rigorous coursework.[15] And some practices are more covert—for example an Office of Civil Rights investigation revealed that one school encouraged Black students to take an ethnic literature course because they would "connect better" with the material.[16] In this case, school personnel systematically rerouted Black students away from courses that admissions personnel valued. An awareness of varying school policies and the possibilities for race- and class-based bias are the first steps to considering students' academic records in context and enacting equitable admissions practices.

However, we found admissions offices inconsistently collected and considered information about school policies. Slightly over half of our admissions representatives said they considered schools' AP policies—all at most and highly competitive institutions. Additionally, most admissions officers learned about schools' policies through business-as-usual means: school profiles, the Common Application School Report, counselor forms or recommendations, and interactions with schools during their recruitment visits. When coupled with (a) the acknowledgment that low-resourced schools face structural barriers to producing profiles that provide the information admissions representatives consider helpful; and (b) admissions representatives are less likely to have meaningful contact with counselors from low-resourced schools, admissions representatives are unlikely to understand low-resourced schools' policies in the same way that they do of high-resourced schools. Only two admissions interviewees recognized this challenge and how they "have no idea" about low-resourced school policies. Another participant elaborated:

> In those situations where you don' t get a profile from the school, we don't even know if there's any restriction [on AP courses] on whether or not a student can be placed in an AP course by recommendation or can they place themselves in it. And when we don't have a profile, nine times out of ten, it is from a lower resource school. And in that case, our counselors are trained to try and get in contact with the school counselor directly . . . so we can get a better understanding of what's offered for the students, without putting them at a disadvantage.

Intentional measures, such as follow-up calls with schools, could help ameliorate the lack of understanding of low-resourced schools' formal AP policies, yet such attempts were only mentioned by representatives from three selective colleges. By relying on asymmetrical information sources (which privilege high-resourced schools) to provide a critical part of the school context, representatives reinforced the status quo and missed an opportunity to fully understand course-taking policies at low-resourced schools.

Beyond consideration for formal policies, not a single participant explicitly discussed other school practices that had the potential for bias, such as tracking, which could make gaining access to rigorous coursework challenging. The lack of acknowledgment of such practices raised the question about what admissions representatives know about race- and class-based biases in school personnel and the ways these biases shaped the opportunities for rigorous course-taking—particularly in schools that were racially and/or socioeconomically diverse.

The processes that determine how students end up in courses are integral to how admissions professionals understand and ultimately judge applicants in selective admissions. Yet, recognition and consideration of these facets was largely absent from admissions officers' decision-making. Some of this information was available through proactive data collection efforts—phone calls, forms, and workshops with counselors. Other processes—like racial bias in recommending students for rigorous coursework—were much more insidious. While some schools proactively looked to provide marginalized students with rigorous academic opportunities (e.g., Equal Opportunity Schools, www.eoschools.org), others created elaborate processes meant to exclude students perceived to fall short of their subjective interpretations of what makes an AP student—many of whom were low-income, Black, and Latinx.

UNEQUAL AND INEQUITABLE: DIFFERENTIAL INFORMATION-SHARING ACROSS HIGH SCHOOL CONTEXTS

Given the limitations of holistic admissions, an acknowledgment of different opportunity structures is necessary but insufficient. At their core, approaches that employ this perspective normalize the unequal distribution of resources and opportunities between high- and low-resourced schools, failing to take meaningful steps to disrupt the structures that create them. Rather than attempting to *account* for differences, equity work requires taking action to *redress* those differences— often in ways that challenge the status quo by allocating a disproportionate share of resources to offset the structural barriers facing schools with fewer resources.

High school visits offer an opportunity for admissions representatives to engage and share information with school personnel and students in a way that is responsive to each school's unique context.[17] However, high school visits are resource-intensive, requiring considerable monetary, time, and human investment. As a result, admissions offices and officers must decide which schools to visit and how much time to allocate to each. Unfortunately, they often prioritize the generation of tuition revenue or commonly used measures of academic prestige, such as standardized test scores, which heavily favor privileged students.[18] By devoting more resources and time to wealthier and whiter schools, institutions perpetuate race- and class-based inequalities in access to college representatives and their institution-specific knowledge about the admissions process.[19] In particular, school visits are essential for the exchange of information about how admissions officers assess rigorous courses (e.g., how AP stacks up against other courses).

Through our conversations with admissions officers, we found two intertwined practices that disadvantaged low-resourced schools. First, we found admissions officers proactively allocated more time to visiting high-resourced schools, consistent with findings from previous studies.[20] Participants justified these decisions by highlighting the additional time that counselors at these schools had, which oftentimes led to extended conversations about the school context and opportunities available for students to pursue rigorous coursework. By contrast, many admissions officers lamented that counselors at low-resourced schools did not have sufficient time to interact with them due to their busy schedules. Because of these perceived time limitations, admissions officers generally planned for and, therefore, spent less time at low-resourced schools, primarily exchanging greetings or dropping off promotional materials before moving on to their next visit. Admissions officers who allocated time based on counselor availability inherently reified the existing structures of opportunity. Rationales that privileged time spent in high-resourced environments represented a missed opportunity to take an initial step towards equity: rather than allocating additional time or efforts (e.g., counselor workshops) to support over-burdened counselors at low-resourced schools, admissions officers rewarded high-resourced schools because they found it easier to share and receive information in those contexts.

Beyond distributing time in an inequitable manner, the second practice that perpetuated inequality was that admissions officers provided different information across school contexts, especially related to rigorous coursework. This practice was often explained as an unavoidable consequence of and in reaction to the different levels of experience, capacity, and knowledge that existed between counselors in different environments. For example, at low-resourced schools, admissions officers reported they primarily answered basic questions that were readily answerable via their institutions' website, such as the minimum AP exam score required to earn credit. Meanwhile, personnel at high-resourced schools posed more nuanced questions, such as which APs a student interested in medicine or engineering should pursue, in order to best advise students seeking admission.

However, admissions officers not only *reacted* to questions posed but also *proactively* determined what information to communicate at different schools. In preparing presentations for low-resourced schools, admissions officers preemptively focused on general college admissions basics, such as defining concepts used in admissions such as a fiftieth percentile. In contrast, when visiting high-resourced schools, they provided specific information about their institution's policies regarding AP courses and exams, for example explicitly naming how many AP courses to take (e.g., nine) or that some APs are preferred (e.g., calculus over statistics). Representing another missed opportunity to pursue equity, admissions officers made assumptions about the types of information best suited to different environments. At minimum, these practices maintained the status quo by providing information that helped high-resourced schools refine (and define) strategic AP course-taking while relegating students and personnel at low-resourced schools to diluted information readily available elsewhere. Thus, rather than engaging in equitable praxis, admissions officers compounded the differences they observed between high- and low-resourced schools through doubly regressive actions and policies.

THE WORDS WE USE: ADMISSIONS OFFICER DISCOURSE ABOUT HIGH SCHOOL INEQUALITIES

In addition to the reallocation of resources, equity requires that admissions officers consider their own identities, experiences, and beliefs in relation to how they approach their work and who they believe is worthy of attending their institution. Admissions work is not a series of objective, insular processes—it is influenced by the beliefs and biases of the individual undertaking the work and the institutional and social environment where they operate.[21] As a result, equitable practices necessitate that admissions officers at selective institutions critically examine their personal and institutional practices, particularly with regard to students from low-resourced and underserved backgrounds. More importantly, they must then take steps to use those reflections to redefine how they approach their work in low-resourced contexts.

Reflecting admissions' historical ties with race and class, selective admissions offices overwhelmingly represent the privileged. Recent surveys indicated that the overwhelming majority of admissions officers identified as white, with estimates ranging from 80 percent overall to 85 percent in executive or leadership roles.[22] Additionally, many admissions officers at selective institutions were alumni of their employer.[23] Such homogeneity generally suggests a lack of diverse perspectives among admissions professionals, and concerningly, research further demonstrated that individuals with these identities had preferences for students from privileged backgrounds. For example, when presented with applicants that had similar academic profiles but different socioeconomic backgrounds, white admissions officers were more likely than their non-white peers to admit students from high-income backgrounds, while admissions officers working at their alma mater showed an even stronger preference for wealth.[24] Most admissions representatives do not come from marginalized communities or have first-hand knowledge and understanding of low-resourced schools—in turn, they are unlikely to advocate for candidates and schools from such communities.

Admissions officers' views are not only shaped by personal identities but also by how diversity and equity are (or are not) discussed, valued, and practiced in their social and institutional environments. For example, Hakkola found that admissions officers employed deficit-based perspectives that framed students from underserved backgrounds as lacking the experiences, knowledge, and abilities required to succeed at their institution.[25] When evoking this particular discourse, admissions officers preemptively deemed these students unfit for admission and devoted little-to-no effort to recruit them to their institution. Thus, admissions officers' discourse about diversity and equity can become the perspectives and narratives that frame their understanding of the world and translate into praxis—from interactions with prospective applicants to the ways they consider an applicant's identities throughout the review process.[26] Many of our participants also discussed differences that exist across schools from deficit-oriented perspectives that positioned marginalized groups as inherently inferior, while normalizing and privileging high-resourced contexts.

"Less Decent" Schools and "Particular Types" of Students

In our data, admissions representatives from selective institutions all used deficit-oriented language to describe low-resourced schools and their students. Similar to the discourse observed by Hakkola, we noticed patterns in admissions officers' language when discussing low-resourced schools that equated school characteristics and/or course offerings to "quality."[27] For example, some indicated they viewed low-resourced schools as "weaker;" and one even used the term "less decent." Admissions officers most commonly pointed to differences across resources as justification for a holistic admissions process, where students' academic participation and performance would be evaluated while considering the opportunities available in their context. As one officer explained, "We fully understand that students don't often have a choice as to which high school they attend. Particularly our low income students, right?" Yet, while holistic admissions could theoretically "accommodate" differences in rigorous course offerings across schools, the assumption that low-resourced high schools insufficiently prepared students for the academic rigors of selective colleges had decision-making implications. Some admissions officers seemed hesitant about the admissibility of students from low-resourced schools in general. As one admissions officer explained:

> We don't want to admit somebody from a low-resourced area just because they have had that kind of disadvantage. They still have to be a competitive applicant, even if we are kind of—I don't want to say lowering the criteria, because we do not have set criteria, but even if we are maybe dropping what we look down a little bit more.

Here, the representative used "criteria" to underscore the idea that students from low-resourced schools did not meet their own internalized bar for admission. An important question to ask within admissions offices is the extent to which criteria used are actually social constructions that reify privilege rather than predict of future success.

Some admissions representatives at most selective institutions also seemed suspicious that AP courses offered by low-resourced schools were as rigorous as APs offered at high-resourced schools. Although AP draws on a nationally standardized curriculum regulated by College Board and despite widespread acknowledgment that standardized test scores favor privilege, admissions representatives critiqued the AP exam performance at low-resourced schools. In one case, an officer shared that they "hate those schools that have moved to an all AP curriculum, definitely those under-resource schools" because students received ones and twos (the lowest possible scores) on the exam. Several other representatives also suggested that AP exam scores helped "confirm" whether the AP course at a school was actually rigorous enough to be part of the AP program.

In addition to viewing students from low-resourced schools as less academically prepared than their high-resourced counterparts, admissions officers also used language that linked a school's opportunities with the character of its students. Many considered the purpose of admissions as assessing student "fit" for their institutional community. With this in mind, the veiled, classed ways some admissions officers spoke about students from low-resourced schools became especially problematic. For example, one admissions representative described students at high-resourced schools as being anxious and overwhelmed from doing too much while claiming that counselors at low-resourced schools asked them "time and time again" to convince students to pursue AP courses. For this officer, only "a few" students at low-resourced schools were eager and willing to challenge themselves with a rigorous college-preparatory curriculum.

Finally, although less common, a few admissions officers verbally expressed pity for students from low-resourced backgrounds. For these individuals, a lack of financial, cultural, or social capital was an insurmountable barrier to the students' success. When discussing what they would change at low-resourced schools, one interviewee lamented, "I would tell them . . . that I'm sorry. I don't—I mean, I guess I wish—I would—education stability, like teacher stability, and feeling safe in their school, and then feeling safe going to school, and feeling that their learning is not for naught," while another wished that the students would "have hope and not be discouraged." Another admissions representative even went so far as to suggest that some students from low-resourced backgrounds would not be able to succeed at their institution, regardless of institutional support provided, because the students' backgrounds had "not given them the tools that they needed" to succeed. The evocation of this language showed that admissions officers sometimes viewed low-resourced schools and their students as lost causes, precluding them from consideration and fundamentally overlooking opportunities to promote equitable access in admissions.

The "Public Service" of "Forgiving" Academically Disadvantaged Students and Schools

Beyond this problematic language regarding low-resourced contexts, we also noted admissions officers discussed their views about equity in their work with limitations. Rather than consider practices that reduced inequalities in access to their institution as a central part of their responsibilities, admissions officers often implied that this work was either going above and beyond their normal duties, or worse yet, not part of their job at all.

Some admissions officers suggested they and their institutions were particularly charitable when they took steps to acknowledge the different opportunity structures present across schools. Rather than stating that they considered a school's resource-level when reviewing applications, some participants felt compelled to highlight this consideration in over-stated terms. For example, one participant framed their institution as "generous" because they did not hold a student's school context against them, while another stated that their institution was "very forgiving" to "students from lower-income, under-represented, first-generation back-grounds." By using this language, admissions officers implied that con-sidering students in the context of their environment was something to be highlighted as exceptional, rather than a normative practice that cen-tered the pursuit of equity.

Similarly, admissions officers described work to promote equitable access, such as programming or workshops designed to assist or support low-resourced schools, in ways that depicted this behavior as outside of their day-to-day responsibilities. In one illustrative conversation, an interviewee highlighted a workshop with low-resourced schools wherein they instructed school counselors on how to fill out profiles and write helpful letters of recommendation as a form of "public service." In this example, the participant believed that providing low-resourced schools with basic information was an exceptional act, rather than a standard best practice. By framing equity-oriented work in this manner, admissions officers afforded themselves an opportunity to selectively engage in such practices—only when convenient or after essential work is complete.

Lastly, some respondents tacitly suggested the ultimate responsi-bility to improve access belonged to low-resourced schools themselves. Despite universal acknowledgment that counselors and personnel in low-resourced schools generally had less time and fewer resources avail-able, some admissions officers stated that these counselors needed to do more to mimic the behavior of high-resourced school personnel. After explicitly acknowledging that counselors in low-resourced environments were much busier, one participant implored them to "just spend ten more minutes" on each individual student who wanted to attend their institu-tion. By requesting a prohibitively large time investment from an already overburdened counselor, this admissions officer avoided equity-oriented work altogether. Such statements allowed admissions officers to place the burden of solution-finding squarely on the shoulders of low-resourced schools and their personnel.

RECOMMENDATIONS FOR EQUITABLE PRAXIS

To be sure, the race- and class-based inequalities in schooling have a long and enduring history in the United States and begin early in the lives of low-income and racially marginalized students. Admissions representatives cannot single-handedly undo centuries of racist and oppressive policies and practices that have and continue to privilege white and affluent students (and schools) in the admissions process. Moreover, individual admissions officers—particularly those situated within colleges dependent on tuition revenue—may feel pressure from institutional leadership to continue allocating time and favor to the high schools that yield full-tuition-paying students. However, for those admissions offices and officers that aspire to become the front line of equity for their institutions, existing admissions practices are insufficient. To this end, admissions officers do have agency.

In this chapter, we identified three issues that hamper the realization of equitable admissions practices and also deny the richness of experiences possessed by students who attend low-resourced high schools. Current avenues for understanding context favor high-resourced schools and leave their low-resourced counterparts woefully overlooked. If institutions sincerely value a holistic approach, they must also center pursuing an understanding of the factors that systematically disadvantage the most marginalized applicants and rectify their in-house practices that systematically privilege high-resourced students and schools.

First, to address systematic gaps in knowledge about policies and practices in low-resourced environments, admissions officers need more information and better training. One possible solution could involve the expansion of the Common App's questions about high school course-taking policies, but this approach would task high school personnel with inputting information. Conversely, admissions offices can deepen their appreciation for how students from low-resourced contexts excel—without burdening these same schools—by intentionally targeting resources to reduce gaps in their knowledge about low-resourced environments. For example, admissions representatives can systematically collect information on course-taking policies and maintain institutional databases that can reduce asymmetries in contextual knowledge during application review. However, equitable admissions praxis must acknowledge more than only formal policies dictate who has access to rigorous courses. Therefore, admissions officers' training needs to include discussion about inequalities in AP opportunities both within and across school environments—and how to think about those inequalities when planning interactions and reviewing applications. After all, holistic review is not just a perfunctory acknowledgment that contexts are unique, but rather that the environments and opportunities therein shape the various parts of a student's application—often in ways that reflect historical and systemic oppression.

Second, to disrupt the calcified patterns of high school visits and regressive information-sharing practices, admissions offices need to expend more resources to develop targeted programming and support services for personnel at low-resourced schools. While a small percentage of our participants discussed such programming, including institution-led workshops and mock application reviews, we noticed considerable room for expansion. We recommend the development of institutional programming that explicitly emphasizes the dissemination of information to low-resourced schools, especially about the role of rigorous coursework in admissions that is institution-specific. Equity work inherently involves increasing the resources devoted to underserved schools at the expense of time spent engaging with high-resourced schools. Indeed, admissions officers should rely upon the abundant, dedicated, and highly trained personnel at high-resourced schools to reach out with questions or advocate for their students as needed.

Although this trade-off might be met with instinctive resistance, admissions officers who aim to promote more equitable access must acknowledge that their current practices actively contribute to the structural barriers that make relationship-building, information-sharing, and recruiting at low-resourced schools seem less efficient. While it may feel more productive to spend the majority of time interacting with the (high-resourced) feeder schools that regularly send dozens of students to one's institution, operating in this manner will never address the unequal opportunity structures that exist across schools. In short, selective institutions and their admissions officers must decide if they place greater value on efficiency or equity. The recent shift to online tours and informational sessions as a result of the COVID-19 pandemic provides a potential opportunity for increasing accessibility into communities that were previously underserved. However, virtual alternatives are no substitute for meaningful interactions and information exchanges at low-resourced schools. In this moment of global change and possibility, admissions offices should resist the return to business-as-usual practices and move beyond deficit-oriented perspectives, seeing equity work as charity, and privileging high-resourced students and schools.

CONCLUSION

Rigorous course-taking, holistic admissions, and selective institutions are generally rooted in beliefs and practices meant to perpetuate dominant groups' existing privilege and power while simultaneously maintaining the subordinate position of those with non-dominant social identities. Although researchers, lawmakers, and education leaders have paid significant attention to making postsecondary education and rigorous courses more accessible for historically marginalized groups, we are a long way from an equitable praxis that will actually begin to redress and ameliorate the historical barriers and resultant gaps. Admissions offices and their representatives are on these front lines. Not only do the majority of admissions officers believe low-resourced students to be less prepared academically and culturally—which has implications for the students' perceived admissibility—but many also do not see themselves as part of the solution to redressing differences in opportunities and resources. Ultimately, if the beliefs about low-resourced schools and the students who attend them do not change, we risk reducing existing practices to a futile exercise in performative charity masquerading as the provision of opportunity.

Advancing Holistic Review Without Standardized Test Scores: A Community Cultural Wealth Approach

EDDIE COMEAUX

CALIFORNIA SERVES AS AN IDEAL CONTEXT for under-standing how low-income and racially minoritized students struggle for access to higher education in a supposedly race-neutral policy context.[1] Los Angeles County, for example, has the second largest population of African American people among the nation's counties, and California has the largest Hispanic and Latino population overall and the fifth largest Black population in the United States.[2] Further, of the more than six million students in California's K–12 public school system during the 2019–20 school year, more than half (55 percent) were Latino and another 18 percent were students of color from other ethnic and racial groups, including Asian (9 percent), African American (5 percent), Filipino (2.5 percent), Pacific Islander (0.5 percent), and American Indian (0.5 percent); the remaining 22 percent were white.[3] Despite the level of racial/ethnic diversity in the state, there is currently a trend toward resegregation in secondary and postsecondary education and a lack of access and equal opportunity for low-income and vulnerable students of color as they transition from high school to college.[4]

These inequalities are perhaps most apparent in the disproportionate rate at which racially minoritized high school graduates gain access to

TABLE 3.1 **Percentage of African American freshman enrollees by UC campus (2018–20)**

Campus	Fall 2018	Fall 2019	Fall 2020
Berkeley*	3.1%	2.8%	3.7%
Davis	3.5%	3.5%	3.4%
Irvine	4.5%	3.0%	2.7%
Los Angeles*	5.8%	6.0%	5.1%
Merced	6.6%	6.4%	7.7%
Riverside	4.9%	4.8%	5.7%
San Diego*	2.4%	3.0%	3.0%
Santa Barbara	3.7%	3.7%	3.4%
Santa Cruz	4.3%	3.5%	4.9%

Source: University of California Office of the President, *Undergraduate Admissions Summary* (Oakland: UC Office of the President, 2020), https://www.universityofcalifornia.edu/infocenter/admissions-residency-and-ethnicity.

*UC flagship campus

the University of California (UC) system. For example, table 3.1 shows the percentage of African American enrollees across the UC system between 2018 and 2020. African American students remain underrepresented at all nine UC campuses.[5] Some of this inequity stems from Proposition 209, approved in 1996. For more than two decades, Proposition 209 has limited UC campuses' ability to consider race as one factor among many others in the admissions review process; as a result, it has had a lasting impact on deserving and high achieving African American students' access to UC, particularly to highly selective campuses.[6] African American students represented a dismal 4.1 percent of fall 2019 UC freshman admission offers, although African Americans comprise almost 6 percent of the state's population.[7] The crisis is worse at some of the system's most selective campuses—at UC Berkeley, UCLA, and UC San Diego, fall 2019 African American freshman admission offers were 3.6 percent, 5.3 percent, and 3.2 percent of all offers, respectively.

Notably, with ongoing public pressures and critical questions raised about fairness, UC implemented a new admissions policy in 2012. Students admitted under this plan must meet one of two criteria: the statewide index (a combination of GPA and test scores calibrated to identify the top 9 percent of students in the state) or Eligibility in the Local Context (ELC), which requires a GPA that places the student in the top 9 percent of their California high school class.[8] The intent of this plan was to widen the applicant pool, eliminate the need for students to take two SAT subject exams, and reduce the number of students guaranteed admission based on grades and test scores alone. Instead, students are comprehensively considered in the context of their educational opportunities and life experiences.[9] The ELC component in particular was designed to recruit qualified students from socioeconomic areas that typically do not send many high school graduates to UC—so called "low-sending" schools. In spite of these policy changes, however, Native American and African American students are still underrepresented at the most selective UC campuses.[10]

As part of UC's ongoing effort to advance access, educational opportunity, and equity, in May 2020 the UC Board of Regents unanimously voted to phase out all standardized testing requirements for freshman applicants. This decision was based on the view that these tests create an unfair barrier for minoritized students and do not tell much about students who enter UC beyond their race and zip code, the education levels of their parents, and, too often, their family income. The decision means that UC will, for the immediate future, proceed with a freshman admissions process absent test scores in the application. Each campus will use high school GPA and a range of other factors, including any recent improvements in grades; extracurriculars; special talents, projects, or achievements; and life experiences.[11] Likely because of this change—and despite COVID-19 challenges—UC had a record number of applications and a substantial increase in California admits for the 2021–22 freshman class, including from low-income students.[12] While the record number of applications is encouraging, this result is not enough.

UC must continue to strengthen and sufficiently advance an admissions system that visibly favors fairness, including by considering additional measures that capture student characteristics with significant relationships to academic success and life outcomes. In particular, admissions officials need to center and leverage alternative forms of capital within vulnerable communities of color; they must account for what Jayakumar and colleagues referred to as *strength-based notions of community*, or what Cooper and Liou called *high-stakes information networks* that students draw upon during their college-going processes.[13] In short, vulnerable communities must be viewed as possessing assets and strengths that benefit students. For example, researchers have recommended measuring alternative forms of capital as well as psychosocial factors, such as intellectual curiosity, perseverance, resilience, and independence.[14] All have the potential to reduce disparate impact across student groups while helping admissions officials understand the whole person in their decisions about whom to admit.

Informed by previous works that explored the problem inherent in how selective UC campuses define and weigh "merit,"[15] this chapter presents stories of UC students of color who were ELC-designated entering college (that is, they did not meet the statewide index) and who demonstrated high levels of academic success as they completed their undergraduate degrees. To date, these types of stories have not been well documented; as such, we cannot fully understand the implications of current conceptions of "merit" or of admissions outcomes that reflect negatively on the future of racial and ethnic equality in the state. Thus, drawing on Yosso's work on community cultural wealth[16], I sought to understand the home, school, and community experiences of UC students who identified as ELC only. I interviewed eleven high achieving UC graduates of color—all had college GPAs of 3.2 or above—about their pathways to college. In the sections that follow, I draw from their stories to describe the alternative forms of capital within communities of color that can be utilized by admissions officials to make more informed and equitable admissions decisions. As well, I demonstrate that the community cultural wealth interpretive framework is useful for holistic review in college admissions. Holistic review looks at the whole student, not just their GPA. For example, UC campuses using holistic review look at a range of factors, including high school course completion, grades in those courses, personal insight questions, extracurricular activities, and so on.[17] No single factor is given a pre-assigned fixed value or weight, and applicants' academic achievements are balanced with other pertinent qualifications in the context of the resources and opportunities available to them.

This research is significant for two major reasons. First, the literature on college access—and on the decisions of admissions officials—has not meaningfully accounted for the wealth of students' own communities or *funds of knowledge* in creating more equitable college pathways.[18] As an example, UC Riverside—prior to their test-free admissions policy—admitted freshmen based on a fixed-weight calculation, and they assigned about 91 percent of the weight to GPA and SAT/ACT.[19] These results therefore fill critical analytical and policy gaps on equitable access to college and the precollege experiences of students of color in California. Second, these findings will help admissions officials at UC and beyond broaden how they define academic success and improve not only their understanding of local communities but also their outreach and broad messaging to schools. Before I turn to the findings, it is useful to have a deeper understanding of the notion of *community cultural wealth*.

VALUING COMMUNITY CULTURAL WEALTH IN ADMISSIONS

Tara Yosso critiqued traditional views of Pierre Bourdieu's cultural capital theory that were narrowly conceived and failed to recognize the community cultural wealth of racially marginalized groups.[20] Yosso expanded on Bourdieu's work, providing a conceptual framework that defined community cultural wealth as "an array of knowledge, skills, abilities and contacts possessed and utilized by Communities of Color to survive and resist macro- and micro-forms of oppression."[21] In her asset-based framework, Yosso outlined six interrelated forms of capital—aspirational, navigational, social, linguistic, familial, and resistant—that communities of color possess but that are too often absent in traditional notions of cultural capital, such as those included in college admissions standards. Admissions officials can and should draw on a community cultural wealth framework because of the cultural wealth and capital in nondominant communities. Moreover, this framework complements and enhances "race-neutral" admissions policies that cannot consider race as a factor in admissions.

According to Yosso, *aspirational capital* refers to the ability to maintain hopes, aspirations, high expectations, and dreams of success, despite perceived structural barriers. *Navigational capital* refers to the ability to navigate "social institutions not created with communities of color in mind."[22] *Social capital* can be viewed as networks of individuals, including family, friends, mentors, and resources available within one's community to navigate educational terrain and achieve desired goals. *Linguistic capital* can be understood as the "intellectual and social skills attained through communication experiences in more than one language and/or style."[23] *Familial capital* includes forms of cultural knowledge nurtured among family, such as shared sense of history or memories. And finally, *resistant capital* refers to "knowledges and skills fostered through oppositional behavior that challenges inequality."[24]

Collectively, these forms of capital within the community cultural wealth framework are useful for understanding how racially minoritized students navigate educational pathways. In particular, a deeper exploration like the one I present next informs a better understanding of how these forms of capital can be acknowledged, valued, and adequately accounted for in college admissions review processes.

THE FINDINGS

To create equitable college pathways and advance the admissions review process, it is valuable to explore the precollege experiences of students of color. More specifically, we must interrogate beyond how multiple metrics within supposedly race-neutral admissions processes actually serve to exacerbate white privilege by over-counting traditional forms of cultural capital.[25] This study seeks to address this problem of what Jayakumar and Page refer to as the failure of admissions to be "racism-conscious," by asserting the need for metrics that honor the racialized experiences of historically excluded groups through valuing community cultural wealth. As I mentioned above, I took on this work by interviewing eleven high achieving African American students who all graduated from UC campuses. In high school, all participants had GPAs of at least 3.6; most were above 3.8, with the highest at 4.1. As well, these students held a variety of leadership positions, earned special school recognition, and were actively engaged in extracurricular activities. None of the study participants were admitted to their first-choice UC campus, namely one of the most selective UC campuses. Below I share and discuss two interrelated themes that emerged from our conversations: family and community as sources of wealth and capital, and preparatory programs that promote college pathways. All names are pseudonyms.

Family and Community as Sources of Wealth and Capital

Study participants utilized support systems and resources in their high schools, and teachers played an important role in their college planning processes. David noted, for example, "A lot of influence came from my peers, and at least two teachers. They were pretty influential and motivating to do well in their classes, or at least [to] be on par when we go off to college." All of the participants reported that their high schools were under-resourced, however, and they also identified family members, local churches, and other local community-based groups as sources of support in their degree aspirations. For example, I asked Maria to describe her family's role in the preparation and decision to attend college:

> I'd describe them as very supportive. My mom always pushed me
> to do my best. My dad, he was also very supportive . . . but it was
> mostly my mom that would actually be, like, on me about my education. She was always very involved in my academics. When I started
> high school, I started, like, slipping. I think it took me some time to

get adjusted to it. So she was, like, really on it. So I feel like all that, like, really helped me to, like, be on it myself—like, to be focused on what I'm doing and trying my best, and having the things that were needed to be able to go to college and obtain my goal, my career goal.

Similarly, Leti highlighted her mother's influence on the decision to attend college:

My mother had us, and after she had my younger brother, she actually decided to go back to school. So maybe I was around the second grade, and I think that was like my first exposure to college. I know she was going back to school because she wanted to better her life, better our lives. . . . We would come to classes with her. . . . My mom did think education was important. So for middle school, I did go to a private school that she put me through. And the education was more rigorous, so I was challenged when I was in middle school. And that was one of the reasons why I wanted to go to college. Because they did influence, we did go on college tours, and they talked about the college process.

Participants also attributed their academic development and success to relationships they established within their local communities. Julu, for example, was driven to do well in school to make his family proud; he mentioned that it was always an expectation to attend college. When asked about local community groups that supported his academic aspirations, he talked about his local church, saying he "volunteered at the church that I went to a lot" and noting that it "helped to support my educational goals a lot." Ana, like many others who participated in the study, talked about volunteerism and community-based work and connected it to her college-going processes: "I did a lot of extracurriculars, like volunteering in my community. . . . Before I had gone to my high school, I had gone to an arts school. So a lot of my extra time was spent . . . teaching piano to other kids or doing recitals. . . . These experiences helped prepare me to transition to college."

Preparatory Programs That Promote College Pathways

These students were aware of the preparation and high-level information required to become college-ready. For advice and guidance about college curricular requirements, they relied on information networks consisting of, for example, family members, teachers, community groups, and so on. College preparatory programs facilitated college-going pathways and provided students with an early sense of what would be expected of them in college. These programs also helped them develop important skills, such as time management, study skills, and writing techniques. Lilly explained that a high school program she participated in "followed" her throughout college:

> They kept track of my grades and stuff, made sure that I was doing well and [what I was] supposed to be doing. So I guess you could say they were my academic support, in the sense of, I knew that I needed to be at a certain place. Because we would report our grades to them every quarter and stuff. . . . They offer a lot of tools that were really helpful to me. . . . They did a lot of career development and stuff. They had networking, and that's how I got this internship. They also helped me with like, interview skills and resume. They do a lot of stuff. . . . I think they were a huge support system for me.

Abraham similarly talked about how his participation in a college prep academy helped position him for a teaching career:

> I knew I wanted to go to college, and I knew I wanted to be a teacher. And so they had an academy that would prepare people to be teachers. . . . With that program, I was able to go to different schools and, like, read to kids, or do different field trips to different colleges. All that stuff kind of, you know, helped me open up my mind to what was coming and whether I did want that. It was also something really good to put on my resume. So that helped me as well to get into college, to be able to say, "I have this experience in this."

Jalil also participated in a program during all four years of high school and said it helped him make sure he met all of the requirements to apply to UC: "I actually had to go there after school, and they would offer tutoring services. They would also make us do, like, certain classes, like extracurriculars. They also assisted me with all my essay writing."

Some participants were able to expand their knowledge base through community college courses. Sara, for instance, said her parents sent her to a community college for "a couple of English classes." She explained, "I would try to improve my education and understanding and then kind of get ahead of the curve as much as I could—or at least catch up in some cases."

WHAT BECOMES EVIDENT

Viewed through a community cultural wealth interpretive framework, these stories illustrate how family members, community-based information networks, and preparatory programs help facilitate college pathways for marginalized students. Earlier researchers had shared similar stories.[26] Here, participants described complex college-going processes during a time of high-stakes UC admissions standards—standards that seldom account for or leverage alternative forms of capital in vulnerable communities. But it is clear that racially minoritized students' communities are rich and multifaceted, and they shape students' college-going aspirations and success.

Family members, for example, provide guidance and motivational support for students' educational goals. As earlier research has also shown, this cultural capital from the family context makes a difference in students' personal development and successes, from preschool through the end of high school.[27] For example, recall how Leti credited her mother's return to school with exposing her at a young age to college life and all its possibilities. This finding dovetails with earlier research showing how family information networks and motivational support can improve the quality of experience for marginalized students.[28]

Furthermore, these high-achieving racially minoritized students were poised to take advantage of resources within their high schools, and, at the same time, identify other community resources to stretch their knowledge base. They identified out-of-school networks, such as local churches and community groups, for guidance and college-related information and resources. Take Ana, for example. She explained that offering piano lessons to kids in her community shaped her college-going identity. Notably, these communities and out-of-school networks were sites of humanness, acceptance, togetherness, and new possibility. Rather than viewing them through a deficit lens, it is important to see them as dynamic, complex, and culturally vibrant.

Beyond local churches and community-based information networks, some students reported involvement in college preparatory programs to facilitate postsecondary success. Lilly, for example, primarily relied on her college preparatory program for her personal and academic needs during college; she characterized the program as a committed and nurturing supporter of her academic goals and obligations. This is consistent with prior studies that found college preparatory programs and training beyond what is available in high schools positively influence students' college-choice processes and academic success.[29] High schools should not, of course, be exempt from fully addressing the needs and interests of diverse learners. Rather, they should find ways to better align and partner with nondominant communities and higher education—something I discuss in the next section.

CONCLUSION AND RECOMMENDATIONS

Racially minoritized students utilize the wealth of their own communities to strengthen their college-going identities. An asset-based framework—as I have used here—helps reframe students' stories and reject the trope that low-income and racially minoritized students do not have agency. It also helps us challenge deficit master narratives about the experiences of minoritized students throughout the schooling process. Racism and other forms of oppression undoubtedly continue to undermine the ability of racially minoritized students to prepare for and actively pursue their college aspirations. These stories, however, describe a reality—and hopefully new possibilities—that college-going resources and support systems do exist in vulnerable communities, and they can be leveraged to create opportunities, including more inclusive and equitable pathways to college. These stories also can and should be valued in evaluation practices and approaches.

The stories I have shared underscore the need for coordinated efforts to imagine ways to activate and operationalize the strengths and community assets that minoritized students bring to campus. Accordingly, based on these students' collective voices—and informed by a community cultural wealth perspective—in this final section I offer several recommendations to facilitate and shape equitable college pathways, including the college admissions review process for students transitioning to UCs (and other institutions) as first-time freshmen.

Develop stronger partnerships between high schools, communities, and higher education.   There are growing examples of authentic school and community partnerships to support student learning (e.g., Communities in Schools program, West Philadelphia Improvement Corps, Harlem Children's Zone). It would be wise for UC (and all universities) to better align with K–12 institutions and nondominant communities to create conditions for enhanced educational preparation and for more equitable pathways to higher education.

Leverage community cultural wealth in admissions review processes.   In its admissions processes, UC can and must move beyond a primary focus on traditional indicators and numeric measures to leverage the community cultural wealth in nondominant communities and to better emphasize psychosocial factors that indicate a strong work ethic, leadership, and commitment to community service.[30] As evidenced by the student experiences I have just described, robust college preparatory programs are important sources of support for minoritized students, and they must be valued and adequately accounted for in the admissions review process. Relatedly, admissions applications should include personal insight questions that more accurately capture the cultural resources that minoritized students develop in their families and communities and bring to the university. In doing so, equity-focused admissions officials can make more informed decisions, and student affairs professionals and campus leaders can identify students early enough to provide appropriate resources and support upon entrance to the university.

Additionally, to provide accurate context to student performance, universities should employ territory managers to serve as application readers. Through an asset-based lens, they can scour applications and highlight the wealth and capital of students in local communities (and their structural challenges) in detail. At present, most UC campuses do not have the necessary support and resources to invest in an adequate supply of territory managers or to ensure the local expertise of application readers; nevertheless, this role is especially important for applicants from low-sending high schools. If readers do not have comprehensive lenses through which to view UC applications, the likelihood they will perpetuate inequities is great. With knowledge of the local context, they can improve their understanding of schools as well as their outreach and broad messaging to those schools, particularly in vulnerable communities.

Provide rigorous reader trainings.   In concert with the previous recommendation, improved admissions review processes and territory management structures should be complemented by rigorous ongoing trainings to mitigate implicit bias. It is important for readers to discuss and acknowledge that implicit bias in the admissions process can work against prospective students. These trainings should discuss the role and value of community cultural wealth and capital that nondominant communities bring to the educational process.[31] Such training has become popular in industry, but its reach in admissions has been low.[32]

Leverage community cultural wealth in hiring practices.   Admissions offices can and should take a fresh look at their hiring practices. They must develop and enact more equity-focused and data-driven approaches when it comes to hiring admissions officials, including readers. Too often, gatekeepers—those in powerful positions who make hiring decisions—assess merit based on qualities ascribed to dominant group candidates.[33] Using a community cultural wealth lens, hiring committees are more likely to view minoritized candidates as assets and to broaden their understanding of successful candidates. This approach has the potential to advance equity and meaningfully respond to structural barriers in the hiring process.

Feature need and vulnerability in admissions processes.   The quality of their precollege experiences and subsequent college success suggest that the high-performing students who participated in this research would have performed well at any UC campus. However, they were all denied access to the most selective campuses. As such, current UC practices preserve a contemporary racial and class hierarchy within the system. Why does this matter? Because the research is clear: Students who attend highly selective institutions increase their chances of higher lifetime earnings after college, access to quality graduate and professional schools, and expanded social networks.[34] In short, this is a serious equity concern. UC can and must consider innovative, data-driven ways to center need, disadvantage, and vulnerability in their admissions processes. For example, in 2013, California enacted a finance system for K–12 education, called Local Control Funding Formula (LCFF), to improve educational outcomes by providing more resources to meet the needs of underserved students. LCFF has advanced equity and improved educational outcomes for underserved students.[35] UC might consider awarding a percentage of high-achieving students from schools that receive LCFF funding from the state admission to their choice of any UC campus to which they apply. This will allow for more high-achieving and deserving minoritized students access to their priority UC campuses.

CHAPTER 4

Inclusion by Design: Structural Equity Practices in Medical School Admissions

SUNNY NAKAE

THE INTENTIONAL RESTRUCTURING of medical education in the early 1900s has lasting outcomes for the composition of today's physician workforce. Elitism, exclusion, racism, and sexism informed the structures and norms for selecting future physicians. While we speak today of underrepresented groups in medicine, the more appropriate term is *historically excluded*. Perhaps an even more accurate term is *purposefully and structurally historically excluded*. Holistic admissions grew out of national consciousness in medical education that diversity in the profession is critical. Despite a majority of medical schools claiming to employ holistic admissions practices, progress in diversifying enrollment has been unimpressive and stagnant. In fact there are fewer Black men in medicine today than there were in 1978.[1] We need to redesign and restructure admissions in order to produce a physician workforce that will meet the needs of our diverse society. If we are to change the downstream impacts of racism, exclusion, and health inequity, we must change the entry points and structures that discourage and exclude minoritized and marginalized groups.

This chapter begins with the historical context that shaped medical education in the United States. Early formations and regulatory systems in medical education formed the pillars of structural racism and exclusion. An array of holistic admissions strategies, tools, and recommended policy changes are presented that include strategies for increasing structural justice to re-imagine admissions in medical education to be more equitable, inclusive, and accessible.

HISTORICAL STRUCTURE AND DESIGN

It is critical to begin this discussion with the historical context that the lack of racial, gender, and socioeconomic diversity in medicine is the product of intentional design. The roots of allopathic (science-based, modern) medicine in the United States are sexist, elitist, and white supremacist. Allopathic medicine practitioners were competing with many philosophies and practice models and wanted a stronger market position.[2] At the time there were no standards for schools or training, as medicine was not yet professionalized.[3] By standardizing and regulating medical education, leaders in early allopathic medicine were able to dominate the market.

There were two elements of this market strategy: the structure imposed by the 1910 Flexner Report, *Medical Education in the United States and Canada*,[4] and the establishment of state licensing boards to regulate training, credentials, and practice.[5] The Flexner Report restricted access to medicine by requiring undergraduate college coursework for entry into medical school. The second element of exclusivity was the founding of the Federation of State Medical Boards in 1912.[6] The board used its wealthy base to gain political clout to pass regulatory laws at the state level that restricted medical practice by requiring licensure. Exams to measure competency and verify credentials began when the National Board of Medical Examiners (NBME) was founded in 1915.[7] Practicing medicine without a license became a criminal offense. While these regulations advanced public safety and offered some protection from "quackery,"[8] it is critical to note that their purpose explicitly included narrowing the field of competition by elevating allopathic medicine as supreme in the market.[9]

There are two elements we can ascertain from the historical lens that clearly apply to today. First, narrowing the gates of entry provided drastic and targeted exclusion. Second, exams play a central role in structural exclusion and reinforce inequities through systems of power and influence. Therefore redesigning admissions today requires examining and expanding entry points and access and addressing the use of exams to structurally disqualify talent.

HOLISTIC REVIEW IN MEDICAL SCHOOL ADMISSIONS

In 2008, the Association of American Medical Colleges (AAMC) and constituent groups began working on holistic review, the practice sanctioned by the Supreme Court in the Grutter decision.[10] Holistic review expanded the focus of selection criteria beyond academic metrics to experiences, attributes, and the background of the applicant.[11] The AAMC launched the Holistic Review Project (HRP) in 2009 with several publications offering guidance to schools on the principles and benefits of holistic review.[12] Since this initial launch, many practices have emerged that have aided schools in working within an acrimonious and restricted legal climate to achieve diversity in their student cohorts, and thus the future physician workforce. Schools that participated in HRP training showed gains in first generation and Latinx enrollment, but not in Black or Native American enrollment.[13] More tools emerged as the HRP model continued to evolve that examined parental education, parental occupation, and an indicator of socioeconomic status.[14]

Medical education admissions practitioners adopted many holistic practices that have been shown to advance diversity of classes across various phases of the admissions process from initial review, interview, and selection to matriculation despite the historical challenges and continued legal setbacks. However, the GPAs and MCAT averages of matriculating students continue to increase. Increased emphasis on holistic practices has led many schools to claim they employ a holistic process without changing structural components that engineer exclusion. The AAMC released a new version of the MCAT ten years after the HRP was founded, doubling down on the exam and the revenue it yields. The use of the MCAT to exclude ethnic and racial minorities and low income students is academic redlining.[15] Students who are well prepared for success are often excluded due to score cutoffs. There is a continued need for more robust practice and more creative, innovative, inclusive strategies to address the structural exclusion created by the early architects of medical education.

The HRP began by defining elements of selection into three areas: experiences, attributes, and metrics.[16] Committees and decision-makers were encouraged to see the intricacies and interactions of a student's environment of home, school, neighborhood, etc. (habitus) in determining their potential for success in a medical career.[17] The focus expanded from assessing the ability of a candidate to complete a medical degree (educational preparation) to evaluating the candidate's potential to contribute to the institution's mission and the medical profession at large. A mission-based lens enabled institutions to consider admissions in the context of broad educational and societal benefits of diversity for the profession as a whole, rather than conferred upon individuals for personal benefit. Admissions committees began weighing the relative achievements of academically qualified applicants more heavily, rather than using more hierarchical, reductive methods for selection. Decision makers considered adversities and hardships relative to overall achievements, thus the concept of distance traveled helped committees recognize the strengths of applicants with average scores who had overcome significant obstacles and resource inequities. Evaluating applicants holistically in context and considering distance traveled became a common practice.[18] Unfortunately at many schools, consideration of distance traveled happens only after applying rigorous cutoffs for MCATs and GPAs. Schools remain cryptic about their cutoffs, which burdens applicants with an expensive application process without knowing at which schools they will receive consideration.

The AAMC began examining outcomes related to MCAT performance and licensing exam performance as part of a strategy to provide schools with data tools to support holistic admissions practice. Outcomes data from nationwide academic progress for students across many scores and GPAs demonstrates that students achieving at least the fiftieth percentile on the MCAT pass the first step of their national licensing exam on the first attempt 97 percent of the time.[19] Despite concrete and robust data demonstrating competencies in future licensure at the fiftieth percentile, medical schools continue to select for higher MCAT scores, suggesting that little has changed structurally in how the MCAT is used.

The USMLEs are an element of elitist competition with residency programs using scores to sort talent for their specialties, despite being advised against the practice.[20] Licensing exams have been shown to have low correlation with clinical performance.[21] Structural exclusion is reinforced by the exam, as students from wealthier backgrounds have more resources to be able to score better, and thus secure more lucrative specialties for residency and practice. In 2022, the USMLE Step 1 exam score reporting changed to pass/fail.[22] The NBME determined that the usage of the pass/fail licensing exam to select talent for medical practice was a misuse of the test. This change is an example of restructuring in medical education to achieve greater equity. Data and tools for holistic practice in admissions and selection begin with a broad consciousness of the role of racism in educational preparation.

RACISM-CONSCIOUS INTERSECTIONAL HOLISTIC ADMISSIONS

Racism-conscious intersectional holistic admissions means schools weigh and examine the entire application and consider the structural vulnerabilities and challenges an applicant may have faced, including but not limited to racism, that may have impacted a student's preparation for medicine. Structural racism is framed as a societal deficit, not as an individual deficit. Students may have very different intersectional experiences depending on their families of origin, their identities, and their backgrounds that may have impacted their preparation in different ways. These practices increase consideration for all candidates with mission-specific selection factors that consider racism as a structural vulnerability, dynamic influence, and intersection, rather than as a monolithic, static commodity or characteristic. Using an intersectional approach can expand consideration for applicants from historically excluded groups.

Structural implementation for racism-conscious intersectional holistic admissions means using education data, census data, and data that informs context to determine a student's potential. Disaggregation and disambiguation are critical, as are the constellations of data that provide a comprehensive view. The AMCAS application contains personal information about the high school an applicant attended and whether they studied at a community college. We can extrapolate if an applicant was born in an underserved county or rural area. Address information can tell us about how structurally privileged or divested a neighborhood is using zip code and census data. We can understand the macro picture of their college experiences by examining graduation data, Pell Grant aid data, and the metrics of past applicants coming from their colleges. Holistic assessment of applicants requires that we use structural data to understand the impacts of systemic racism. Practitioner tools are also critical in reshaping and widening the gates for medical education.

TOOLS AND INPUTS FOR HOLISTIC PRACTICE

Restructuring medicine to be more inclusive begins with dynamic tools and processes, which many schools claiming to practice holistic review have failed to redesign and question. Medical school admissions is a multiphased process with a high degree of variety across schools, but all schools conduct interviews. There is vast room for improvement and innovation among current practices in medical school admissions.

Multiple Mini Interviews

Individual one-on-one interviews have long been the norm in medical education admissions.[23] The validity of traditional interview scores is fair to moderate as a selection tool.[24] Schools began using multiple mini interviews (MMIs) in the early 2000s when the practice emerged from McMaster University.[25] MMIs consist of several stations of interactions, tasks, paired tasks, questions, or problem solving scenarios presented to applicants in a timed exercise. Applicants have a set amount of time to read a prompt, and then a limited amount of time to respond. Every applicant rotates through the same stations over the course of the interview experience. MMIs use raters instead of interviewers to score applicants based on their performance at the station. The raters also make comments on the performance of the applicant relative to the station's task. The scores for each session's group of candidates are then averaged, with a z-score provided for each candidate. This design allows for the bias of the session to be encapsulated within the group of candidates and raters participating for that session. The z-scores diversify and distribute bias and mitigate the impact of any one rater/station on an applicant's score. MMIs are entirely separate from the application, so biases that may enter due to experiences or metrics from the application are restricted in the MMI process.[26] MMIs have been shown to increase the diversity of the applicant pool, especially when weighting schemes calibrate admissions processes separate from other application elements.[27]

MMIs may be improved as part of holistic practice by using standardized interviewers who are paid, trained raters. Currently most schools use faculty, staff, or student volunteers to conduct stations and these volunteers have varied levels of skill and proficiency in conducting MMIs. Due to time constraints, scheduling challenges, personnel shortages, and tight budgets, admissions teams often utilize individuals who may not administer the MMI stations consistently. Sometimes little attention is paid to the diversity of the raters, which can have a negative impact on candidates from historically excluded groups by introducing stereotype threat. Using paid, standardized raters may provide an opportunity to ensure a diverse panel making for a more equitable experience for applicants. MMIs may be integrated into the selection process with or without comments from raters. When scores are utilized without comments, bias can go unrecognized and unchecked. Reviewing and monitoring comments from a trained core of raters makes addressing bias and inconsistencies more possible. Another tool of expanded consideration is better data curation, namely masking and indices.

Curating Information

Holistic review methodologies require that practitioners consider when and where in the process applicant information should be visible and considered. The application is dense and has academic data, demographic information, personal comments, and experiences. Admissions processes usually include phased approaches that determine a threshold for academic qualifications. After this initial phase, metrics should be masked so applicants are chosen based on their qualities and characteristics that committees deem mission fit and have the potential to contribute to the profession of medicine as a whole. Most schools fail to mask metrics at subsequent phases. This introduces anchor bias and may be one reason why average MCAT scores have continued to rise despite claims of widespread holistic review.

Schools doing traditional 1:1 interviews may also offer one or more of them as masked interviews, where the interviewer does not receive information about the candidate in advance.[28] Curating information through phased approaches and masking provides applicants an opportunity to present themselves without prejudice (positive or negative) to the interviewers or selectors. Masking data elements at various phases is an effective strategy that should be more widely used to mitigate the bias of overweighting MCATs or GPAs. Data curation tools also include the use of innovative, institution-specific indices.

Indices

The use of indices can decrease structural biases and help schools curate data strategically according to mission. With the raw data from the AMCAS application, schools can design their own systems that examine service hours, medical exposure hours, employment, Pell Grant eligibility, citizenship status, language skills, and more. The demographic fields available on the AAMC's common application (AMCAS) are robust and continue to increase with each iteration.[29] Schools may use data curation to calculate GPAs that focus on the most recent coursework or specific courses rather than total GPA or total science GPA. Indices may also combine MCAT scores, science credits, GPAs, and other data implements that contextualize applications more fully. Some schools have key distance traveled elements, such as speaking a language other than English in the childhood home or coming from a single parent household, that appear as flags within their tools to remind committee members of these aspects of applicant journeys. These mission factors can also be combined into an index or weighted strategically to ensure priority in early phases. Geographic markers via county flags for birthplace, childhood home, current residence, or high school may help establish a more robust picture of how an applicant's environment has shaped their preparation. Schools with regional service missions may select for, and/or prioritize, applicants with area ties or experiences. In addition to indices, admissions practitioners may also implement processes that help ensure more equitable outcomes by distributing roles and decisions across the process.

Phased Decision-Making

Phased decision-making via committee processes is another way that admissions practitioners can advance better outcomes with regard to representation of women and other groups historically excluded based on race or income. Rather than have one person decide on interview invitations, schools may utilize a screening process where there may be more than one person evaluating the merit of an application using a standardized tool. Creating more sophisticated tools can enable schools to examine patterns of selection and bias within their committees and sub-committees. If data are not collected throughout the process, retrospective examination of bias is impossible. Holistic review ushered in a new era that called for studying the process itself to continuously improve outcomes related to student body diversity and equity practice.[30] In addition to holistic review strategies and tools, many schools are also integrating more holistic approaches to recruitment and preparation that account for the challenges applicants face in meeting requirements for admission. Programs that offer solutions to structural racism are critical.

Access Programs

One promising strategy is pathway preparation programs that retain talent from the applicant pool that is highly qualified, yet below the metrics threshold. These bridge programs add additional preparation and resources to allow students who have demonstrated commitment, talent, and potential to continue progress and enter medical schools. Some of these programs do not include the MCAT,[31] while others have modest MCAT thresholds.[32] Still others provide test preparation and resources to attempt to address the structural vulnerability of students that have been unable to surmount these obstacles on their own. These programs use observable performance-based metrics to select students and have high rates of success.[33]

Postbaccalaureate Programs

Postbaccalaureate (PB), or postbacc, programs have demonstrated that they enhance diversity and meet the needs of underserved communities, and are another effective strategy for increasing access to medical education.[34] The success of PB programs should not be examined without the larger context of higher education that renders a motivated, talented group of students who have completed their undergraduate studies ineligible or not competitive for medical school. Not surprisingly, PB programs attract students historically excluded from medicine and students who are typically older, as many of them have experienced resource inequities that created challenges with academic performance. These students have been shown to serve underserved patients at higher rates than their non-PB program counterparts.[35] Committee training is another area that holds promise for improving the holistic practices of committees.

Bias Training

Admissions practitioners have been calling for unconscious bias training as a strategy for reducing the impact of bias on selection.[36] Data show that committees who engage in unconscious bias training are more likely to be aware of these biases and mitigate them during selection or interview than committees that have not engaged.[37] We need to move beyond bias awareness to bias mitigation practice, where committees recognize how bias manifests in the deliberation and selection process and take responsibility for correcting it in real time.[38] Continuous practice and attention toward mitigating bias in admissions processes remains critical in shaping medical education and widening the gates of opportunity for historically excluded groups. Another recent innovation in holistic admissions tools are situational judgment tests.

Situational Judgment Tests

Situational judgment tests (SJTs) have been used in business and other professional disciplines for many years.[39] SJTs have shown promise in helping schools identify candidates with strong reasoning, judgment, problem solving, and professional values.[40] CASPer is an SJT developed in Canada and was shown to be effective in predicting performance on the professional licensing exam for Canadian physicians.[41] CASPer has a very low correlation with academic metrics and has been shown to constructively measure preparation areas other than GPA and MCAT.[42] Some SJTs are multiple choice, while others, like CASPer, are open-ended, timed responses and scored by raters, making them similar to MMIs. Score gaps by race, ethnicity, gender, and income are narrower for CASPer. The CASPer test is less expensive than the MCAT ($12 vs. $320) and applicants view video-based scenarios, which mitigates the confounds of reading speed and comprehension. These elements increase access to medicine by assessing constructs unrelated to academic preparation that are important in professional competency. The mission focus for an institution may be to increase providers for underserved communities, thus a school may wish to elevate communication skills or the assessment of problem solving and compassion in their admissions process once academic preparation thresholds are met. SJTs provide an opportunity for greater mission alignment while expanding the gates of consideration for historically excluded groups. Beyond existing processes and practices employed by schools, we may also examine broader structural solutions to increase access to medical education.

FUTURE DIRECTIONS

Discontinue Use of the MCAT

During the COVID-19 pandemic many schools had to relax their policies due to restrictions and applicants not being able to take the MCAT.[43] A few schools went test optional,[44] and all schools were forced to change their in-person interview practices to online, video conference platforms.[45] This increased access and equity in the process by reducing cost, despite introducing some new challenges related to Wi-Fi access and private space for video calls. I worked with premedical students who may not otherwise have applied that were successful in obtaining admission during the 2020–21 cycle. One student was working two jobs and was unable to make time to study for the MCAT, but she had very strong grades. She applied and received three acceptances with robust financial aid offers. Were it not for test-optional flexibility due to COVID, she would still be studying to surmount the MCAT hurdle while working and living in a two-bedroom apartment with nine family members. In the wake of these admissions decisions there are opportunities to test the utility and necessity of the MCAT in predicting student performance within similar groups at the same school. For the first time in history, there is a significant increase in matriculants who were selected without MCAT scores at multiple institutions. Beyond widening the gates through discontinuing standardized exams for entry are ideas to expand the opportunities for historically excluded groups by replicating successful, existing models.

Create More HBCU Medical Schools

A recent article detailed the impact of the use of the MCAT in admissions calling it "academic redlining" and called for the MCAT to be discontinued.[46] Still more authors are calling for the creation of another HBCU medical school in order to meet the workforce need for physicians from historically excluded groups.[47] Over the years the HBCUs have shown that they have lower MCAT averages for admitted students, yet similar graduation and board passage rates.[48] These successful outcomes demonstrate that, in addition to coaching and support, an environment explicitly supportive of racial identity has a positive impact on performance and outcomes. The racism within the environment by virtue of being few in number can impact a student's performance. The HBCU medical schools play a vital role in the nation's physician workforce with today's four schools graduating more Black physicians over the last ten years than the top ten predominantly white medical schools combined.[49]

Addressing access and equity in medical education remains critical due to medicine's history of purposeful, structural exclusion. Holistic review processes and practices must address structural equity in order for medical schools to dismantle the white supremacist roots of medical education. Representation in medicine is critical as the population of the United States becomes increasingly diverse. As we forge ahead, continued creativity, courage, and innovation are needed to redesign and reimagine admissions structures and processes to ensure that medicine attracts and retains a talented, dynamic, and diverse physician workforce.

CHAPTER 5

How Not to Level the Playing Field: Why Test Prep Falls Short

JULIE J. PARK

THE COVID-19 PANDEMIC significantly weakened the SAT/ACT's grip on US higher education. As the pandemic surged, one by one, elite institutions that many believed would embrace "test optional"—Harvard, Yale, Princeton, and Stanford, among others—issued press releases suspending the mandatory submission of SAT/ACT scores. The vaunted CalTech even went so far as to pilot the elimination of SAT/ACT scores, asking that applicants forgo sending in scores altogether. High school students nationwide breathed a collective sigh of a relief, but the future of standardized testing in college admissions remains uncertain. Some institutions will become permanently test-optional, and others may go back to requiring the test, as has been the case for certain institutions such as the University of Georgia and the University of Florida during the 2021–22 admissions cycle.

As institutions weigh next steps to take in revising admissions requirements, understanding the underlying contexts that shape inequality around the SAT/ACT is critical. One of these contexts is the test prep industry, which has sprung up to prepare students for standardized college admissions tests through classes or tutoring. Students may take test prep in a variety of settings, from college outreach programs to classes for students looking to improve an already strong score.[1] Even if SAT/ACT-optional admissions becomes permanent at many institutions, test prep will still be a sought after resource for students seeking to distinguish themselves through their scores. Despite institutions establishing their own assessments or making testing optional, the test prep industry will morph to meet the continuing needs of anxious students and help them conquer a new set of admissions requirements. The admissions arms race is not going away, even with new sets of criteria.

Some individuals have argued that test prep is actually a mechanism to promote opportunity by giving some students the chance to receive extra preparation for the test and gain an advantage in the competitive admissions cycle otherwise dominated by elites.[2] Following that logic, a common prescription to redress the inequality in standardized tests both in college admissions and K–12 is to "expand test prep," with the idea that simply allowing all or at least more students to participate in test prep will level the playing field.

I disagree strongly with this perspective. In this chapter, I will present research that demonstrates how the test prep industry is largely an agent of inequality, both reflecting and exacerbating inequities affecting K–12 and college admissions. Even in a "test optional" era, I will argue, admissions officers and other evaluators must proceed with great caution: the unequal benefits derived from test prep even when access is expanded should give admissions gatekeepers much pause in the utilization of scores and the overreliance on test prep as a policy solution to advance equity. The unequal resources, opportunities, and socialization that students receive completely negates the idea that the SAT/ACT or any standardized test is "standardized" in any meaningful way.

To provide context, I first explain the test preparation industry in further detail and will document patterns related to race, class, and prior achievement, addressing research on how certain populations have disproportionate access to such resources. I then address research illuminating inequities that persist even when students have the opportunity to take test prep, explaining why universal test prep is an inadequate solution to address inequities in standardized tests. I discuss implications for certain populations, particularly East Asian Americans, and explain why recognizing the influence of test prep is critical to understanding the applicant pool in highly selective admissions. I then comment on the importance of understanding inequality in test prep beyond the SAT/ACT, given the role of high-stakes testing in admissions to elite public/private high schools, gifted education, programs within the university, and the possibility that institutions will develop their own assessments for admissions. I conclude by noting how the values communicated by the veneration of test scores, and the accompanying test prep industry, are out of sync with the values that higher education claims to prioritize such as preparing students for citizenship and leadership in a diverse democracy. Altogether, much of the time dedicated to standardized test preparation could be better spent elsewhere.

UNDERSTANDING THE TEST PREP INDUSTRY

For many years, the SAT/ACT has been a high stakes gatekeeper in a college admissions system already stratified by race and class.[3] Unequal access to SAT/ACT test preparation services is a key barrier to college access, and the rise of SAT/ACT prep during the 1990s coincided with other services that wealthy families began leveraging in the college admissions process, such as private college coaching.[4] SAT/ACT prep services typically cost anywhere from hundreds of dollars on the lower end to thousands of dollars for private tutoring, making them considerably out of reach for most lower-income and middle-income families.

While an entire test prep industry exists to give its partakers a leg up on standardized tests and college preparation, not all groups engage test prep at the same rate. While test prep is naturally more common among affluent families, within East Asian American communities, it is particularly prevalent, even for lower- and middle-income families. For example, among a national sample of first-year college students, low-income Korean Americans actually took SAT/ACT prep at rates that were higher than affluent Whites (46.2 percent versus 42.0 percent).[5] Zhou and Kim note that higher rates of participation within East Asian American communities reflects the influence of the ethnic economy, an ecosystem made of businesses, media outlets, and civic institutions that cater to immigrant communities.[6] The ethnic economy facilitates participation in SAT/ACT prep first, by providing the very SAT/ACT businesses that cater to the ethnic community; second, by facilitating the flow of information around education through mixed-income social capital networks (e.g., via ethnic churches and other community institutions); and third, by socializing people into the idea that taking SAT/ACT prep is seen as "normal" and even expected. Overall, higher participation in test prep from this population is caused by a number of complex factors, versus the reductionist idea that Asian Americans simply "work hard," or are more intelligent in any sort of way.

These complex factors help explain the relatively high rates of test prep participation by some East Asian Americans. However, the population itself is heterogeneous, and inequality still affects rates of test preparation for different ethnic subgroups. For example, while 42.0 percent of all Chinese Americans took SAT/ACT prep, the participation gap between low-income and high-income Chinese American students was almost 20 percentage points—a bigger gap than the one existing between low-income white, Black, and Latinx students and their same race/ethnicity, high-income counterparts.[7]

Undoubtedly, access to SAT/ACT and similar types of supplemental educational opportunities is a vital issue. Most low-income students of color experience significant economic isolation, meaning that they will have limited access and ability to leverage information networks that facilitate the flow of college-going knowledge, attuning them to the ins and outs of applying to college.[8] College outreach programs try to compensate for this information gap, and thus many outreach initiatives offer test prep as an integral component of preparing students to be college-ready.[9] Reflecting this trend, Black students take test prep at a surprisingly high rate, likely due to participation in college access programs.[10]

However, there is evidence that suggests that SAT/ACT and other types of test prep are limited in their effectiveness for most students, particularly for students who perhaps need it the most. Thus, increasing equity in this area is more than just an issue of expanding access. As will be discussed later, test prep within such programs does not appear to be an adequate solution for leveling the larger playing field, and researchers have documented how groups do not benefit equally from test prep, even with higher usage.[11]

THE LIMITED BENEFITS OF SAT/ACT PREP FOR THE GENERAL POPULATION

All tests operate under the veneer of objectivity, which promotes the assumption that everyone has the same opportunity to succeed on the test.[12] Some may acknowledge inequality in access to test preparation services, but express that all students would be able to demonstrate similar levels of performance if test preparation services were widely expanded. While often well-intentioned, these messages can have disastrous effects for public policy, as exemplified in the battle over the future of the Specialized High School Admissions Test for New York City's elite, selective public high schools. Billionaire Ron Lauder poured money into defeating Mayor Bill de Blasio's initiative to get rid of the SHSAT, and then with former Citigroup chairman Richard Parsons, gave about $750,000 to fund test prep for Black and brown students. The act reflected the persistent belief that the playing field can be leveled, and that test prep is the answer to remedy persistent inequities. Unfortunately, the numbers of Black and brown youth testing into the city's selective high schools continues to be far below the numbers who enrolled in the 1970s, and in 2021, only eight Black students tested into the revered Stuyvesant High School.[13]

Why is test prep often proposed as a silver bullet, fix-all policy solution for inequities in standardized test performance, diverting attention from interrogating the validity and usefulness of standardized tests as gatekeepers? Advertising can be seductive. The test prep industry often advertises the impact of its services: "Boost your score by 300 points!" Businesses may prominently display lists of the college destinations of past customers, making families think that an elite college destination is within reach if they can only fork over hundreds, if not thousands, for test prep services. However, in a summary of the research on SAT prep, Briggs notes that effects are considerably less than the "hundreds of points" that private SAT prep providers like to boast.[14] Effects appear to be fairly modest, in the area of 10 to 30 points per section. In a randomized controlled trial of College Possible, an outreach program that includes extensive ACT preparation, Avery did not find significant differences in ACT scores between treatment and control group participants.[15] He suggests that it is possible that control group participants found other ways to prepare for the ACT, but his findings are consistent with the work of Briggs[16] and others.[17]

One example of how the actual gains of test prep trails the hype is the much-publicized collaboration between Khan Academy and College Board to offer free SAT/ACT prep utilizing Khan Academy's popular online delivery system starting in 2014. As described by journalist Paul Tough, "Official SAT/ACT Practice" allowed students to receive customized practice questions and online lessons specifically tailored to their skill level.[18] The initiative was supposed to be a major breakthrough, leveling the playing field and giving especially low-income students the same opportunities to prepare for the test as their upper income peers.

In 2017, the results were announced to much fanfare: on the surface, the Khan Academy/College Board collaboration was a triumph, where students who used the service for 20 hours or more increased, on average, 115 points. That gain was consistent across race and socioeconomic status. However, a deeper look unveiled that the gains were not as widespread as one might think. First, students who did not use Khan Academy at all still gained, on average, 60 points on the SAT/ACT over the course of a year, which could likely be attributed to their growth in age. Second, less than 1 percent of the students invited to link their Khan Academy and College Board accounts actually studied 20 hours or more, meaning that usage rates were extremely low. Similar to what Briggs found, the actual "effect" linked with the Official SAT/ACT Practice, even for students who studied for 20 hours or more (once again, a tiny percentage of the overall group to which it was offered), was more likely in the ballpark of about 55 points total on the SAT, or 20–30 points per section, given that on average students gained 60 points without the curriculum.[19] Ironically, MIT's Dean of Admissions cited the Khan Academy program as one rationale for why MIT decided to reinstate mandatory submission of test scores, in essence arguing that the program created a level playing field for students.[20]

UNEQUAL BENEFITS OF TEST PREP: THE RICH GET RICHER

Still, in a system that heavily weighs SAT/ACT scores, even total point gains of 30–50 points—on the SAT, moving a score from a 1520 to a 1570, for example—can be a form of currency when students are seeking any means to differentiate themselves. Average gains may be slimmer than the "Increase your score by 300 points!" claim commonly peddled by the test prep industry, but they can still be a way for students seeking any advantage to distinguish themselves. Also, students with higher levels of prior academic preparation may experience larger gains than the average of 30–50 points, making test prep an even more attractive option for students who already score well on standardized tests.

Tough called the Official SAT/ACT Practice program run by College Board and Khan Academy an example of the "rich get richer" effect, wherein students who already had a level of advantage in the admissions race were further advantaged. As one deeper look into the data unveiled, "Among students who spent any time practicing on Khan, those who are Asian, male, and with more educated and higher income parents spent more time on Khan," meaning that these were the students who disproportionately benefited from the Khan Academy tutoring.[21] As Tough put it, "Official SAT/ACT Practice was consistently reinforcing the privilege of precisely those students who already enjoyed lots of advantages in applying to college . . . their collaboration was not leveling the college-access playing field at all. It had made it more uneven than ever."[22] Overall, Official SAT/ACT Practice had limited utility in making a meaningful difference in test scores for the vast majority of students.

Research helps shed light into why Asian/Asian American users were more likely to benefit from Official SAT/ACT Practice. When disaggregating by race, Byun and Park found that East Asian Americans were the only group that had significantly higher scores with any form of test prep, and their higher scores were only linked with one format: taking a prep course.[23] Byun and Park uncovered other unique trends related to participation in SAT/ACT prep. Besides confirming other studies that document a higher rate of participation by Asian American students in general,[24] they found that Asian Americans were the only group where higher prior achievement positively predicted participation in SAT/ACT prep classes.[25] It is possible that many of these students are taking SAT/ACT prep to get a competitive edge, making a strong score even stronger.[26]

In contrast, prior academic achievement was negatively associated with receiving SAT/ACT tutoring for white, Black, and Latinx students,

suggesting that SAT/ACT prep (via tutoring at least) plays a more remedial role for these groups.[27] This point is easily overlooked by individuals
who view the higher rate of test prep among Black students as evidence
that test prep is broadening opportunity for these groups. For example,
New York Times columnist Jay Caspian Kang critiqued the University of
California (UC) system's move away from the SAT/ACT. Referencing
research on higher rates of participation in SAT/ACT prep for Black
students, he described test prep as "relatively innocent" and noted, "If
anything, test prep seems to be a way that middle-class and poor Black
students and the children of recent East Asian immigrants can gain an
advantage over white students, not the other way around."[28]

However, it appears that East Asian Americans and students with
higher prior achievements are the ones able to gain an advantage, and
not low-income Black students. In another study, students who attended
high schools where a higher percentage of students took Advanced Placement classes were more likely to take SAT/ACT prep and also had significantly higher SAT/ACT scores.[29] Findings suggest that students who are
already well prepared gain the most from SAT/ACT prep courses, although
there are independent effects associated with race/ethnicity that persist
even when controlling for prior achievement. Altogether studies suggest
that the benefits of SAT/ACT prep are not consistent across race/ethnicity
or high school context. Student experiences in SAT/ACT prep generally
differ markedly if some students are taking it as a more remedial measure, while others participate to receive a competitive edge. Further,
there are layers of structural inequality that surround students and shape
everything from their prior socialization with standardized tests to
their very understanding of the SAT/ACT. For example, in studying low-
income students in Chicago Public Schools, Deil-Amen and Tevis found
that their mainly Black and Latinx participants had little understanding
of the ACT.[30] They struggled to interpret the meaning behind their test
scores and also did not realize that one could actually prepare for the ACT
and potentially boost performance through taking the test again.

As noted earlier, East Asian Americans experience unique structural conditions—high availability of test prep through ethnic economies and social capital networks that make test prep seem like a normative behavior.[31] These conditions are layered on other conditions like relatively greater access to higher quality K–12 public education, including higher rates of attendance in integrated schools than other communities of color.[32] While not all East Asian Americans are able to access these resources and networks, together they form a potent combination of forces that socialize youth early on into the idea that standardized tests greatly matter and thus are worthy of a tremendous investment of time, money, and energy. Furthermore, many East Asian American youth have parents who emigrated from Asia, or are familiar with test prep culture in Asia, where such activities are highly normative. East Asian American parents who are immigrants will generally be more familiar with an admissions system based on a single, high-stakes test score (versus holistic review), and thus may be particularly invested in stressing the importance of standardized tests and test prep to their children. Altogether, these conditions help explain why they seem to uniquely benefit as a population when it comes to test prep.

Admissions officers would be well-advised to look beyond the single metric of a score received and understand the layers of complexity that likely influence its formation. Given that East Asian Americans, the affluent, and students with higher prior levels of academic achievement have greater access and payoffs from standardized test prep, it is clear that test prep does anything but level the playing field. Also worthy of attention, media coverage highlights the troubling trend of white, affluent students being able secure extra time to take the test by getting a diagnosis for a condition needing accommodations (e.g., attention deficit disorder), a trend that is particularly apparent in wealthy suburbs and also came to light during the "Varsity Blues" admissions scandal.[33] Altogether, existing evidence underscores the limited utility of standardized tests in accurately assessing student achievement and potential.

THE NEED FOR CHANGE

Test scores and test prep have ramifications beyond direct admissions to an institution, and many students will likely feel obligated to submit test scores due to many institutions signaling that scores are needed to qualify for certain programs. Test scores are often considered for entrance into opportunities like honors colleges and programs, specific majors (e.g., engineering, business), consideration for special awards, "merit" scholarships, or other financial aid, and graduate school admissions (e.g., MCAT, GMAT). In one example, the University of Illinois, Champaign-Urbana went test optional in the 2020–21 year and continues to do so, yet in the same year, the website for the Honors program at the same institution reads (as of June 2021) "How Do I Apply? You don't have to! We'll use your application for admission for most honors programs, reviewing your GPA and test scores and considering your essay responses very carefully." Other institutions more directly state that test scores are not needed to apply for their honors programs or scholarships, but continue to send somewhat mixed messages about whether students should submit scores. (See for example the Ohio State University–Columbus, which was test-optional in 2020–21 and 2021–22, but states "We recommend applicants take the ACT or SAT/ACT and submit test scores if they are available, as we believe that standardized test scores provide useful information and predictive value about a student's potential for success at Ohio State.") At the University of Illinois, Champaign-Urbana, the website as of September 2021 read "[test scores] may also be a factor when it comes to scholarship and aid decisions," which may make students applying for financial aid feel pressured or obligated to submit scores.

These dynamics suggest that many families will still likely invest significant time and financial resources in test prep, especially if institutions continue to send ambiguous messages about test scores being connected to aid. For all of the good, or possibly mixed intentions in colleges going SAT/ACT optional, test prep and the supplemental education industry in the United States is here to stay, widening an already troubling level of inequality. I describe intentions as being possibly "mixed" due to the likelihood that many colleges and universities will embrace their SAT/ACT score averages increasing under test-optional, which almost makes the SAT/ACT in itself a meaningless metric. The same structural conditions that affect SAT/ACT prep permeate the use of individualized tutoring and supplemental education programs that upper-middle class parents secure for their children from an early age, predating kindergarten in some cases.

Regardless of whether institutions require or consider the SAT/ACT or not, the same "prep" industry—catering to the SAT/ACT's replacements and/or other programs meant to bolster academic competitiveness—will continue to permeate the American landscape, perpetuating and exacerbating inequality. In many cases, the use of college test prep is just the pinnacle of a lifetime of cumulative advantages secured by parents to give their children any possible opportunity to get ahead, with the byproduct being that the rich continue to get richer. At the end of the day, not only would Black, Latinx, Indigenous, Southeast Asian American, first-generation, and low-income students benefit greatly from the eradication of the "prep" industry, but so would other populations. Ironically, the populations that have supported the test prep industry for so long—whites, East Asian Americans, and the affluent—have experienced tremendous stress, anxiety, and pressure associated with actually partaking in test prep. System reform is needed that acts in the best interests of all parties involved, advancing both equity and mental well-being for students and their families.

CONCLUSION

Altogether, test prep is both reflective of existing inequality, as well as a contributor to the unequal playing field in college admissions. Even with the change to test-optional or even with the eradication of testing requirements at some institutions, inequality in the US admissions landscape is still pernicious and deep-seated. The test prep industry will remain as a fixture for many pursuing selective college admissions, be it preparing students for new institution-specific assessments, preparing students for graduate admissions, or even old-fashioned SAT/ACT prep. While on average, gains attributed to SAT/ACT prep are slim, they can play an outsized role for those who are already experience some level of privilege in the education system. Further, pouring millions of dollars into the expansion of test prep in the illusion that it will somehow level the playing field for low-income and historically disenfranchised young people is an inadequate policy response to a much bigger problem.

Indeed, instead of focusing the conversation about what is gained in test prep, a pertinent dialogue would be to shift the focus to what is lost: time that could be spent developing special interests and talents, time invested in other forms of learning and activities that hone critical thinking, time serving one's community, and time building relationships with friends and family. If higher education espouses goals related to fostering citizens prepared to contribute to a diverse democracy, is test prep and the overarching regime of standardized testing that results from the admissions requirements (or expectations) set by colleges themselves contributing to that goal? Indeed, Tough detailed circumstances wherein institutions prioritized the enrollment of white, affluent students who tested well, but these same students did little to realize their potential once they actually got to college.[34] The test prep industry sends the message that it is "getting in" that matters, versus what students actually do to develop their talents and goals upon college entry. Altogether, institutions would do well to eradicate standardized testing altogether and to take a deep look into the college application preparation industrial complex and what it does to exacerbate inequality. Even without standardized tests, college applications are still profoundly susceptible to, and reflective of, inequality. If colleges really want to live out their values, admissions reform is greatly needed.

PART II

Considering Different Approaches to the Work in Admissions Offices

CHAPTER 6

How Are Admissions Decisions Racialized?

Julie R. Posselt and Steve Desir

AN UNCOMFORTABLE TRUTH ABOUT ADMISSIONS, one not often openly discussed, is that it is as much in the business of exclusion as it is of granting access. Its fundamental task is selecting from among a pool of applicants who vary on many dimensions, to decide whom to admit and whom to reject. These decisions do not occur in a vacuum. They are affected by the standard practices of the admissions office (or a professional school or graduate program, as the case may be), and they are subject to institutional and public policies (e.g., published application requirements and Supreme Court precedent). Decisions are also a function of individual judgments about how applicants should be evaluated and informal but widely held ideas about what makes a "good" letter of recommendation, test score, personal statement, record of extracurricular involvement, or applicant altogether. That admissions decisions are racialized through these varied influences is perhaps a second uncomfortable truth about admissions.

We therefore want to propose in this chapter the importance of scholars and practitioners addressing race in individual judgment, organizational practice, and formal policy alike, in order to combat racism as a systemic problem in admissions decisions. Glenn Harris, president of Race Forward and publisher of the prominent news site *Colorlines*, defines systemic racism as "the complex interaction of culture, policy and institutions that holds in place the outcomes we see in our lives."[1] In admissions, to discuss racism as systemic means recognizing that we hold in place racially disparate outcomes not only through the biased judgments of individuals (i.e., micro level), but also through standard organizational practices (i.e., meso level), and postsecondary institutions' cultural values and policy environment (i.e., macro level). As scholars who are deeply engaged with admissions professionals, we have seen to date more attention to questions around affirmative action policy and individual biases than attention to the host of routine practices embedded in our organizations that also contribute to inequities. Unveiling and countering these practices is critical to developing a response to racism that is systemic—as racism itself is.

To recognize systemic racism in admissions as something we can begin to manage, we present research at the micro, meso, and macro levels. Table 6.1 lays out levels and ways that racialization affects admissions and selected interventions for nudging the system toward equity. After introducing key concepts, subsequent sections are organized around the rows in table 6.1: these are levels at which research offers us perspective into the racialization of decisions as well as possible interventions toward racial equity. We argue that inequalities are reflected and recreated in admissions decisions through three contexts of racialization: individual judgment that is contaminated by implicit and explicit racial

TABLE 6.1   **Framework for Examining and Intervening on Racism in Admissions Decision-Making**

Levels of Analyzing Admissions	Racialization Processes Affecting Decisions	Selected Interventions for Racial Equity
Individual judgment	Implicit & explicit biases manifest social stereotypes	Confront overt & covert manifestations of racism in decision-making contexts
Organizational policy & practice	Evaluative criteria with racial disparities and meanings	Reveal & decenter whiteness in admissions preferences
Law & public policy	Legal prohibitions on consideration and conversations about race	Reinstate race-conscious admissions as lever for reparative/ corrective justice

biases that reflect stereotypes; *routine organizational practices and policies*, including reliance on criteria that reinforce racial disparities and racist assumptions; and the policy environment, particularly *legal prohibitions* on the consideration of race and such policy's ripple effects. Our concluding section describes actions and reflections for admissions professionals toward aligning their everyday work with the promotion of racial equity and justice.

To fully address the manifestations of systemic racism in admissions and recruitment, practitioner and research communities will need to work together to review and reconstruct some long-standing policies and practices. We have been inspired by and continually learn from our research-practice partnerships with individuals and organizations working to improve undergraduate and graduate admissions. They have unveiled for us—and we hope to reflect back to you—the myriad steps involved in evaluation, decision-making, and other organizational routines in admissions. Together, these steps constitute what we have described with coauthors Theresa Hernandez, Aireale Rodgers, Cynthia Villarreal, and Lauren Irwin, as a "repertoire of practices" that typically impede equity, but which can be reimagined and reconstructed for positive change.[2]

Our hope is that readers will come to see changes to admissions practice not only in terms of avoiding wrongs (i.e., actions that reinforce the fallacy of race and racial hierarchy), but also as levers for socially just professional practice. In addition to applying lessons from this chapter to admissions work, we invite equity-minded readers whose work is in other functional areas of higher education (e.g., advising, teaching, institutional research, to name a few) to use our multilevel framework for racialized admissions to break down the causes and consequences of racial inequities that may be reinforced through routine activities. So much of what we do in higher education involves a combination of individual judgment, organizational practice, and public policy.

KEY CONCEPTS

Before proceeding, we want to offer introductions to two key concepts that frame the discussion: racialization and equity. Scholars of race define *racialization* as the process of assigning racial meanings or associations to facially neutral qualities, practices, or identities.[3] Some things—for example, athletic ability, academic intelligence, school quality—have become associated with race in the minds of the public or actors in higher education. When this occurs, people may mistakenly think and act as if the associations are real and thereby reinforce race and racial associations as real. These racial meanings and associations often lead to discourses that naturalize inequality and absolve institutions and the practitioners within them of any responsibility.[4] It is a vicious cycle that needs to be broken.

Organizations are social actors that participate in racialization through what and whom they value. Institutions of higher education and their units are what sociologist Victor Ray calls racialized organizations.[5] For example, the college admissions office operates through a complex set of seemingly neutral routines, some of which perpetuate racial inequality—especially when combined with the policy context and individual professionals' biases and discrimination. While in principle admissions is designed to facilitate the enrollment of students who meet a university's goals and objectives, what—and indirectly whom—admissions values in practice has also reflected racism in society and reinforced race-based patterns of exclusion in higher education and the labor market.[6] Indeed, while much of the discourse surrounding admissions frames the persistent underrepresentation of racially minoritized students as a challenge of access, unequal access is itself an expression of system design.

A straightforward example is standardized admissions tests, which have layers of racialization: the SAT emerged directly from the eugenics movement.[7] Through the increasingly widespread awareness of race/ethnicity-based score differences, the historical use of tests to subvert desegregation mandates, and the risks of racial stereotype threat that come with taking these tests, more and more people think of tests as racist, as racially biased, or as tools of race-based exclusion. The racial meanings that standardized tests have come to take on in the minds of stakeholders have contributed significantly to their delegitimization, particularly in a historical time when colleges and universities publicly express commitments to diversity, equity, and inclusion. Standardized tests will be explored more fully later in the chapter along with other racialized practices (e.g., responding to student email inquiries; scheduling high school recruiting visits; and adhering to field-wide norms about college prestige), but are offered here as just one example of how the history of college admissions is far from equitable or race neutral.[8]

Equity is a process of reconfiguring structures, cultures, and systems to close gaps and empower historically marginalized and excluded groups.[9] We propose that a conceptualization of equity attuned to racial justice may include (1) corrective justice for the educational debt owed to descendants of enslaved people and other minoritized populations who have been excluded from education;[10] (2) confronting both overt and covert forms of racism embedded in institutional policies and practices;[11] and (3) decentering and making visible whiteness.[12] To seriously address the fact of inequities, we need to confront the direct and indirect processes through which our professional practice makes and remakes racial inequalities. Pursuing equity in practice means attending to and intervening on the layers of racialization in our practice as professionals, which we discuss next.

RACIALIZATION IN ADMISSIONS DECISIONS THROUGH INDIVIDUALS, ORGANIZATIONS, AND POLICY

With these definitions in mind, the core of this chapter will break down current research about ways that admissions decisions are racialized and what we can do about it. We will discuss patterns and potential interventions at three levels: individuals, organizations, and policy. Scholars have argued that individuals in admissions contribute to unequal enrollment in selective colleges and universities through decisions marred by bias and by executing inequitable organizational practices.[13] We discuss these issues first in a section about individual judgment that reflects racial biases, and what can be done about those biases. Then, we present research about the use of racialized admissions criteria and organizational routines that reinforce racial disparities. As universities take steps toward generating revenue and climbing in the rankings, for example, they normalize organizational routines that privilege wealth and whiteness in their applicant pool. They also downplay recruitment from high schools and colleges that graduate significant numbers of Black, Latinx, and Indigenous students. To the extent that responsibility for evaluations and decisions lies with individuals within organizations whose practices can be changed, readers will see that research indicates there is a lot that can be done to promote equity. However, the work of decision-making is also affected by broader forces that need to be acknowledged and negotiated. Public policies surrounding affirmative action, for example, constrain what it means to be "race-conscious" when looking at files. As we will discuss, this has had a chilling effect on higher education professionals' discussion of race generally.

Individual Judgment Manifests Social Stereotypes

Research on the presence of racial bias in admissions processes is drawing attention to the role of individual decision-making in the reproduction of racial inequality. Admissions officers across the country make judgments on a daily basis, and these judgments cannot be easily separated from the interlocking systems of oppression that produce racial stereotypes. Because admissions systems often provide considerable discretion to individual decision-makers, room for personal biases based on stereotypes is part and parcel of admissions decisions.

Among the layers of judgments involved in reviewing an application, assessments of an applicant's school quality and academic rigor, as well as perceptions of their ability, admissibility, and likelihood to succeed may be influenced by a reviewer's social position and identity.[14] For example, in a study on the impact of admissions officer diversity on admissions decisions, a national sample of 311 admissions officers participated in a simulation where they reviewed three fictional applicant files.[15] The team of researchers found that admissions officers from minoritized backgrounds were more likely to admit low-SES applicants. In admissions processes, personal biases about the educational experiences of and the opportunities available to Black, Latinx, or Native American students can lead to negative evaluations of students from stigmatized groups.

In a study of the role of implicit bias in medical school admissions, researchers administered the black-white implicit association test (IAT) to all members of the Ohio State University College of Medicine admissions committee. The researchers found that admissions committee members displayed significant racial bias.[16] While research has not specifically measured implicit bias in admissions decision-making, its presence challenges the race-neutral discourse that many universities use to describe the admissions processes.

Another important study has documented intraracial discrimination among admissions counselors—that is, preferences for some applicants over others within a particular racial/ethnic group. Sociologist Ted Thornhill studied the email response patterns of 517 white admissions decision-makers who received fictitious emails from Black high school students displaying varying levels of commitment to antiracism. Thornhill found that white admissions officers were 26 percent less likely to respond to emails from Black students who espoused a commitment to antiracism.[17] The reduced responsiveness to Black students who actively resist racism raises critical questions about a tendency to pursue diversity in ways that ultimately uphold the status quo.

Collectively, these studies highlight how individual judgment may reflect racist thinking, in ways that aggregate over many admissions officers and applications to contribute to patterns of racial inequality in higher education. We share this research about the presence of biases in admissions judgments not to cast aspersions on admissions officers' commitments to equity, but rather to demonstrate that admissions decision-making is not immune from, but rather is influenced by, the same biases that are present in many other contexts.

A developing literature is tracking experiments in managing implicit biases. Training that raises awareness of racial biases appears to be a starting point, but it is less effective than training that encourages perspective taking and individuation (i.e., recognizing one's own views as distinct from social norms). Also beneficial are opportunities that train participants to recognize moments of bias as habits of mind that need interruption like other negative habits.[18] Outside of the admissions context, research also documents the potential of longer term reduction of racial bias in education through the use of rubrics and evaluation protocols that focus attention and provide structure to individual judgment.[19] Findings about structured review as a means of bias management take us to the next level of decision-making: admissions criteria and other organizational standards of practice. Although individual admissions decision-makers have freedom to exercise judgment, normative expectations established by their institutions contribute to how decisions are made on a day-to-day basis.[20]

Admissions Criteria and Organizational Practices with Racial Disparities and Meanings

Formal and informal admissions standards, which are determined by colleges and universities, have made it extremely difficult for people of color to gain access to selective institutions. Such standards reflect culturally ingrained beliefs about excellence, merit, and fit with clear racial implications. High school math and science curriculum, grades, and college entrance exam scores, for example, remain among the strongest predictors of admission to highly selective colleges, but they are unequally distributed by race (and socioeconomic status).[21] Structural inequalities in K–12 education, such as unequal access to advanced high school and math coursework, contributes to these criteria operating as racialized barriers.

The relationship of SAT/ACT scores and probability of enrollment in the most selective colleges/universities has strengthened over time, which compromises access for minoritized students because high SAT/ACT scores are not evenly distributed across race and SES.[22] The documented disparities in standardized test scores have made these tests, both requirement of scores for application and reliance upon scores in admissions, a lightning rod in the evolving discussion of inequities in admissions. In 2021, the University of California system eliminated SAT/ACT score requirements and settled a lawsuit brought against it by a coalition of students, advocacy groups, and the Compton Unified School District, arguing that "by basing admissions decisions on those tests, the system illegally discriminates against applicants on the basis of their race, wealth and disability."[23] A parallel push to eliminate GRE score requirements for graduate school admissions has also been underway due to similar race and gender disparities.[24] At both undergraduate and graduate levels, disruptions to testing infrastructure and the test-preparation industry during COVID-19 have rapidly accelerated the number of institutions that have done away with standardized test score requirements. Whether this wave represents a permanent change remains to be seen.

There are other ways that admissions decision-making practices and enrollment management routines may be racialized. In one study, selective colleges judged institutional fit as one of the most important criteria, second only to academic metrics.[25] However, the profile of who is judged to "fit" historically white institutions and specific majors within them has been affected by colleges' preferences for activities and experiences that wealthy, white people disproportionately have access to and engage in. Examples include forms of both academic preparation, such as prior training in Latin and Greek languages in order to major in Classics, and extracurricular involvement, where "exceptional performance" in athletics favors wealthy students who have opportunity, specializations, and various supports.[26] Standardized tests may have received the lion's share of public and research attention to date, but it is clear that many formal and informal criteria need to be reassessed and reinterpreted for more equitable outcomes and repertoires of admissions practices.[27]

Standard recruitment practices shape the pool from which admissions decisions are made, and these practices can also reflect racial bias. Salazar, Jaquette, and Han studied the off-campus recruitment activities of fifteen public universities and found that admissions officers, in their desire to improve admissions yield, primarily recruited from well-resourced high schools in predominantly white communities.[28] In this study, high schools that had high concentrations of Black, Latinx, and Native American students were less likely to receive an out-of-state recruiting visit after controlling for other factors. What admissions officers count as a desirable high school to visit, their study shows, is racialized in ways that likely reduce applications from racially minoritized students.[29]

As with strategies for managing individual implicit bias, research is still developing about the efficacy of specific changes to admissions standards and practices as levers for equity. Holistic, individualized review is widely advocated, for example, but understanding about what it means in practice varies widely. An experiment by Bastedo and colleagues found that holistic review in undergraduate admissions that contextualizes key criteria increases the probability of admitting applicants with lower socioeconomic backgrounds.[30] At the graduate level, evaluation of a research-practice partnership of universities that are prohibited from practicing affirmative action found STEM PhD programs that revisited their standard practices, reduced reliance on or eliminated GRE requirements, implemented rubrics, and contextualized applicant information significantly increased the number and share of students from minoritized backgrounds who applied, were admitted, and enrolled.[31] Other studies that have measured the impacts of eliminating test score requirements alone have come to mixed findings about impacts on racial composition of admitted and enrolled students.[32]

Legal Prohibitions on Considerations and Conversations of Race

Public policy sets the boundaries for organizational practice, and admissions is racialized at the policy level through laws in eight states and Supreme Court precedent that limit whether and how colleges and universities can account for race in the admissions process. These laws affect how they consider individual students' race or ethnic background and how universities construct diverse entering classes. This discussion represents an extension of the previous section, because these policies directly constrain race as an admissions criterion. The policy environment also has indirect effects on the public and professional discourse about race and admissions.

The US Supreme Court's decision in *Regents of the University of California vs. Bakke* in 1978 is perhaps the single most important federal case law precedent. In Justice Powell's decision, SCOTUS ruled that colleges and universities cannot predetermine the racial composition of an incoming class before application file review, either through quotas or by setting aside a specific number of seats for students from historically underrepresented groups. However, "race or ethnic background may be deemed a 'plus' in a particular applicant's file, yet does not insulate the individual from comparison with all other candidates for the available seat."[33] So important was the ruling in this case that Justice Thurgood Marshall, the only Black member of the court, commented, "I doubt that there is a computer capable of determining the number of persons and institutions that may be affected by the decision in this case."[34]

Justice Marshall was correct. Research demonstrates that the *Bakke* case and legal environment associated with subsequent cases and state bans on affirmative action have cast a long shadow on admissions and all of those whom admissions policy touches. These decisions have had direct effects on practice and have changed how admissions professionals and the public talk and think about relationships between race and admissions. Public discourse about why we should consider race in the first place and professional discourse about race in admissions offices have shifted and narrowed through the increasingly restrictive policy environment. In *Bakke*, the Supreme Court ruled that affirmative action could not be used to remedy the present effects of past injustice, but only more narrowly to achieve the educational benefits of a diverse student body.

The Supreme Court has reaffirmed this precedent through the *Gratz* (2003), *Grutter* (2003), and *Fisher* (2013, 2016) cases. Legal history by Garces convincingly traced three sociocultural threats to race-conscious admissions back to *Bakke*'s discursive shift from equity to diversity: (1) the decoupling of diversity goals from the problem of persistent racial inequities, (2) discourse of affirmative action as "reverse discrimination" that diminishes attention to systemic inequities that inspired affirmative action, and (3) portrayal of race-conscious policies as compromising merit, and therefore diversity as compromising educational quality.[35] These developments have undermined public support for race-conscious admissions and fueled arguments for state-level affirmative action bans.

Additional research by Garces and Cogburn documented indirect effects of an increasingly restrictive legal and policy environment for considering race.[36] Their interviews with admissions and other professionals revealed that perceived threat of litigation has a chilling effect on any discussion of race:

> The law not only banned the consideration of race as a factor in admissions, it effectively silenced their conversations around race and racism, thereby rendering efforts to address racial diversity less visible and making individuals who have sought to promote racial diversity feel less empowered. The law also raised concern that it has undermined perceptions of the institution's commitment to racial diversity.[37]

In their research, we see how policy has systemic effects beyond limiting race as a criterion in the evaluation process. Policy constrains the very way that the admissions community acts, talks and, increasingly, thinks and feels about the place of race in admissions. Whether the Biden administration's attention to racial equity at the federal level, as indicated by the Executive Order he signed on his first day in office,[38] may have ripple effects that begin to create a more open conversation on these matters has yet to be seen.

MANAGING RACIALIZATION: IMPLICATIONS FOR ACTION AND REFLECTION

In a society where race is one of the primary ways that people experience and interpret the world and organize themselves, it is no surprise that we can find racial meanings laced through individual judgments, organizational decision-making practices, and public policy that shapes admissions practice and discourse. Confronting the overt and covert manifestations of racism in the admissions office requires attention to racialization at multiple levels. With our conceptualization of equity as reconfiguring of structures, cultures, and systems in mind, we would like to leave readers with a series of questions to guide assessment of their current practice. We hope they will devise plans of action that reconfigure organizational structures and professional practices, and manage individual biases and public policies toward improving access to higher education and all the benefits that it confers.

Individual Level Considerations

How are admissions professionals structuring their work to minimize the risk of implicit bias?   Recognizing that awareness of bias is one of the most important steps toward mitigating it, practitioners can examine how they are structuring their review process to manage risks. Naming the conditions under which implicit bias is most likely to be activated (i.e., when cognitively burdened, when working quickly, when hungry or tired) is a first step. Building equity checks into one's own work when it occurs under such conditions may also support more equitable judgments. For example, when responding to emails from prospective students, it may be useful to have an email template that can be adapted to individual messages, rather than counting on one's energy in the moment to equitably write responses. When reviewing large batches of files, using evaluation rubrics and knowing when to take breaks to manage fatigue is important. Building in pauses during the admissions cycle to conduct an equity check where you examine the racial/ethnic composition of who is advancing to the next stage of the process can raise attention to the phases in the process through which students from minoritized backgrounds are disproportionately being eliminated.

How are admissions professionals using the agency they have in their roles?   While the actions of individual decision-makers can and do help maintain inequalities, actions can also disrupt them. Thoughtful engagement with colleagues and advocacy for more equitable policy and practice can themselves become routine practices. Posselt documented how admissions committee members simply articulating counterexplanations for their colleagues' racialized associations of low GRE scores with "risk" and "belonging" when they came up in deliberation proved to be a powerful act, particularly when other members of the committee would vocalize their support for these counterscripts.[39] Racial meanings are socially constructed, which means they can be reconstructed; in practice, this includes both active affirmations of Blackness and its value for our institutions, and questioning associations that reinforce preferences for whiteness.

Organizational Repertoires of Practice

On what grounds are we excluding? How may our routines and policies racially exclude, even if our individual judgment is vigilant to bias?   Situated between the parameters of the law and the agency that accompanies individual admissions officers' judgment, changing routine practices are a promising space for changing racialized organizations and the implicit patterns of exclusion that emerge from admissions work.[40] For too long, standard practice in colleges and universities has been to rely upon admissions criteria and recruitment preferences that privilege students from already overrepresented populations. To build a repertoire of equity-advancing admissions and recruitment practices will require making visible how beliefs that reinforce white privilege and anti-Blackness are ingrained in current preferences and practices.

What does it look like to bring a focus on equity to the policies and structure of the admissions office?   We hope to have shown that in a society where opportunities to gain the experiences and knowledge that admissions decision-makers find desirable are unequally distributed by race, it is not enough to simply extricate bias from assessment of individual elements of the application, or even to be more cognizant of whiteness. Equity requires systemic change, including a deeper reconstruction of the organizational infrastructure for admissions: its personnel, recruitment priorities, and positioning within strategic enrollment management goals (that may be at odds with advancing equity).[41] We know, for example, that the judgment and social identities of admissions decision-makers are intertwined.[42] Who is at the decision-making table and their norms for interacting with each other are therefore angles for change that are distinct from, but related to, the official criteria in use.

Policy Interventions

Policy creates the foundation for organizational regulations and structures in admissions, which are themselves foundations for individual professionals' actions and decisions. Interventions at the institutional and public policy levels may be more difficult to execute because they are rooted in bureaucratic and political power structures, but they cannot be ignored. Admissions has been—and could be again—part of a societal project of reparations that corrects injustices that continue to exclude racially minoritized students in higher education. Here, the history that preceded the *Bakke* case is instructive: in an address to the graduates of Howard University in 1965, President Lyndon B. Johnson stated that civil rights are "not just [about] equality as a right and a theory but equality as a fact and equality as a result."[43] During the Civil Rights era, university presidents, admissions directors, and policy makers came together to advance policies and practices that expanded access and opportunity for racially minoritized groups.[44] Leaders such as Carl A. Fields and Alden Dunham at Princeton and Walter Leonard at Harvard devised recruitment and admissions practices that were responsible for the largest increases in the enrollment of Black students in their respective institutions. President Richard Nixon issued the executive orders responsible for affirmative action.[45] Before that, Lyndon B. Johnson and John F. Kennedy pursued a legislative agenda that provided a series of carrots and sticks that motivated university presidents to adopt practices that would increase the enrollment of Black students. These examples of public policy working in concert with university practice to change higher education can serve as models for admissions leaders today who are interested in advancing racial equity. For example, in a time of reductions to higher education funding, legislators may wish to consider performance-based funding mechanisms that tie funding to the enrollment of groups that have been traditionally underrepresented and underserved in higher education.

CONCLUSION

The conduct of admissions is situated within apparently contradictory social realities: colleges and universities claim the educational benefits of diversity, and even want to portray themselves as racially diverse, but their admissions practices and professionals, the law, and the broader priorities of higher education reproduce and maintain a racially stratified higher education system.[46] We believe that recognizing this tension is the first step toward actions that bring racial justice to the admissions profession.

When we fail to pay attention to the processes of racialization in college admissions, it becomes increasingly challenging to address their consequences for enrollment and degree attainment. Patterns of enrollment by race in institutions at different levels of selectivity highlight what has been called the "racial polarization" of the higher education system.[47] The most selective colleges and universities have also enrolled the highest percentage of white students.[48] Black students, despite increased levels of baccalaureate attainment over the last forty years, still only account for 6 percent of incoming graduate students at universities with the highest level of research activity.[49]

In selective private and public universities alike, recruitment and admissions are primary mechanisms through which racial disparities in enrollment are protected and measures of prestige are constructed.[50] Admissions decision-makers and the organizations in which they work therefore hold enormous influence. As we introduced in table 6.1 and have discussed through the chapter, admissions decisions are racialized at multiple levels: individual biases shaped by societal stereotypes, criteria and organizational practices that reinforce preferences for white students and whiteness, which all occur in a policy context that is not conducive to racial equity.[51] Equity-minded change requires purpose, attention, and the courage to acknowledge and address the multiple manifestations of racism. In the journey of changing how we look at and think about individual applications, design and implement activities over the admissions cycle, and deliberate evolving norms and values the ability to step outside of prevailing norms and narratives around race is critical. We hope this chapter has been a useful tool in taking that step.

CHAPTER 7

Criminal Records and Higher Education Access: A College Application Experiment

ROBERT STEWART

CRIMINAL RECORDS ARE A PERVASIVE, acutely restrictive feature of American society.[1] They can limit access to employment, public assistance, housing, intimate relationships, family planning options, and civic participation.[2] These restrictions can perpetuate cycles of crime, inequality, and lost opportunity, especially for low-income people and people of color. For many people who have direct experience with the criminal legal system, a college degree represents a potential pathway to mitigate and even overcome these barriers. To be sure, college attendance and completion are associated with lower rates of unemployment and higher relative earnings, but it can also encourage desistance (abstaining from criminal activity) for system-involved people.[3]

Through college, system-impacted students can access otherwise unavailable social and professional opportunities and develop human capital.[4] Higher education is also a potentially compelling mechanism for reducing future criminal activity.[5] Although there are unfortunately no rigorous causal studies of the relationship between higher education and desistance, compelling observational and quasi-experimental studies of the effects of prison education suggest that participation in secondary and postsecondary education inside and outside of prison are associated with positive outcomes, including lower recidivism and higher employment and earnings.[6] Further, higher education may facilitate desistance by serving as a bridge to cultivate social bonds with peers who have similar aspirations and role models, develop self-efficacy, and acquire employable skills.[7] Education likely reduces some crime by increasing earnings and the quality of employment, which could help counterbalance the negative effects of criminal justice involvement on employment, earnings, and mobility.[8]

Yet most colleges require applicants to disclose detailed criminal history information as part of the application process, and surveys of admissions administrators suggest that applicants are being rejected on the basis of their records.[9] Thus, the benefits of higher education may not accrue for applicants with criminal records. The increasing scrutiny of criminal records in college admissions is especially consequential for groups most subject to the criminal legal system, particularly young Black males. In 2019, Black males accounted for 8 percent of American residents age 18–24, less than 5 percent of the entire undergraduate population, and 32 percent of people incarcerated in state and federal prisons.[10] Considering the historic underrepresentation of Black Americans, especially young Black males, in higher education and their overrepresentation in justice-involved populations, criminal history disclosure requirements could raise additional barriers to racial progress and undermine an institution's diversity, equity, and inclusion efforts.[11]

Students who have been subjects of the criminal legal system are thus confronted with a distinct Catch-22: to gain access to the benefits of a college education that could mitigate the collateral consequences of criminal punishment, they must first successfully overcome those consequences to get into college. In this chapter, I draw from a field experiment on college admissions to test how reporting a criminal record affects the likelihood of rejection.[12] I find that a felony record, while not a categorical disqualifier, can become a major impediment to college access, especially for Black applicants. I conclude with a discussion of the implications for educational attainment, equity, and reentry.

CRIMINAL RECORDS AND
COLLEGE ADMISSIONS

The use of criminal history disclosure requirements (CHDs) in the college admissions process has only recently gained attention from scholars, advocates, and policymakers. During the planning process for this study, I reviewed undergraduate applications for the Fall 2015 term from more than 1,300 colleges and universities in the United States.[13] Overall, 71 percent of applications reviewed (79 percent of private colleges and 58 percent of public colleges) required applicants to disclose criminal history information. Further, colleges that have more competitive admissions (according to Barron's) are more likely to have CHDs on their applications, with nearly 86 percent of "Most/Highly Competitive" colleges to just 56 percent for "Less/Non-Competitive" colleges.[14] Colleges with higher crime rates, that consider race/ethnicity in their admissions process, are highly residential, and suburban are also more likely to include CHDs on their applications.

Many previous admissions innovations (e.g., college admissions departments, standardized testing, essay requirements, merit-based aid, affirmative action policies) began at mostly elite institutions and spread through the rest of the field, motivated by competition, normative goals, and legal uncertainty.[15] Colleges also form group relationships with those perceived as similar in status, such as football conferences, to protect or gain status, but also to provide a platform through which to share and compare policies, procedures, and practices.[16] The widespread incorporation of CHDs onto admissions applications was likely the result of a similar diffusion process.

Higher education institutions ask their applicants about criminal history information for a variety of reasons. Publicly and in surveys, college administrators claim these questions are geared toward preserving campus safety. According to a 2011 survey of college admissions administrators, the most prevalent reasons cited were reducing violence, protecting against liability, reducing illegal drug use, and reducing nonviolent crime.[17] However, there is no evidence that criminal history questions on college applications are effective tools for reducing campus crime.[18]

Further, the effectiveness of criminal history application questions for soliciting accurate criminal history information has not been demonstrated empirically. For most institutions, these questions rely at least initially on self-reported information from the applicant.[19] These responses are usually only verified if the applicant indicates that they do have a prior criminal conviction.[20] Otherwise, the application continues to move through the process unfettered. Put another way, these questions are susceptible to inaccurate responses and are poor predictors for future criminal behavior or college misconduct, a claim that has been borne out by empirical research. For example, a University of North Carolina task force found that current students were named as the suspect in 532 of the 1,086 campus crimes reported between 2001 and 2004.[21] Twenty-one of those students had a prior criminal history, but only eight of those twenty-one students had disclosed their criminal record on their application.[22] Later, UNC expanded their use of background checks to a larger population of applicants, but a recent review of the new policies similarly did not find any reduction in campus crime.[23]

A team of public health researchers, led by Carol W. Runyan, found similar outcomes. They conducted a survey of graduating seniors at a large public university and matched admissions and student conduct records.[24] They did find that students who self-reported precollege criminal legal system involvement were somewhat more likely to engage in misconduct while in college (though the bulk of that misconduct were marijuana or alcohol violations). But, according to Runyan and colleagues, criminal history disclosure questions on college applications "poorly predict which students will have disciplinary action in college and demonstrate that few of the students with disciplinary action during college reported criminal behaviours at the time of their application."[25]

Under the surface, colleges may have been motivated to adopt these practices out of concerns for legal liability and reputational preservation.

Although negligent hiring cases concerned with hiring people with criminal records have been successful in many contexts, to the best of my knowledge there has not yet been a successful negligent admissions case in which a college was sued for admitting a student with a criminal record who later went on to victimize another student on campus.[26] Legal uncertainty in an era of risk aversion and mitigation may provoke many colleges to take a hardline approach to students with records and lead to significant discrimination in admissions, not dissimilar to the labor market.[27]

Reputational risk is also a concern that might motivate colleges to adopt these policies and to apply significant scrutiny to applicants with records. Colleges have long been concerned about reputation and status, particularly compared to peer and more elite institutions. Higher education institutions market themselves to potential students and donors using various indicators, such as rankings, diversity, admissions ratios, and labor market outcomes through promotional materials and media representation.[28] It has also been common for colleges to invoke campus safety in their marketing strategies, though it is unclear whether those strategies are effective.[29] Nevertheless, colleges that are particularly attuned to reputational preservation (e.g., more competitive and/or elite colleges) may be more apprehensive about admitting students with criminal records.

It is difficult to predict which groups might be most in jeopardy of being rejected if applying to college with a criminal record. Previous studies that focus on criminal record and race discrimination in the labor market have suggested a "racial hierarchy" with white applicants without records serving as the baseline.[30] This hierarchy might extend to the higher education context wherein similarly situated Black applicants would be rejected at a higher rate than their white counterparts. Then again, colleges tend to consider and prioritize race differently than employers, though it is unclear whether this is as true for less selective colleges.[31] In recent years, however, an increasing number of states have banned race-conscious admissions policies through statute or court action, so the effect of race on college acceptance might be mitigated.[32]

THE EFFECT OF DISCLOSING A FELONY RECORD ON ADMISSIBILITY

To test whether disclosing a felony record affects admissibility, I conducted an audit study on college admissions. Audit studies have become an important methodology in the social sciences, particularly in discrimination studies.[33] In the most basic terms, an audit study is a field experiment in which an attribute (e.g., criminal record or race) is randomly assigned to one tester application within a pair of very similar or nearly identical tester applications to test the effect of that attribute on the outcome of interest. Traditionally, all information conveyed by the tester applications would be fabricated by the researchers.

Total fabrication would, however, be quite difficult in the college admissions context since applying to college requires a variety of official documentation (e.g., transcripts, test scores), many colleges have transitioned to digital admissions document transmission processes, and criminal record data are generally public and easily verifiable. I instead recruited real people through several methods, including Craigslist ads, local and student newspaper ads, email announcements, word-of-mouth, and partnerships with local nonprofits. Eleven months of recruiting efforts generated a list of approximately 25 possible participants with felony records and more than 450 possible participants without criminal records who met the basic qualifications (18–25 years old, graduated from high school/GED, taken the ACT). From these possible participants, I successfully recruited two well-matched pairs of male testers based on GPA, high school transcript, ACT score, age, and high school.[34]

These pairs served as the basis for the tester profiles. Each profile included tester-specific information (e.g., high school transcript, ACT score information, and other information that I would not be able to fabricate) and unique contact information (e.g., unique email addresses, street addresses, phone numbers with voicemail boxes, and social media accounts). I also created sets of generic profile attributes that could be randomly assigned within each pair, including extracurricular activities, volunteering information, essays, and employment information.

Within each pair, one tester (which I will refer to as the *Record tester*) had a real low-level felony record (a third-degree burglary or aiding simple robbery), and that student was also slightly better qualified academically relative to the tester without the record (the *Control tester*). The assumption was if an admissions reviewer were to compare the applications head-to-head without considering the felony, the Record tester applicant would be evaluated as a slightly better student (and thus more likely to be admitted) than the Control tester applicant. These matched pairs were reviewed by six admissions counselors at different colleges to confirm that, but for the felony, the Record testers were the more competitive applicants within each pair. I also calculated admissions index scores using formulas from seven different college systems to further ensure that, within each pair, the Record testers were always the better of the two students on paper. This matching strategy should therefore provide a conservative estimate of criminal record discrimination by design.

All of the testers were B-/C+ students, so I limited my sampling frame to only include colleges categorized as "Very Competitive," "Competitive," "Less competitive," and "Non-Competitive" by Barron's *Profiles of American Colleges*.[35] The race of the applicants was randomly assigned to each tester pair-college combination (i.e., [1] Black/no-criminal record and Black with a criminal record or [2] White/no-criminal record and White with a criminal record) regardless of the actual race of participants. That is, the same tester pairs both checked "White" on applications at one subsample of colleges and both checked "Black" at another subsample of colleges. I also randomly assigned essay responses, employment history, and other information.[36] I left the field with 280 completed tests.

Results

Starting with the descriptive results, which includes colleges that do and do not require criminal history information, the proportion of applicant profiles rejected by race and felony record status is shown

FIGURE 7.1 **Rejection Rate by Race and Felony Record Status**

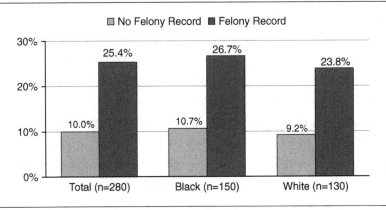

in figure 7.1. Tester applicant profiles that disclosed felony records (the dark gray bars) were rejected overall roughly 2.5 times more than their counterparts that did not disclose felony records (the light gray bars)— even though between the two the Record tester applications had slightly better academic qualifications. This pattern holds when looking at both race groups individually. Though Black applicants in both record conditions were rejected at slightly higher rates, the difference between the Black and White applicants with records is not statistically significant.

In figure 7.2, the sample is disaggregated by whether there was a criminal history disclosure question on the application, which results in an even larger gap between applicants that disclose a felony record. When Record applicants had to disclose their felony record, their rejection grew to three times the rate of the Control applicants without records. But when they didn't have to disclose their records, their rejection rate dropped precipitously. In fact, it's lower than the rate of the applicants without records, which suggests that when the felony was not considered, the Record applicants were slightly more competitive than the Control applicants.

I ran additional statistical models (in this case, mixed effects logistic regression) to predict college rejection while controlling for variation between colleges and applicant factors. I included a slate of institutional and applicant characteristics, including institution type, enrollment,

FIGURE 7.2   **Rejection Rate by Criminal Record Screening and Felony Record Status**

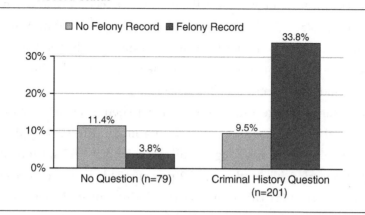

FIGURE 7.3   **Predicted Probability of Rejection by Race, Record, and Criminal Record Screening**

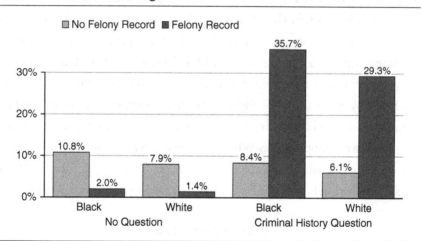

diversity, proportion receiving Pell, admissions competitiveness, campus crime rate, and more. I also interacted felony record status with whether there was a criminal record disclosure requirement to isolate the relationship between whether an applicant has a felony record and whether they had to disclose that record when applying. For ease of interpretation, figure 7.3 presents the results as predicted marginal probabilities of rejection by race, record, and criminal record disclosure requirement, holding covariates constant at their means. Overall, when applicants identified as White, they were somewhat less likely to face rejection than when they identified as Black. For both race conditions, the predicted probability of rejection was slightly higher for Control testers at schools that did not require criminal history disclosure, but the predicted probability of rejection was under 11 percent for all conditions.

Applicants with records, who again were better qualified than their non-record having counterparts, faced a much different application environment. When applying to colleges without CHDs, their probability of rejection hovered around 2 percent. This low rate of rejection is to be expected for this group, as the design ensured that the tester applicants presenting records should have been somewhat more attractive to admissions officials than the tester applications without records. But the likelihood they would be rejected jumped significantly for both race conditions when they had to disclose their criminal records, from less than 2 percent up to 29 percent when identifying as White and from 2 percent up to 35.7 percent when identifying as Black. More remarkably, compared to their counterparts without records, when applicants with felony records had to disclose their records, they were more than four times as likely to be rejected (4.3 times when applying as Black and 4.8 times when applying as White). In short, disclosing a felony conviction presents significant obstacles to overcome for all applicants, but Black applicants with felony records face the greatest likelihood of rejection.

Recommendations

In this chapter, I examined how criminal history disclosure questions on college applications can become serious obstacles to college admission for system-involved applicants. I conclude with a few recommendations for college admissions officials and policymakers. The first and arguably most empirically supported recommendation is to simply "Ban the Box" (BTB). The basic BTB higher education policy, adapted from the labor market, would remove any criminal history disclosure requirements for admission.[37]

Based on concerns regarding barriers to reintegration and the racially disproportionate effects of the justice system, the Obama administration pushed this issue to the forefront when they released a report urging colleges to reevaluate and reconsider their admissions policies regarding criminal history questions.[38] Following the release of that report and the efforts of local activists, the State University of New York System's Board of Trustees (SUNY) voted to remove the criminal history box from SUNY's application.[39] Louisiana became the first state to pass and enact a college BTB bill in 2017 for its public colleges, followed by Maryland wherein the Maryland General Assembly overrode a veto in early 2018 to enact its own college BTB bill.[40] And in August of 2018, The Common Application announced that it would no longer include a criminal history question on its main application component, though members colleges can continue to require criminal history information on their supplemental applications.[41]

There has been some concern about these reforms as recent evaluations of "ban the box" (BTB) initiatives that restrict criminal history questions on employment applications have identified potential adverse effects on Black men without records.[42] However, the present analysis may provide some initial reassurance that such adverse outcomes are less likely in the higher education context. Because the audit design included both colleges that required criminal history information and colleges that did not, I am able to directly compare how the Record and Control testers fared under each condition. I did not sample on whether a college required criminal history disclosure, so I caution that this comparison is not perfectly interpretable and should be understood as exploratory. Looking again at figure 7.3 to explore whether applicants—particularly Black applicants—without records were harmed by removal of criminal history information from college applications, I find there are small differences within race in the probability of rejection for colleges with and without the box. However, these differences within race are not statistically different from each other. Although I again caution that I did not sample on whether colleges required criminal history information, I did not find evidence suggesting that Ban the Box in higher education admissions would have a pronounced adverse effect on outcomes for Black males.

If an institution nonetheless chooses to require college applicants to disclose criminal history information, college decision-makers might consider the implementing the recommendations of the "Fair Chance Admissions Practices," as outlined by the US Department of Education.[43] For example, college administrators should be deliberate in crafting detailed policies that guide admissions professionals when reviewing applicants with criminal records.[44] Policy elements to consider include identifying specific offenses or offense types of concern to the institution, detailing procedures for reviewing applications that disclose criminal history information, and providing applicants with information about review the process and how to appeal adverse decisions.[45] Colleges might also consider a two-part admissions process wherein an applicant's criminal history is only considered after a conditional offer of acceptance is made following an initial admissions decision, which would save time, effort, and resources for admissions professionals and applicants.[46]

CONCLUSION

Higher education has classically been viewed as a pathway to foster employability and enhance social mobility, but these benefits may be out of reach for system-involved applicants if their college prospects are systematically curtailed because of their criminal records. This is particularly salient for those who face disproportionate exposure to the criminal legal system, such as young Black males. For the 70 percent of colleges that request criminal history information on their application forms, it is perhaps time to reconsider these practices, with particular attention to how they might conflict with other institutional goals such as diversity, equity, and inclusion.

CHAPTER 8

Intensifying Pressures, Increasing Pitfalls: Exploring Ethical Hazards in College Admissions

NATHAN F. HARRIS

AMERICAN COLLEGES AND UNIVERSITIES confront a crisis of public confidence. Over the past decade, public opinion surveys have revealed mounting skepticism about higher education. In 2018, the Pew Research Center reported that 61 percent of adults believed that higher education was headed in the wrong direction while Gallup found that barely half of adults—51 percent—believed that attending college was "very important."[1] In particular, young adults increasingly express doubts about attending college. In 2013, Gallup found that 74 percent of adults aged 18–29 believed that attending college was "very important," but this figure dropped to 41 percent in 2019.[2] The same surveys indicate that dampening perceptions about higher education stem from concerns about admissions, especially frustrations with narrowing access to higher education.[3]

Worse yet, Operation Varsity Blues further eroded public trust in admissions. In March 2019, the Federal Bureau of Investigation (FBI) exposed a conspiracy in which wealthy parents committed fraud to secure spots for their children at prominent universities.[4] When announcing key arrests, Andrew Lelling, US Attorney for Massachusetts, characterized the conspiracy as evidence of the "widening corruption of elite college admissions."[5] In the aftermath of arrests, commentaries called for a reexamination of ethics in college admissions.[6] Dr. Jerome Karabel, a sociologist and historian of admissions, criticized the "taken-for-granted" prevalence of special treatment for privileged applicants, highlighting that prosecutors differentiated between "illegitimate" practices such as falsifying transcripts and "legitimate" practices such as donating money.[7] Karabel argued, "the deeper scandal is what is legal. . . . [That] a U.S. attorney could cite [donating money] as an entirely legitimate practice, reveals the underlying pathology."[8] In response to the scandal, college and university presidents disclosed their own concerns about admissions practices. A survey sponsored by the American Council on Education found that 19 percent of presidents "strongly agreed," and another 52 percent "somewhat agreed," that admissions practices undermined public trust in higher education.[9] This survey also revealed that 67 percent of presidents either "strongly agreed" or "somewhat agreed" that unfair external influences advantage some students in admissions.[10]

Despite the audacity of Operation Varsity Blues, concerns about ethics in admissions are not new. The history of admissions features numerous eras of increased competition for students that stimulated new recruitment practices and raised corresponding apprehensions about ethics.[11] The founding of the National Association for College Admissions Counseling (NACAC), for example, emerged from discussions among administrators who recognized a need to develop standards for recruiting students and awarding scholarships during the Great Depression.[12] In the 1970s, scarcity supplanted surplus across higher education, recasting the work of admissions officers from counselor to marketer at many institutions, which spurred questions about the ethics of emerging recruitment practices such as contracting third-party recruiters and discounting tuition beyond need-based aid.[13] Throughout the 1990s and 2000s, the increasing sophistication of enrollment management raised ethical concerns about promoting early decision, courting parents as donors, applying need-aware and need-blind practices, and distorting institutional data to improve institutional rankings.[14] To address ethical hazards, the associations that represent admissions, including NACAC and the American Association of Collegiate Registrars and Admissions Officers (AACRAO), have long published codes of ethical conduct for practitioners.[15] Codes of conduct constitute essential elements of ethical infrastructure in organizations by emphasizing espoused values and norms, but codes often offer insufficient detail to inform most practices and processes and overlook competing environmental and organizational pressures, which creates cynicism about commitments to ethics.[16]

A rich examination of ethical hazards in admissions, therefore, should explore the effect of organizational dynamics and environmental pressures on decision-making inside and outside of admissions. Today, admissions offices confront pressures to achieve critical yet competing institutional objectives—generating revenues, curbing tuition discounting, protecting if not enhancing prestige, recruiting amidst declining cohort sizes, diversifying representation on campus, and adjusting to new norms for recruitment.[17] Among many objectives, the pressure to generate revenues tends to dominate because missing enrollment targets creates budgetary shortfalls for institutions.[18] While a small set of prestigious colleges and universities aim to improve (or at least maintain) their positions in rankings, a larger group of institutions confront existential pressures about enrolling enough students to generate sufficient operating revenues to avoid deficit—or worse yet, closure.[19] These high stakes can blur ethical lines inside and outside of admissions offices. David Hawkins, NACAC's executive director for educational content and policy, argues, "The business of admissions continues to be volatile. . . . It creates a very intensely competitive environment . . . and it can drive institutions right up to the line and even going across it to behavior that could be considered unethical and potentially even illegal."[20]

In this chapter, I aim to advance conceptual and methodological perspectives for investigating ethical hazards in college admissions. First, I frame three admissions practices as ethical hazards—offering incentives for applicants to enroll, providing special treatment for high-profile applicants, and leveraging demonstrated interest. While other admissions practices warrant examination as ethical pitfalls, such as gaming waitlists and reporting for institutional rankings as well as privileging legacy, donor, and athletic applicants, the three profiled practices constitute a set of emerging, enduring, and everyday ethical dilemmas in admissions. This framing of ethical hazards reflects conceptualizations of unethical behavior, which is defined as actions or decisions that are "morally unacceptable to the larger community," but extends beyond conceptualizations of corruption, which is defined as the "illicit use of one's position or power for perceived personal or collective gain."[21] Second, I introduce the concept of bounded ethicality, which explains how individuals overlook the ethical implications of their decisions, as a framework for interpreting ethical hazards in admissions. This concept, along with its corollary of ethical fading, posits that unethical behavior stems from cognitive biases more than rational calculation. Third, I explore methodological considerations for investigating ethics in admissions, including specifying several opportunities for future research such as surveying administrators inside and outside of admissions and leveraging freedom of information laws. Ultimately, this chapter reminds scholars, institutional leaders and guardians, admissions practitioners, and policy makers that the potential for misconduct in admissions pervades colleges and universities because stakeholders inside and outside of admissions might not be able to comprehend the ethical implications of their decisions while pursuing competing priorities.

SURVEYING ETHICAL HAZARDS
IN COLLEGE ADMISSIONS

Practice #1: Inducing Early Commitments

While Operation Varsity Blues captured headlines across the country in 2019, many admissions professionals were more focused on a dispute between NACAC and the United States Department of Justice (DOJ). In 2017, the DOJ's Antitrust Division launched an investigation into NACAC's practices, particularly three provisions in its *Code of Ethics and Professional Practices* that prevented offering incentives to encourage early decision applications, recruiting first-year undergraduate applicants who had committed to other institutions, and recruiting transfer students from previous applicant pools.[22] The DOJ framed its investigation as championing consumer choice, claiming that NACAC's guidelines restricted competition, thus inhibiting opportunities for students to court offers from multiple institutions.[23] In September 2019, NACAC voted to remove sections from its guidelines that pertained to these concerns; in response, the DOJ filed a consent decree with NACAC, ending its investigation.[24]

Immediately, this shift in guidelines altered recruitment practices at many colleges and universities. Within an admissions cycle, some institutions began enticing students with once-prohibited perks, including: Albion College in Michigan encouraging students to submit deposits by sponsoring an "Early Deposit Sweepstakes," which raffled perks such as room and board for a semester and an annual parking pass; Colorado Christian University offering numerous incentives such as $1,000 annual scholarships, preferred housing assignments, early class registration, and travel vouchers to encourage students to submit their deposits by December 1st; Daemen College in New York offering early decision for the first time, enticing applicants to apply by guaranteeing tuition rates for four years upon acceptance; and Reed College in Oregon encouraging students to apply early decision by guaranteeing placement in their first- or second-choice residence hall.[25]

The rapid adoption of these recruitment practices reshapes the ethical landscape of college admissions. Despite the DOJ's intention to protect students, admissions leaders fear that the shift in recruitment practices will constrict student choice. Early decision practices have long flourished at selective colleges and universities due to their enviable market position, but less selective institutions can now entice students by coupling bountiful perks to early decision. In advance of the DOJ settlement, Todd Rinehart, NACAC's president and vice chancellor for enrollment at the University of Denver, cautioned that eliminating restrictions on incentives could distort the decision-making of applicants, explaining, "instead of making an informed choice to apply early to their No. 1 college, some students will apply early somewhere just because they were offered special incentives."[26] With respect to extending recruitment periods, one retired admissions leader argued, "you have to look at this process from the standpoint of a 17-year-old kid. . . . Our focus should be on how to make this process less stressful and more meaningful for students, who should not have colleges badger them after they've decided which college they're going to."[27] Moreover, Rinehart argued that offering incentives to induce commitments from students will stabilize enrollment (and revenues) for some institutions, but privilege high- and middle-income students because low-income students need to compare the financial aid packages offered by multiple institutions.[28] This shift in practice renews an enduring question across the profession—are admissions officers counselors or "wranglers"?[29]

Practice #2: Admitting Unqualified "Special" Applicants

Before Operation Varsity Blues captured headlines, scandals at the University of Illinois and University of Texas exposed the extent to which colleges and universities extend special treatment to marginal— and even unqualified—applicants because of their personal connections to elected officials, prominent donors, and university administrators and trustees. Over the past decade, media reports and surveys have revealed that this form of preferential treatment in admissions is commonplace.[30] At the University of Texas, former president Bill Powers responded to allegations of offering special treatment to connected applicants by characterizing it as standard practice at "every selective university."[31] Similarly, at the University of Illinois, former president Joseph White contended that abolishing this form of special treatment would be "a real departure from the way things are done in great universities both public and private."[32]

The "clout" admissions scandal at the University of Illinois (UI) illustrates how colleges and universities enact preferential treatment in admissions. In May 2009, the Chicago Tribune exposed how UI administrators developed a secret admissions process for "special interest" applicants with connections to political officials as well as university trustees and donors.[33] In response, Illinois's governor launched a commission to investigate admissions practices at UI, especially at the Urbana-Champaign campus (UIUC). This investigation found that throughout the 1980s and 1990s, UIUC administrators had maintained a "watchlist" of special interest applicants.[34] Over the 2000s, this watchlist morphed into a "shadow admissions process" in which administrators reviewed—and reversed—denial decisions of admissions officers.[35] In 2009, for example, administrators reversed admissions decisions for thirty-three applicants—all but one of whom were white applicants who hailed from affluent suburbs.[36]

The shadow process for special interest applicants featured several key elements. UIUC Chancellor Richard Herman steered the process. While serving as UIUC's provost in the late-1990s and early-2000s, Herman fielded queries about special applicants because undergraduate admissions reported through the provost's office; but Herman continued this work after becoming chancellor in 2005, despite no longer overseeing admissions.[37] Admissions officers, for example, could not deny special applicants without informing him.[38] Chancellor Herman also convened secret meetings with the associate provost of enrollment management and the executive director of governmental relations to review the status of special applicants before admissions notification dates.[39] During these meetings, this clandestine group of administrators debated whether to reverse denial decisions for special applicants. To deflect attention from counselors at feeder high schools, most special applicants were deferred or waitlisted until summer, except for those who were admitted through the actual admissions process.[40]

Over time, the initial watchlist morphed into a formal clandestine routine for several reasons. First, over the 2000s, UIUC began receiving more special applications because of increasing cohort sizes and the affordability of in-state tuition.[41] Amidst increasing applications, an absence of coordination between senior administrators and admissions officers created embarrassing episodes with high-profile sponsors, including sending a rejection letter to the grandchild of a former governor without any alert to the former governor.[42] Second, UIUC confronted a precarious economic and political environment. In the early 2000s, UI experienced consecutive midyear rescissions totaling $75 million as well as cuts in state appropriations totaling $130 million.[43] In its FY2010 budget proposal, UI administrators described the institution's budget as "significantly eroded," which created "extreme stress" for the institution.[44] Third, the implementation of a new enrollment management system enabled administrators outside of admissions to access detailed data about special applicants.[45]

My analysis of email messages between administrators and trustees about special applicants and testimony from the state-sponsored investigation reveal that administrators rationalized their participation in the shadow admissions process for four reasons, even twisting improper behavior into noble actions. First, administrators aimed to appease key stakeholders. UI President Joseph White described the shadow process as a way to "respond courteously" to stakeholders, averting "complaints" that UIUC was "a big, faceless bureaucracy."[46] Second, administrators wanted to create educational opportunities for students. Dr. James Stukel, a former UI president, described the shadow admissions process as "a vehicle" for promoting access for under-represented students.[47] Third, administrators aimed to protect deserving applicants. Terry McLennand, Assistant Director of State Relations, argued that special applicants reported "very competitive" test scores that would have earned admission had they attended different (and less competitive) high schools.[48] Fourth, administrators wanted to shield the admissions process from external interference. Chancellor Herman characterized himself as "the buffer" between admissions and other stakeholders such as trustees, donors, and political officials.[49] Ultimately, the scandal prompted the resignation of UI's president, UIUC's chancellor, and seven of nine UI trustees over summer and fall 2009, raising a critical question about safeguarding ethics in admissions—how can institutions promote ethical admissions practices if misconduct originates from administrative suites and boardrooms?

Practice #3: Privileging the Privileged Through Demonstrated Interest

The image of an equilateral "iron" triangle has been used to describe three objectives that guide student recruitment.[50] First, admissions offices sustain if not enhance the academic reputation of their institutions. This objective often translates into recruiting students who report higher class ranks and scores on standardized tests, which signals higher student quality (and informs rankings). Second, admissions offices generate tuition revenues that fund academic operations, which prompts recruiting applicants who pay full tuition such as higher-income, out-of-state, and international students. Third, admissions offices assemble a diverse class, recruiting students who represent different interests, talents, geographies, and demographic and socioeconomic groups. The image of an equilateral triangle, therefore, misrepresents the recruitment admissions priorities of many institutions because generating revenue and enhancing reputation often outweigh promoting access and diversity.[51]

The recruitment strategies adopted by many institutions illustrate these trade-offs among competing institutional priorities. Admissions offices recruit applicants through many activities, tracking attendance at on-campus, off-campus, and virtual events; and many institutions calculate a "demonstrated interest" score from this data, which signals an applicant's likelihood to enroll if admitted.[52] Students can demonstrate interest by participating in prevalent recruitment activities: attending college fairs, on-campus information sessions and tours, and online information sessions; meeting with admissions officers at high schools; interviewing with admissions officers, alumni, or faculty; emailing or calling admissions offices; accessing digital content from admissions emails or institutional websites; and applying via early decision.[53] Increasingly, private and public institutions consider demonstrated interest when making decisions about applicants. Among respondents at more than 2,000 four-year colleges and universities, 19 percent described demonstrated interest as a "very important" or "important" consideration in decisions, while another 35 percent reported that demonstrated interest is "considered" in decisions.[54] Notably, at highly selective private institutions, 26 percent described demonstrated interest as a "very important" or "important" consideration and another 48 percent reported that it is "considered."[55] By considering demonstrated interest, admissions offices admit applicants who are more inclined to matriculate, which increases yield rates while decreasing acceptance rates, which enhances institutional reputation.[56]

One prominent way that students demonstrate interest is applying via early decision. With early decision, institutions offer students an earlier decision timeline in exchange for only applying early to their institution and agreeing to commit upon acceptance.[57] The practice of early decision offers clear benefits for institutions. Along with extending the reading period for admissions officers, colleges and universities can increase their yield rate by securing commitments from students early in the admissions cycle.[58] One recent analysis found that the average yield rate for students admitted through early decision was 90 percent, but only 25 percent for all students admitted by the same institutions.[59] For these reasons, many selective private institutions admit substantial proportions of incoming classes—even upwards of half or more—through early decision.[60] Some students also benefit from early decision. The acceptance rate for students applying via early decision, for example, tends to be much higher than for students applying via regular deadlines at selective private and public institutions.[61]

Not all students, however, benefit from these prevalent admissions practices. Demonstrated interest tends to benefit affluent and white students because they are more likely to attend high schools that institutions visit for recruitment and live near areas that attract off-campus recruitment events as well as possess the financial means and family support to coordinate expensive and time-consuming campus visits and obtain knowledge about admissions practices.[62] Similarly, early decision tends to benefit privileged students, despite some depictions framing the practice as a means for diligent applicants to secure enrollment at dream schools.[63] Research demonstrates that early decision advantages white students who hail from more affluent and educated households because they are more likely to obtain private college counseling, attend high schools that have lower counselor-to-student ratios and more rigorous curricula, and disregard competing financial aid packages from different institutions.[64] Scholars and policy makers have long characterized demonstrated interest as inequitable, but might this practice also be deemed as unethical as more institutions explicitly articulate diversity, equity, and inclusion as institutional priorities?[65]

CONCEPTUALIZING UNETHICAL BEHAVIOR AS COGNITIVE ERROR

The three profiled practices—incentivizing early commitments, providing special treatment for high-profile applicants, and leveraging demonstrated interest—underscore the extent to which environmental pressures and organizational dynamics shape ethical decision-making in admissions. Traditionally, ethical behavior was described as a rational calculation in which "good" and "bad" individuals enact different behaviors due to differences in moral character.[66] This conceptualization, however, understates the effect of broader social context, including environmental pressures and organizational dynamics, on individual behavior, especially in forging notions of "right" and "wrong" amidst competing choices.[67]

In recent decades, the field of behavioral ethics has recast misconduct as the product of cognitive biases more than individual traits, exploring the extent to which individuals are even capable of understanding the effect of social context on their ethical reasoning. From the idea of bounded rationality, which asserts that cognitive limitations impede the ability of individuals to process information and comprehend situations, the concept of bounded ethicality explores when individuals fail to enact their espoused ethical values.[68] Individuals, for example, tend to overlook accumulating environmental pressures that distort their ethical decision-making.[69]

From this perspective, the concept of ethical fading posits that individuals ignore the ethical implications of decisions when engrossed by other considerations. By framing decisions in non-ethical terms—increasing revenues, decreasing expenditures, attaining metrics—individuals fail to notice that decisions even include ethical consequences; and by failing to acknowledge these implications when framing decisions, the ethical dimensions of decisions fade from subsequent consideration.[70] Specifically, environmental and organizational cues trigger self-deception mechanisms that narrow the decision frames of individuals, which privileges interpretations of situations that ignore ethical implications.[71] In fact, individuals can construe situations in ways that enhance their ethical self-image by overstating the magnitude of situational factors.[72] These tendencies help to explain why otherwise ethical individuals engage in misconduct, only recognizing their transgressions in hindsight.

The self-deception mechanisms that trigger ethical fading are common features of organizational life. First, euphemisms, or linguistic disguises intended to mask unethical behavior, foment ethical fading.[73] By employing euphemisms—for example, referring to firing as "rightsizing" or sexual harassment as "banter"—individuals sanitize unethical behavior.[74] Second, the "slippery slope" phenomenon triggers ethical fading.[75] Individuals tend to notice abrupt shifts in work routines, but miss incremental alterations.[76] The gradual escalation of transgressions explains why individuals often miss misconduct that seems obvious in retrospect.[77] Third, outcome bias shapes ethical fading. Individuals are more likely to notice and question misconduct when actions generate suboptimal outcomes for organizations or themselves than when behavior leads to positive results.[78]

EXPLORING THE EFFECTS OF ETHICAL FADING IN COLLEGE ADMISSIONS

The concept of ethical fading offers a rich framework for investigating ethical hazards in admissions, including the practices presented in this chapter. First, environmental factors shape ethical perceptions of admissions practices, anchoring the decision frames of administrators inside and outside of admissions in critical outcomes such as generating resources and protecting reputations. In the University of Illinois scandal, administrators rationalized preferential treatment as stewarding relationships with critical stakeholders who supported the institution through donations or appropriations. Chancellor Richard Herman, for example, deemed the shadow admissions process as necessary to "secure" the institution's "broader interests."[79] Due to this framing, administrators overlooked the ethical implications of interfering with admissions decisions. Similarly, environmental factors likely shape how administrators inside and outside of admissions frame demonstrated interest. Intense competition for applicants anchors recruitment strategies in optimizing metrics associated with generating revenues and enhancing prestige, which overshadows ethical considerations such as promoting diversity and equity, even as institutions increasingly articulate these values as strategic priorities.[80] Due to similar pressures, some institutions now offer once-prohibited incentives to entice applicants before National Signing Day, prioritizing securing enrollment—and corresponding revenues—at the expense of distorting the decision calculus of applicants.

Second, euphemisms can distort ethical reasoning. The University of Illinois scandal reveals that administrators evoked numerous euphemisms to describe the shadow admissions process. Administrators continued to characterize the shadow process as a "watchlist," disguising its purpose. Administrators also sanitized their involvement by employing positive language such as acting "courteously," not wanting UI to seem like a "faceless" institution, and providing "relief valves" for "qualified" applicants. Instead of undermining admissions practices, administrators rationalized their involvement as meeting the needs of stakeholders and creating educational opportunities for deserving applicants.

Euphemisms also distort the ethicality of recruitment strategies. The label "demonstrated interest" presumes agency and choice; students elect to demonstrate interest, which frames participation as an expression of commitment and intent. Yet this label masks the inequalities of demonstrated interest. By contrast, alternative labels such as "demonstrated opportunity" or "accumulated opportunity" cast different meanings, describing the practice in terms of opportunity more than interest. Different monikers evoke different ethical interpretations. With new recruitment guidelines, euphemisms likely shape ethical perceptions, even if the swift shift in practices fostered immediate ethical reflection. By characterizing incentives as "sweep-stakes" in which applicants win "prizes," institutions enact a framing effect that overlooks the extent to which students forfeit the opportunity to consider a wider range of choices by submitting deposits earlier than traditional deadlines.

Third, the gradual escalation of transgressions can obscure ethical awareness inside and outside of admissions offices. In the UI scandal, the incremental development of the shadow admissions process blurred decision points that might have prompted administrators to consider the ethical implications of their actions. If tracking high-profile applicants was ethical, so was meeting to discuss them; if meeting to discuss special applicants had been ethical, so was meeting to reconsider denial decisions. In hindsight, administrators acknowledged that reversing admissions decisions was unethical, yet the incremental escalation of offering special treatment hindered their capacity to comprehend the consequences of their actions in the moment. Similarly, the adoption of demonstrated interest over the late-1990s through the 2000s and 2010s, coupled with pressures to decrease acceptance rates, probably blurred occasions for administrators inside and outside of admissions to consider or reflect on the ethical implications of using demonstrated interest in admissions decisions.[81]

ENHANCING AWARENESS OF ETHICAL HAZARDS IN ADMISSIONS

How might colleges and universities apply insights from ethical fading to confront ethical hazards in admissions? Institutions can establish new structures and cultures that address ethical hazards by considering the environmental, organizational, and psychological factors that shape decision-making. In this effort, senior administrators should assume instrumental roles due to their unique positional power and perspective.[82] Through their words and actions, senior administrators such as presidents, provosts, and deans can promote and model ethical awareness as an organizational competence that guides decision-making.[83] Institutions need senior administrators to espouse ethical conduct in public at convocations and commencements and to promote structures and cultures that embed ethics into decision-making behind closed doors.[84] Conversely, senior administrators run the risk of condoning misconduct when they ignore or dismiss ethical hazards throughout their institutions.[85]

To buffer admissions from ethical hazards, colleges and universities can develop and implement new policies and structures. To mitigate preferential treatment in admissions, for example, institutions can create a "firewall" around admissions offices by prohibiting and monitoring external inquiries about applications. After its scandal, the University of Illinois adopted this approach, stipulating that only students and their guardians, spouses, and school counselors can contact admissions to discuss applicants; other "third-party" individuals such as university trustees, administrators, faculty, lobbyists, and donors as well as government officials and business and civic leaders are prohibited from contacting admissions about applicants.[86] University officials can redirect curious (and cunning) constituents by recommending that they encourage students to contact admissions with questions about their applications. To strengthen these policies, institutions can implement supporting procedures such as specifying that the admissions office will document inquiries from third parties, contact institutional ethics officers about inquiries, and publish annual reports that disclose the number and nature of inquiries. These policies and structures serve as explicit cues for individuals inside and outside of admissions that frame third-party admissions inquiries as ethical hazards.

In addition to adopting procedural remedies, colleges and universities can design interventions that apply the lessons of ethical fading to develop more ethical institutional cultures. Notably, institutions could develop more robust ethical training programs to animate and address ethical hazards in admissions. Training programs, which could be framed as multi day retreats, would engage staff in admissions as well as other stakeholders such as the president, the provost, deans, and senior staff in advancement, athletics, and government relations as well as trustees and faculty leaders. The programs would explore the environmental, organizational, and psychological factors that shape institutional decision-making inside and outside of admissions, identify and acknowledge ethical hazards in admissions at their institutions, and begin to address these hazards.

The content of this training program would extend well beyond summarizing institutional policies and espousing ethical norms. First, after orienting participants to key elements of the institution's ethical infrastructure (such as codes of conduct), the program would detail competing priorities that shape admissions policies and practices at the institution such as generating revenues, enhancing reputation, and diversifying enrollment. During this review, participants would interpret the competing pressures and trade-offs confronting admissions and articulate how their own work shapes admissions policies and practices. Second, the program would then introduce participants to traditional and emerging conceptualizations of ethical behavior. This content would explore the key tenets of bounded ethicality, particularly the self-deception mechanisms that trigger ethical fading, which would illustrate individual challenges with comprehending ethical implications in decision-making.

Third, with this institutional background and conceptual foundation, participants would apply insights from ethical fading to identify examples of ethical hazards in admissions at their institution. In group discussions, participants would examine potential outcome biases that privilege certain admissions practices, potential examples of incremental shifts in admissions ethical hazards in admissions, including investigating hazards from different perspectives. The chair of the board of trustees, for example, could be asked to describe how the *Chronicle of Higher Education* might write an exposée about the institution's approach to navigating ethical hazards in admissions, anticipating quotes from different stakeholders; or the president could be asked to describe the competing environmental pressures that influence decision-making inside and outside of admissions, but from the ethical perspective of the director for undergraduate admissions. To end the program, participants would identify ethical hazards in admissions at their institution. Instead of dismissing or ignoring these hazards, participants would begin to develop an action plan for addressing them, identifying steps for different stakeholders to consider. Albeit time- consuming, a comprehensive training program that engages numerous institutional stakeholders would stimulate awareness about ethical hazards in admissions and reveal fresh opportunities to reframe the ethicality of admissions policies and practices.

In addition, professional associations in higher education could explore new ways to address ethical hazards in admissions. Professional associations assume essential roles in establishing ethical standards across practices that compromise ethical values, and potential euphemisms that mask the extent to which admissions policies and practices harm stakeholders, especially students. In these discussions, participants would explore questions that further stimulate critical reflection about industries.[87] Despite its recent lawsuit with the Department of Justice, the NACAC continues to promote ethical practices through its *Guide to Ethical Practice in College Admission*, which articulates specific values (e.g., access and equity) and specifies "recommended practices" that promote these values.[88] NACAC, along with the AACRAO, could enhance their codes of practice by including additional ethical hazards such as preferential treatment in admissions. Professional associations in admissions, along with other associations in higher education such as the American Council on Education (ACE), could also explore new opportunities to collaborate with institutions to design and deliver more robust ethical training programs for stakeholders inside and outside of admissions that aim to enhance ethical awareness (as outlined above).

CONCLUSION

Inside and outside of admissions, policy recommendations tend to characterize ethical transgressions as individual failings that can be fixed by adopting more stringent rules.[89] This chapter advances an alternative thesis, underscoring that the potential for ethical misconduct in admissions pervades colleges and universities, particularly as institutions confront intensifying economic, political, and social pressures. David Hawkins, NACAC's executive director for educational content and policy, offers a sobering reminder, arguing "when competition is at an all-time high, institutions can, and likely will, be driven to all sorts of different practices, some more desperate than others."[90] These competitive pressures create ethical hazards inside and outside of admissions offices; presidents, chancellors, provosts, deans, and trustees are just as likely to emerge as culprits as admissions officers. The psychological realities of ethical fading only complicate the ability of individuals to identify hazards in admissions while working to advance institutional strategic interests.

By investigating and interpreting the environmental, organizational, and psychological factors that shape decision-making, scholars in higher education can help colleges and universities confront ethical hazards in admissions. The challenge for institutions, particularly their senior leaders, is not eliminating the pressures that foment hazards, but establishing structures and cultures that encourage candid reflection of these tensions.[91] By exploring the ethical implications of admissions practices in public forums and behind closed doors, institutional leaders and guardians can promote ethical awareness in decision-making.[92] This enactment of espoused ethical values in everyday settings reorients scholars, institutional stakeholders, and policy makers to pragmatic conceptualizations of leadership that explore how fixating on pressing imperatives such as securing resources can undermine organizational integrity, thus jeopardizing organizational mission over time.[93] By adopting grittier interpretations of leadership, colleges and universities can begin to strengthen ethics in admissions and repair public confidence in higher education.

CHAPTER 9

More than Marketing: Professional Development and Learning to Integrate Diversity

DOUGLAS H. LEE, JOANNE SONG ENGLER,
JESSICA M. HURTADO, ALI RAZA,
AND OIYAN A. POON

IN EDWARD BLUM AND ABIGAIL FISHER'S Students for Fair Admissions (SFFA) v. Harvard legal complaint filed in 2014, SFFA claimed that race-conscious admissions practices unfairly discriminated against Asian American applicants to the university, which annually rejects over 95 percent of its applicants. In the United States District Court's 2019 ruling, Judge Burroughs found no evidence of anti-Asian discrimination in the College's practice of race-conscious holistic admissions. In 2020, a panel of federal judges in the First District US Court of Appeals unanimously affirmed Burroughs's ruling, finding no evidence of anti-Asian discrimination in the University's limited race-conscious admissions practices. At the time of writing this chapter, Blum has filed an appeal to the US Supreme Court, which has yet to decide whether the nine Justices will hear the case.

As a team of researchers committed to racial equity and interested in how race-conscious holistic admissions practices work, we have been heartened by lower court rulings in favor of diversity and its educational benefits. We have also been intrigued by Judge Burroughs's opinion, which raised important questions about college admissions practices.

In particular, the judge noted that "training would likely benefit from conducting implicit bias trainings for admissions officers, maintaining clear guidelines on the use of race in the admissions process."[1]

We are not legal experts and cannot comment on whether Judge Burroughs's questions about staff training and guidelines for race-conscious admissions are relevant to the legal questions at hand. However, as social scientists, we are interested in taking up two questions from Judge Burroughs's opinion. First, what does professional development and staff training related to racial diversity generally entail? Second, what organizational imperatives does professional development and staff training serve in admissions offices that practice race-conscious admissions?

Research on college admissions is often focused on the evaluation and review processes and the inequitable outcomes of those practices. Scholars have interrogated different admissions routines, norms, and outcomes, including analyses on organizational cultures in admissions offices,[2] holistic review practices and outcomes,[3] test-free/test-optional policies,[4] recruitment practices,[5] and the politics, effects, and benefits of race-conscious admissions.[6] Some have interrogated how the racial identities of admissions office staff can affect admission outcomes for applicants along economic class.[7] Others have pointed out the potential promise of equity checks and audit studies to improve the bias mitigation in holistic admissions practices.[8] In this chapter, we explore the existing norms of professional development and training related to racial diversity and what organizational purposes they serve, to offer recommendations for how professional learning can be shaped.

In this chapter, we draw from an analysis of interviews completed in 2019 with fifty admissions professionals who have extensive experiences managing and practicing race-conscious holistic admissions at seventy selective (i.e., 35 percent or lower admit rates) colleges and universities.[9] In these anonymous individual interviews, we asked each person to walk us through the work required to enroll a new cohort of students each year, and how race was considered through their daily tasks throughout a given cycle. We also intentionally prompted partic-ipants to share about how training and professional development were incorporated into their organizational practices and norms, because we wanted to know whether and how staff were prepared to consider race in their work.

All fifty participants, at some point in their interviews, expressed personal commitments to racial diversity and explained that their employers also publicly communicated commitments to diversity. As such, we expected to find that organizational leaders would prioritize the learning and development of skills among staff needed to do admissions work—including recruitment, reading (i.e., evaluation of files), shaping, and yield—in a way that would rigorously include race in legally limited (i.e., narrowly tailored) ways.

It is notable that these interviews were completed in 2019, during the year the Department of Justice announced their Operation Varsity Blues investigation, which was at the forefront of many public discourses related to college admissions that year. Although we wondered if partici-pants would shy away from sharing about their work, we found the oppo-site. Admissions professionals we interviewed seemed grateful for the opportunity to share their reflections and observations about how they did their work, day in and day out. Our final interview was completed in November 2019, a few short months before the March 2020 COVID-19 pandemic shutdowns. By late summer 2020, it was clear to most colleges and universities that they could not responsibly require students to sit among crowds to take the SAT or ACT, as admissions offices began their processes to admit and enroll a class for Fall 2021. Without test scores, admissions offices have had to adjust their practices. However, based on our ongoing conversations with research partnerships and relationships with admissions leaders, we do not believe that professional development and training practices have substantially changed due to the pandemic.

In the remainder of this chapter, we present what we learned about professional development and training from our interviews with admissions professionals. We draw on the CHAT-IT (cultural historical activity theory and institutional theory) framework to recognize how staff in admissions offices teach and learn with each other to do the work expected by their organizations. Given time constraints, marketing and sales goals, file reading demands of admissions staff, and political contexts, professional development and training related to racial diversity was limited. Office-based learning programs about racial diversity and equity were generally sporadic and limited to one to three hours per year or every other year. More importantly, deep learning about how to integrate concepts learned from these diversity-related sessions into their work routines seemed absent. With this in mind, we end this chapter with recommendations for possible strategies and approaches to make racial diversity more than just an institutional value in marketing materials.

PROFESSIONAL DEVELOPMENT: "ALL WE DID WAS ALL GO AROUND IN A CIRCLE AND SAY WHAT WE LIKED AND DIDN'T LIKE."

Organizational leaders presumably design and offer formal and informal professional development and training to support and guide the work, daily routines, and meaning making of staff members to align with team goals. Admissions offices serve various functions within larger organizations of colleges and universities, including marketing to prospective students (and their families), collecting and organizing data submitted by students for the evaluation (or reading) of applicant files, selecting students in shaping a class, and working to yield a class of enrolled students aligned with a given institution's values, priorities, and organizational needs, among other responsibilities.

To offer a framework through which to understand professional development and staff training in admissions offices, we draw from the framework of CHAT-IT, which brings together concepts from cultural historical activity theory (CHAT), which is a sociocultural theory of learning, and institutional theory (IT) from organizational studies.[10] Following CHAT-IT, we recognize professional development and training for admissions staff members as learning activities that shape how "individuals negotiate meaning and where communities develop, reify, and transform common practices" in admissions offices, which are formal organizations.[11] According to CHAT-IT, it is important to acknowledge the historical and social contexts that have shaped organizations and their activities. Drawing from this framework, we consider how professional development activities, informed by larger contexts, shape staff college admissions office members' learning about their work responsibilities and organizational expectations. How do admissions offices teach their staff to do the work of admissions, through professional development and training activities? How and what do admissions professionals learn to consider related to race and racism in their work? We start with an assumption that organizational leaders design professional development and training for staff in response to broader social, historical, and cultural contexts for admissions.

Through our interview study, we learned two key things about professional development and training in admissions office organizations. First, professional development and training are limited in scope, depth, and time, due to political and financial pressures that create a time crunch on admissions staff time. Even though many admissions professionals we interviewed claimed that they and their offices cared deeply about intersectional racial equity, the lack of time and intentional attention to these stated values seemed to suggest that their organizations did not demonstrate these expressed commitments through their allocations of time and energy. It made us wonder why and led us to consider plausible explanations and our second finding about professional development. The prevailing political context and cloud of fear over possible litigation and misinformation about federal case law can also lead leaders to feel hesitant about intentionally designing sustained organizational activities, including professional development activities, to address race and racism to facilitate deep changes in their organizations.

"It's always a time factor": Time Limitations

A key barrier to trainings that many participants identified was the lack of time due to the heavy workload of admissions officers that exists year-round. There is no time, even between when admissions decision letters go out and recruitment for the next class begins. Before decisions are finalized, admissions staff are already recruiting for the following year's class. Recruitment for application submissions and for yield, reading, and shaping (i.e., finalizing the desired cohort to admit and recruit to enroll) all occur simultaneously throughout the year.

Within this context of overlapping workflows and time scarcity, the majority of participants talked about a "training day" or a retreat lasting three days to one week, with new staff spending additional time learning how to read and evaluate applications. This training included how to understand and evaluate myriad data points ranging from the transcript (curriculum, course rigor, and grades), test scores, recommendation letters, essays, and cocurricular activities. In preparation for "reading season," offices often began training staff by reviewing the prior year's admissions cycle goals and outcomes as well as learning about updated institutional priorities. Additionally, the training for "reading season" focused mainly on how to review the applications to determine whether or not applicants met the admissions requirements and were a good "fit" for their specific institution. They worked on how to read and evaluate application files using the office's rubric in a constituent relationship management (CRM) online platform, such as Slate.

Generally, this training for reading season occurs in the early fall, as the offices begin receiving applications. As one participant explained:

> We do a reader training that looks different every year depending on
> who's new and who's not. [For new staff] our calibration was to this

institution. And then for the following two years, we had the same staff, so reader training was updates, refreshing, that stuff. There's opportunity to make [training] more robust, but I will also say it's always a time factor. Early decision is helpful because it's a little slower paced. It's a smaller pool. Regular decision just sneaks up on you and all of a sudden, you're ahead one day, behind the next and you didn't even realize.

Like many others, this interview participant expressed that lack of time made it difficult to design and implement more robust training, beyond how to read and identify files that align with institutional priorities. Moreover, as this quote illustrates, training to identify desired characteristics among applicants (e.g., leadership, persistence, curiosity, etc.) calibrated readers to applicants in early admission stages including Early Decision (ED), Early Action (EA), student athlete applicant files. We suspect that admission reader norms are generally established each year through calibration activities aimed at matching institutional priorities with an overwhelmingly majority white and wealthy applicant pool each year, for past research has demonstrated that these populations are generally whiter and richer.[12] As another participant explained, the process of calibrating for "fit" between an applicant and institution, through training and ED/EA season, was:

A little bit of a self-perpetuating culture. If we were really unsure of a student's fit, we would get a perspective of a current student, "Could you see this person living in your dorm? Could you see this person in your classroom? Could you see this person hanging out with anybody that you know on campus and being a productive member of the community here?" And that was always really helpful when we were unsure and wanted to get that student perspective to bring back to the committee and consider in the selection process.

Consequently, it is possible that this practice norms characteristics of whiteness and wealth as central to determining the "fit" of a student, placing different students at a disadvantage. We might be less troubled if we knew that office staff engaged in meaningfully designed professional development and training that integrated deep learning about evaluation practices to be mindful of racial diversity. Due to a lack of time, some offices did not offer training to address diversity and equity, as one participant shared: "We have not done a formalized implicit bias training. Training is not our strong point here, and we know it. . . . When I first started here almost everyone here had been here for a gazillion years, and they were basically like, 'I don't know. Figure it out,' and I did."

Preparation for "reading season" did not often offer learning and guidance on how to evaluate applications for the consideration of intersectional racial diversity—myriad ways learning dispositions and characteristics (e.g., curiosity, persistence, etc.) might show up in different students. For example, one participant shared, "in my first year, all we did was all go around in a circle and say what we liked and didn't like. And that was it. And that was like, shouldn't we be talking about what we should be doing in spite of these things, instead of just having a general conversation."

Like others, this professional pointed out how few intentional engagements about diversity and bias were in their offices. Some participants shared that their offices would invite staff from cross-cultural centers on campus or faculty to engage in one-hour programs once a year with their staff about different population demographics. In general, these learning programs were not as important as training days and retreats focused on reading in CRMs.

Some shared concerns over the lack of intentional teaching and learning in their office about admissions work and diversity. According to one participant,

for so many admissions officers, they don't understand the significance or the importance of what they're doing. Because in their mind, they're just trying to get through it. They're trying to get through the files. They're not always necessarily being trained to think about the individual behind that application that they're reading or the context in which they're coming from. And so, if there was a way for them to be able to see that before they're just talked to about context, I think that would make the process a lot easier.

Admissions staff were often prompted to consider the "context" of education and opportunities each applicant had access to.

"Context" was the key construct to understanding diversity of race, ethnicity, class, and other social identities among applicants. As social scientists, we wondered whether and how admissions personnel were learning to review and evaluate applicant files for social identity contexts, even at a cursory level. None of the interview participants discussed their approaches to considering diverse contexts and how they learned to do this in their offices.

Across interviews, participants expressed personal values for diversity and equity. Many also asserted that their institutions shared these commitments. However, these values and commitments did not seem central in their experiences with professional development and training activities. If resource allocations, including time and effort, represent investments in values, the technical practice of reading in a CRM to identify "fit" between applicants and the institution was the most important institutional commitment. What could explain this incongruence between expressed principles and resource allocation? One explanation is the political culture of fear over possible litigation.

"Not touching it with a ten-foot pole": Fear of Litigation

Through many of our interviews, participants expressed how ongoing litigation was affecting their work. For example, one participant shared:

I think with a change in leadership and in the context of the current case in the news, there actually was a shift. We can say that we still have these same [institutional] priorities and ways of approaching

the applicants, but less of it should be on paper in terms of not necessarily getting pretty specific instructions to not refer to students
on race or ethnicity in our write-ups about them unless it was something that really made sense in terms of describing how they wrote
about it in their own essays.

All documents (e.g., training documents and materials), emails, and data
analyses, among other texts and artifacts, can create paper trails that can
be deposed in lawsuits. A fear of litigation has caused many institutions
to be wary of how they even discussed race. For example, when asked
whether training about race went beyond learning about "test score gaps
or just racial disparities in testing," one participant shook their head "no,"
and explained:

> It's really like, ad hoc conversations. . . . [T]his is my passion, so I will
> have conversations with people about it. But there has never really
> been like, a, you know, conversation, institutionally, where we are
> getting, we are being told like, you know, "This is a priority because,
> X, Y, Z," you know. It's kind of more just like, "This is why I think
> they do it, but I don't know." I think that at my previous institution,
> because of you know, specific circumstances to the university where
> there needed to be conversations about race-conscious admissions,
> it was talked about a little bit more. But only within the context of
> legal [parameters].

According to this person, there were few to no intentionally designed
learning opportunities to understand how race and racism are part of
students' educational and socioeconomic contexts. Without intentional
learning, staff were left to figure out for themselves why and how race
should be considered as one of many factors in the review process, in
accordance with federal case law. Another participant explained:

> I think a lot of schools don't do anything around implicit bias train-
> ing or cultural understanding whatsoever. Even at this conference

I was at, they asked us to do a session . . . and they called it the Sensitivity Training. And I was like, "How about we start with not calling
it Sensitivity Training? Because that insinuates that you have to get
on the defensive about something." So we changed it. Participants
walked away being like, "That really helped me because we don't have
these conversations in my office and I've already had challenges and
now it makes me feel better that I'm not just living on an island by
myself." But I think many offices are just like, "Not touching that."
Especially if they're public institutions. Many of them are like, "Not
touching it with a ten-foot pole."

As this participant explained, admissions offices seem fearful of engaging in intentional professional development programs in their offices,
especially if they are at public institutions, because of the threat of
litigation.

Lawsuits like *SFFA v. Harvard*, *SFFA v. Yale*, *SFFA v. UNC-Chapel Hill*,
SFFA v. UT Austin, in addition to federal investigations pursued by the
Trump Department of Justice, have created a chilling effect in the political climate for admissions organizations and their work routines. Some
research has found that within this political climate and social context
hundreds of colleges and universities have ended considerations of race
in limited and legal ways in their admissions processes.[13] The chilling
effect, likely amplified by the increasingly hostile environment for teaching and learning about race and racism, as seen with the backlash against
Critical Race Theory in 2021, may prevent some offices from designing
and implementing professional development programs to help admissions personnel learn about how race and racism are embedded in social
contexts that shape their organizational activities in relation to prospective students.

Although we are not legal experts, we do not believe that current federal case law should be interpreted to mean that learning about race in
the context of college access and admissions work should be limited in

any way. On the contrary, Justice Kennedy's ruling in *Fisher v. UT Austin* (2016) suggests that assessments of campus environments using qualitative and quantitative data are necessary to justify the consideration of race as one of many factors through holistic review. Therefore, much more can be done to intentionally design and implement professional development programs for admissions office staff to understand how race and racism are related to their work and daily routines.

RECOMMENDATIONS: MOVING TOWARD AN EQUITY CENTERED PRACTICE

What does it mean to value and commit to equity in admissions work? Through our interview study of fifty admissions professionals, we found few had experienced professional development or previous educational training, in college or graduate school, to help them engage deeply in research and theories about race, intersectional racism, education, and college access. Yet, all of these are key concepts in assessing student contexts in holistic admissions.

In this chapter, we identified two key barriers to professional development and organizational learning that centered equity and diversity. First, there is a time crunch in admissions work that many expressed as a core challenge. Participants seemed to view equity and diversity as an additional task, rather than as institutional values to be operationalized and integrated into daily organizational routines. Second, fears of litigation and political hostilities targeting diversity and equity efforts have led some admissions leaders to avoid these topics. Therefore, many expressed deep individual and institutional commitments to these values and a reluctance to engage and operationalize them in their work. Paradoxically, such an avoidance of dialogue, learning, and training related to best practices and legal frameworks for race-conscious admissions work can undermine institutional goals for diversity and facilitating its educational benefits.

This leads to our first of four recommendations. Work with organizations like the EdCounsel or the Lawyers' Committee for Civil Rights Under Law, in conjunction with university or college counsel, to learn what is and is not allowable under current federal and state case law. In our conversations with legal experts in this area, we believe that misinterpretations of what is and is not legal are rather common. In addition to Judge Burroughs's ponderings about diversity training, the 2016 Supreme Court ruling in Fisher points to the importance of both qualitative and quantitative evidence to identify whether a campus needs to continue considering race as one of many factors to advance diversity and its educational benefits. Working with legal experts who are also immersed in admissions work can help with implementing robust practices that are within the bounds of legal parameters. Staff need to learn about the evidentiary basis for race-conscious holistic admissions, possibilities in its practice, and how diversity is necessary to advance the educational mission of their postsecondary institution.

Second, professional development and training should focus on concepts of intersectional racial diversity and educational context and help staff understand admissions as evaluation work. As Posselt and colleagues[14] pointed out, "The backgrounds, training—or more pointedly, lack thereof, and work of faculty and others tasked with admissions decisions each impact evaluation and selection processes and, by extension, the outcome." Because most admissions professionals do not enter the field with advanced or specialized training, they need to learn necessary skills on the job. It isn't enough to value diversity and equity. Specifically, admissions professionals need to learn about how social dynamics, including intersectional racism, shape unequal K–12 pathways to college—the student contexts that are so central to holistic admissions. Such skills need to be integrated into how staff review and score files in their CRM systems. Admissions staff should develop and apply inquiry skills, guided by a framework of intersectionality, like how research scholars learn to apply conceptual frameworks to their research projects.

In admissions work, institutional priorities constitute the framework for evaluation and decision-making. If diversity and equity are truly institutional priorities, they should be included as a lens for evaluation and decision-making aligned with legal bounds. In training, staff should be continuously learning and integrating relevant research and theories into their work.

Relatedly, the hiring, training, and promotion of admissions professionals should center skill sets needed in the work of admissions offices beyond sales and marketing aptitude, including investigative data analysis, assessment, evaluation, all through a lens of equity and diversity. Although many professionals expressed that they cared about diversity and equity, it often seemed like there was a line between learning to evaluate files and these values, especially given how little attention professional development and trainings centered these notions. These offices should dismantle this line. If the campus cross-cultural center or a faculty member is invited to share about their expertise on intersectional inequalities in college access and campus climate, how is what staff are learning going to inform their work and daily routines of reading, recruiting, shaping a class? How is the design of learning in the office encouraging a process of sensemaking for deep change? Sensemaking is a collective or shared process of learning among people that allows individuals to wrestle with new information or organizational change and to adapt their work routines.[15] Sensemaking helps individuals and organizations navigate through uncertainty and ambiguity. Too often, it seemed that if an office engaged in learning about diverse communities and students, there was little to suggest there was an accompanying process of conscious and purposeful sensemaking and organizational change. Without organizational review and change in routines, staff can default into dominant norms that reproduce inequities.

An incorporation of sensemaking begins with an intentional space for individuals and teams to engage in necessary self-reflection and organizational reflection, to identify and plan for change for more equitable processes. Some key methods include scheduling ongoing and widespread organizational evaluative conversations that extend and apply a one-day or one-hour diversity training to interrogate organizational routines. It is not enough to have training at the beginning of the admissions cycle and then expect admissions officers to have a solid understanding of equitable practices and how to properly implement these practices when reviewing applications. Unless learnings are applied systemically, change will be hard to achieve. Because systems thinking to interrogate and change organizational routines can trigger individual guilt, individuals that make up an office may need to process through emotions of culpability. In unlearning and learning how systems reproduce inequalities, some will react in ways that defend organizational practices under scrutiny from change.

Fourth, because professional development and trainings—no matter how well designed—are limited in their effectiveness, we encourage admissions organizations to engage in a practice of equity checks[16] as an approach to regular systems review for change. The social contexts of admissions, which is a place of high stakes decision-making in postsecondary institutions, need to be regularly reviewed with available data. When asked whether there were routine checks for biases in the evaluation of application files, many shared that they trusted that the collegial nature of their offices or having senior staff read with or after junior staff was enough to ensure against biases. They did not seem concerned that perhaps junior staff might not feel empowered to raise concerns or that routines led by senior staff might be the very things reproducing inequities.

Only a handful of participants shared that their offices had used data analytics to check for outliers in the reading and scoring of files. When we met with a group of admissions professionals to present and discuss preliminary findings, and asked why data checks were so rare, the consensus was that it would create a paper trail that could be subpoenaed if their institution were to face a legal complaint from a disappointed student denied admission. Paradoxically, as we have pointed out, this avoidance of data analysis can allow for the reproduction of inequities as well as leave open the door to litigation.

In addition to recommendations to practitioners, we want to end by encouraging research scholar colleagues to consider engaging in research-practice partnerships with admissions professionals and organizations. Fellow scholars have often asked us how we were able to collect so many interviews with admissions professionals. Quite simply, many of us have been in dialogue with admissions leaders and present at various practitioner conferences for many years. Some of us are scholar-practitioners who are both admissions leaders and past admissions practitioners. We are in relationship and dialogue with professionals in the field, and have learned that many admissions practitioners want to do better and change their systems of work and the field of admissions. We encourage more researchers to recognize how scholarly inquiries can be strengthened for pragmatic impact if we engage in more critical understanding of how admissions work from those who are in the field.

Admissions professionals play a critical role in shaping institutions of higher education and organizational leaders have a responsibility to support the work of their staff. The admissions profession employs many who believe in the power of higher education to transform lives and express deep commitments to values of diversity and equity. Yet there is little evidence of ongoing and robust professional development and training to help them translate and effectively operationalize these values. Fear of litigation and political backlash should not hinder the field from learning and imagining new ways to improve admissions systems.

PART III

Considering New Models for Admissions Practice and Research

Flipping a Coin for Equity: The Potential of Lotteries for Selective College Admissions

DOMINIQUE J. BAKER, MICHAEL N. BASTEDO, AND AMANDA ADDISON

EVERY SPRING, SELECTIVE COLLEGES INFORM the majority of their applicants that they were denied admission to their university. With admittance rates for the most selective schools hovering in the single digits, receiving a positive decision may feel akin to winning the lottery. There are several well-noted economic and social benefits to attending more selective institutions, including increased salaries, access to top graduate schools, and better job prospects.[1] This is especially true for students with fewer economic resources or racial groups underrepresented within higher education generally and more selective higher education specifically.[2]

On the surface, the admissions game appears to be one that rewards individual merit and success. Admitted students are often congratulated for their hard work, intellectual valor, and extracurricular accomplishments. However, researchers have noted that the playing field is not equal. Admitted students are overwhelmingly white, wealthy, and well-connected. Critics blame the admissions process for maintaining the status quo, by being intentionally opaque, inequitable, and in recent years, open to abuse through the bribing of college officials. To address these issues, many critics offer a "radical" but simple alternative—an admissions process conducted by lottery. In this chapter, we will present arguments for and against admissions lotteries, discuss the previous research, and describe the results of a new study that examines the potential impact of admissions lotteries on institutional diversity.

Admissions lotteries have been proffered many times over the years as a solution to the inherent issues of highly selective admissions. Each time the idea is proposed, however, it is presented as a ground-breaking solution to a longstanding problem. For example, New America, a Washington, D.C. think tank, put forth a "radical" proposal in 2019 to conduct a lottery for college admissions that would be more democratic than holistic review, eliminate legacy and athletic preferences, and ensure "colleges and universities increase social mobility."[3] The design of the lottery is very unclear—selective colleges would be required to participate in a "lottery-based admissions system" with a minimum requirement for SAT or ACT scores to enter. New America goes as far as suggesting that the federal government withdraw all funding—including financial aid and research dollars—from institutions that refuse to participate. National Public Radio described this proposal and others like it as "out-of-the-box ideas" that could shake up admissions to elite institutions and hiring practices at the corporate level.[4]

But the concept of an admissions lottery is neither new nor novel. As early as the 1960s, scholars proposed lotteries as a way to combat rising competition for limited spots at elite schools. In 1964, political philosopher Robert Paul Wolff offered a scathing critique of the admissions "rat-race" in the journal Dissent.[5] He argued that selective colleges, namely those in the Ivy League, should admit students via a lottery. By randomly assigning students who met a minimum academic threshold, institutions and students could focus on teaching and genuine intellectual inquiry. Otherwise, Wolff feared rising competition for spots would cause students to become conformists who cared more about grades than learning for its own sake.[6] In 1969, education researcher Alexander Astin recommended a lottery as a way to expand educational opportunity, particularly for students of color.[7] Neither Wolff nor Astin provided great detail on how a lottery would work.

In fact, college admissions lotteries have been suggested frequently by scholars, policy intermediary organizations, reporters, and others. In the past five years, scholars such as Dalton Conley,[8] Matt Feeney,[9] Fabio Rojas,[10] Barry Schwartz,[11] and Natasha Warikoo[12] have each recommended lotteries. In the policy world, lottery recommendations come from across ideological and partisan spectrums. Lottery advocacy comes from organizations like New America, the left-leaning think tank mentioned previously, and from representatives like Frederick Hess, the education policy director of the right-leaning think tank American Enterprise Institute.[13] Reporters also suggest that lotteries could improve college admissions. For example, Alia Wong, writing in The Atlantic,[14] and Ginia Bellafante, writing in The New York Times,[15] both advocate for the potential benefits of lotteries to improve selective college admissions.

More than fifty years later, lotteries are still being suggested as an alternative to traditional admissions processes. Why is this the case? It is a consistent solution to a set of consistent problems within the realm of highly selective admissions. First is the issue of transparency in the process. For as long as selective schools started seeing thousands more applicants than seats, observers have been perplexed by how institutions go about choosing an incoming class. Many students find the holistic review process, which considers academics, extracurricular activities, and school context, among a host of other student details, to be confusing and anxiety provoking.[16] The competition for spots and uncertainty of whether a student measures up are decades-old problems. A lottery would increase transparency and simplicity because it would, in most designs, publish a clear academic threshold and then rely on simple random chance.

Second, the highly selective admissions process has been accused of maintaining the status quo, rather than increasing diversity in higher education. As evidenced by Astin's treatise on selective admissions in the 1960s, racial and class bias have been long-held concerns.[17] The admissions process is often accused of protecting privilege, by over-representing white students and giving preference to students with family connections to the university. Princeton sociologist Dalton Conley argues "a lottery would single-handedly end debates over affirmative action, legacy admission, and preference for student-athletes."[18] Proponents state that a simple lottery could make the process fairer and more transparent, as well as increase diversity. To address concerns that students would not have to be particularly good but just lucky,[19] some suggest a weighted lottery that preferences those with higher grades could be used to offset any concerns over the academic reputation of an institution being negatively impacted by a lottery.[20] While proponents argue that lotteries address these two long-term issues within college admissions hypothetically, few researchers have explored the feasibility of a lottery in practice.

WHAT DO WE KNOW ABOUT ADMISSIONS LOTTERIES?

Is there any evidence that a lottery would produce more fair and equitable outcomes from college admissions? The answers depend on if we analyze what happens in theory or practice. In practice, lotteries have had limited use and even fewer instances of success in higher education. Two early examples of lotteries in American institutions, Federal City College in 1969 and the University of Illinois in 1970, did not have success with using a lottery for admissions.[21] As Rebecca Zwick points out, although the Federal City case was deemed difficult to evaluate due to other issues plaguing the college at the time, the University of Illinois case was a clear failure. After rejecting over 800 qualified candidates through the lottery, the institution was met with a public outcry for not admitting what critics felt were the best students in the state. The chancellor swiftly reversed the decision and admitted those they previously rejected. Around the same time period, the admissions lottery process for medical school in the Netherlands was criticized for being "immoral" and letting students' fate be decided "by a game of chance."[22] The lottery was eliminated after further public outcry over a highly qualified candidate who was rejected three times.

There have been limited studies on lotteries in selective higher education settings in the United States, and what we know is based on simulations of what would happen if lotteries were implemented using historical data. Carnevale and Rose explored the effect of eliminating affirmative action by simulating five different "race-neutral" admissions schemes, one of which included a lottery.[23] In their study, they analyzed data from two longitudinal studies from the US Department of Education (ED), focusing on 146 of the most selective colleges in the United States from 1979 to 2000. For the lottery simulation, they set a minimum academic threshold of an SAT score of at least 900 (math and verbal combined). This cutoff was somewhat arbitrary, but the authors explained that it was chosen because it is a close approximation to what the NCAA sets for student athletes.

Proponents of lotteries for the purposes of increasing diversity may take pause at the findings. Carnevale and Rose's simulation showed that the share of Black and Latinx students declined in the lottery, though socioeconomic diversity substantially increased.[24] In terms of academic readiness of the pool, they posited that college performance would suffer, predicting that a minimum bar of a 900 on the SAT would cause college graduation rates to decline. A simple solution could be to increase the SAT cutoff (which on its face could be considered "race neutral" but would have racial implications), but how would an institution decide the threshold and what component (grades, test scores) to use? Furthermore, setting minimum academic qualifications would undermine one of the goals of holistic admission, namely to evaluate all students based on many factors considered in context,[25] and place more emphasis on testing, possibly creating more stress for students who will focus even more on achieving certain scores for admission.

In a similar study, Rebecca Zwick conducted an admission lottery simulation using an SAT test-score threshold of 1000 (math and verbal combined) and a minimum GPA of a 2.8 (B-average).[26] She wanted to see how the demographics of college enrollees in her dataset would differ based on the lottery thresholds. The findings of the lottery simulation did not produce enrollment demographics that were radically different from the traditional methodology. When using just the SAT score as the lottery threshold, the race, gender, and socioeconomic makeups of the actual enrollees and the simulated enrollees were nearly identical. The class composition did see a slight two percentage point increase in Black, Latinx, and Indigenous students when GPA was factored into the threshold. Like Carnevale and Rose, Zwick predicted lower graduation rates of students in the simulation based on the wider range of academic credentials of students in the lottery.[27]

A NEW STUDY

In a recent study, Baker and Bastedo conducted a simulation of an admissions lottery for selective colleges.[28] They found that the type of admissions lotteries generally described by proponents would not, on their own, create more equitable entering classes at selective institutions. The authors used two different nationally representative datasets from ED, one tracking students who first started tenth grade in 2002 and one tracking those who first started ninth grade in 2009. The study was able to use the pool of students who reached twelfth grade as a proxy for individuals who could be eligible for a college admissions lottery.

Both datasets allowed the researchers to explore different academic criteria for lottery eligibility (i.e., college entrance exam scores [SAT/ACT] or high school GPA). We recognize that both college entrance exam scores and high school GPA are the result of years of students' interactions with larger structural forces like racism and sexism. There are real, pernicious disparities in these measures of academic achievement.[29] Still, the majority of proposed college admissions lotteries use one of these measures, so it was necessary to include them in a simulation (see Table 10.1). This created ten groups of lottery-eligible students, those who cleared the threshold for college entrance exams (two groups: above the twenty-fifth percentile of enrollees, above the fiftieth percentile of enrollees), for high school GPA (four groups: above the twenty-fifth percentile of overall GPA; above the fiftieth percentile of overall GPA; above the twenty-fifth percentile of academic, weighted GPA; and above the fiftieth percentile of academic,

TABLE 10.1 **Thresholds of Lottery-Eligible Students**

Eligibility Type	Thresholds Based on Enrollee Data
College entrance exam	25th percentile in SAT units
	50th percentile in SAT units
High school GPA	25th percentile overall GPA
	50th percentile overall GPA
	25th percentile weighted, academic GPA
	50th percentile weighted, academic GPA
Exam & GPA	25th percentile in SAT units & 25th percentile weighted, academic GPA
	25th percentile in SAT units & 50th percentile weighted, academic GPA
	50th percentile in SAT units & 25th percentile weighted, academic GPA
	50th percentile in SAT units & 50th percentile weighted, academic GPA

Source: Dominique J. Baker and Michael N. Bastedo, "What If We Leave It Up to Chance? Admissions Lotteries and Equitable Access at Selective Colleges," *Educational Researcher* 51, no. 2 (2022), 134–45, published online 2 November 2021. https://doi.org/10.3102/0013189X211055494.

weighted GPA), and those who cleared both thresholds (four groups: all combinations of the college entrance exam and academic, weighted GPA). The datasets also allowed students to be followed into college enrollment, providing researchers the opportunity to see who actually enrolled in highly selective institutions (like Harvard University or Stanford University) or selective institutions (which included the highly selective institutions but also included institutions like Grinnell College or the University of Georgia) based on Barron's rankings of admissions competitiveness.

The authors examined the potential impacts of an admissions lottery in two ways. First, following prior simulations of college admissions lotteries, the authors compared the demographics of students in the pools of eligible students for the lottery to the demographics of students who actually enrolled in either selective or highly selective institutions. These demographics included race/ethnicity, gender, parental income, and parental education in addition to other characteristics focused on collegiate financial aid eligibility. Using twenty-fifth percentile overall GPA as an example, the intuition behind this analysis was that randomly selecting the admitted students from all twelfth graders with a GPA of at least 3.21 (the twenty-fifth percentile in the data following ninth graders in 2009) means that the demographics of the randomly selected students would be roughly similar to the pool of students that were drawn from (based on the principles of random selection).

The slight wrinkle in this intuition is that the randomly selected sample from a larger population will have roughly similar characteristics of that larger population only across a large number of repeated samples. Because of that, it is not actually true that a single sample drawn from a larger population will reflect that larger population. For example, if a person holds five playing cards, with four being black and one being red, and randomly selects two of those cards, they would either end up with two black cards or one red and one black card (even though the likelihood of winding up with a red card from a random draw would be quite low). Therefore, even though black cards make up 80 percent of the cards in the total card population, a single randomly selected sample from that population would wind up with black cards representing either 50 percent or 100 percent of the population. But what if we repeatedly draw two random cards? If we did that five times, we might get the following:

1. Black, Red (50 percent black)

2. Black, Black (100 percent black)

3. Black, Black (100 percent black)

4. Red, Black (50 percent black)

5. Black, Black (100 percent black)

If we average across the five random draws, we see that the share of black cards is 80 percent, the same share that was in the population.[30] Therefore, for the intuition behind the first simulation of lottery admissions (used by prior researchers) to be correct, one must look across repeated samples for the characteristics of the samples to approximately reflect the characteristics of the population, though, from sample to sample, the ratio of black to red cards will vary.

Using this math in our context, let's say Stanford University had over 50,000 students apply and 30,000 of those students had a high school GPA that was at least the twenty-fifth percentile in the United States. In that lottery-eligible pool of 30,000 students, 10 percent are Black. Stanford randomly samples 1,200 of those students to be admitted for the fall of 2021. There is no guarantee that Black students would be 10 percent of the single, 1,200 person sample. Since the theory behind random selection requires repeated samples, while a single year would not have 10 percent of students be Black, looking across 100 years of the 1,200 student random samples would reflect that 10 percent. Therefore, Baker and Bastedo, in their second simulation analysis, randomly sampled students from the pool of lottery-eligible students 1,000 times in order to explore the variation in student demographics across individual samples (akin to the variation in demographics from admission cycle to admission cycle).

Simple admissions lotteries, on their own, were not able to increase the diversity of the entering class of students. When looking at the simple comparison of the demographics of the lottery-eligible pool and the students who enrolled at either highly selective or selective institutions (analysis #1), students of color were underrepresented in all lotteries, low-income students were either underrepresented or did not increase, and men were underrepresented in GPA lotteries. Turning to the exploration of repeated samples (analysis #2), the authors found similar outcomes. In fact, the variation was wide enough that in several years an admissions lottery would likely yield only 1–2 percent of admitted students being Black or Latinx (especially in lotteries including college entrance exams as a minimum bar).

The authors also explored if stratifying the sampling, randomly drawing a certain number of students from within categories, would help admissions lotteries to increase the diversity of the entering class. While Baker and Bastedo were unable to explore racial stratification (due to data limitations), they were able to explore gender and income. When stratifying by gender, there was no clear evidence of a shift in the race or income of entering students. When stratifying by income, the study found better income representation but no shift in the race of entering students, echoing prior research.[31] These explorations further demonstrate that the best admissions practices for increasing racial or income diversity likely must incorporate race or income, respectively.

IMPLICATIONS FOR POLICYMAKERS AND PRACTITIONERS

Admissions lotteries would produce the simplicity and transparency that many higher education observers crave from a system that is highly complex and tends to reproduce social and educational inequality. Unfortunately, admissions lotteries with minimum bars for grades and test scores simply do not produce more equitable outcomes than current practices. Minimum bars for grade-point averages, weighed or unweighted, substantially reduce the proportion of men—in some simulations, the proportion of men reduces to almost one-third of the class. The proportions of low-income students either fall or remain relatively stable. Minimum bars for standardized tests substantially reduce the proportion of students of color; in our simulations, the proportion of Black and Latinx students falls to 1–4 percent of the incoming class.

These would be devastating changes to the diversity of our selective colleges and universities. Why do we not see the increases in race and class diversity that many advocates would expect? In our view, this is essentially a cognitive and statistical bias. When you imagine the beneficiary of a lottery, you might imagine a low-income student, or a disadvantaged student of color, who is dissuaded from applying or who just barely misses the criteria for admission at a selective college. What is rarely imagined is the large number of wealthier, overrepresented students who would also be attracted to a lottery and have similar educational credentials. You could imagine that these students could easily pour applications into a lottery, far overwhelming the number of underrepresented students with the same qualifications.

Unfortunately, we believe many also simply misunderstand the true depth of educational inequality and stratification in secondary education by both race and social class. Low-income students and students of color are massively overrepresented among students with low standardized test scores, such that even minimum bars for SAT or ACT scores exclude them from consideration. To compensate, underrepresented students above the bar—and there are many of them[32]—would have to participate in lotteries far above the average for other students. Unfortunately, there is no reason to believe this would occur—wealthier students would, as they always have, have better information, resources, belief, and motivation to participate in potential lotteries. A student from a wealthier family may see a lottery as an equal chance to attend, while a low-income student might well see a university that remains wealthy, exclusive, and has a very high sticker price that they cannot possibly afford to pay.

Without underrepresented students participating in lotteries at substantially higher rates, the only other option to increase equity in the entering class would be lotteries within certain groups of students, often referred to as stratified random sampling. As the study from Baker and Bastedo shows, lotteries that explicitly incorporate income do appear to shift the economic diversity of the entering class. While the authors could not test whether the same is true for race due to data limitations, it is unlikely that an admissions lottery could be conducted within racial groups, due to standing legal precedents banning quotas in college admissions.

Many observers may also fail to realize the very substantial differences in high school achievement between young men and women. A recent meta-analysis of grade differences shows girls having about 6.3 percent higher grades than boys in high school, with a gap of 3.1 percent in STEM courses.[33] Because college admissions is a winner-take-all scenario where marginal differences in credentials can make an enormous difference, this has very substantial implications for any GPA-based lottery. Given that women remain underrepresented at the most selective colleges despite those strong grades,[34] some may not bemoan these results. However, it is unlikely that institutions will be eager to institute lotteries that create such stark gender disparities, as institutions frequently argue that students of any gender may be less attracted to their campuses.[35]

It has been suggested that one potential solution is to use holistic review as a first read on applications, and then use a lottery thereafter to determine who will actually be admitted. This has some appeal, as it maintains the use of holistic practices while also avoiding the "distinctions without a difference" that so many find frustrating about selective college admissions. However, the main benefits of a lottery are simplicity and transparency, both of which will be eliminated by the use of holistic practices in the "first cut." And for those who long for admissions policies that avoid litigation—like *Fisher v. University of Texas, Students for Fair Admissions v. Harvard*, and the like—the opportunities for these court battles will remain if the subjective nature of holistic admissions is retained.

We also need to consider why lotteries may be so unappealing from an institutional perspective. The public often views admissions as serving only one purpose—to select a new incoming class for the university. But it serves many other purposes as well, including communicating institutional values and priorities, socializing students to the new campus, and starting a lifelong relationship between the student and their alma mater. Institutions argue that this lifelong relationship is crucial to maintain student commitment and dedication to the university, and not least of all, for the development potential of students after graduation. Admission to a selective college is a source of joy and connection, a moment of exultation for students and the impetus of countless YouTube videos of positive admissions decisions. Through holistic admission, the university is sending a clear message: "We want you." Now imagine the alternative result of an admission lottery—the message is not "we want you," but "you have been admitted." How different will the connection between students and institutions become when students are admitted by a faceless lottery? That is a scenario that few institutions who depend upon the goodwill of their graduates are eager to face, above and beyond the inevitable furor from the American public that would result.

The desire for admissions lotteries is driven by good faith motives to improve and simplify the college admissions process. However, we must consider the real-world impacts of these potential policies on student equity and diversity, as well as the public, institutional, and legal environments that admissions offices must navigate. Holistic review is the result of political compromises among the many stakeholders to which universities must adapt and respond—demands for fairness, equity, reputation, status, resources, and legality. Until these environmental factors shift, we are more likely to see change and adaptation of existing holistic review practices rather than the adoption of lotteries or other externally mandated admissions practices.

CHAPTER 11

Direct Admissions: Proactively Pushing Students into College

JENNIFER A. DELANEY AND TAYLOR K. ODLE

What stands in the way of going to college? Cost and confusion.
—Chuck Staben, Former President, University of Idaho

In an unprecedented move, the state of Idaho decided to automatically admit all high school graduates to its public universities. Enrollment rose.
—Kasia Kovacs, *Inside Higher Ed*

REIMAGINING THE COLLEGE ADMISSIONS PROCESS

College access in the United States is best characterized as an "unequal opportunity," where wide gaps in college enrollment and attainment by income, race, and geography have persisted for much of the twenty-first century.[1] One important barrier to equitable college access by race, income, and geography is the college search, application, and admissions process. Indeed, evidence suggests that the current "traditional" admissions system increases equity gaps.[2] To explore postsecondary options and apply to college, students face a gauntlet of unclear and uneven information, multiple steps toward preparation, postsecondary institutions with varying application and admission requirements, and administrative hurdles—all of which rely heavily upon social and cultural capital.[3] Conceptually, a simplification of this process benefits students by removing barriers to college search and choice, and previous interventions seeking to reduce these "frictions" have been shown to increase the likelihood of college application and enrollment.[4] Such policies that eliminate barriers to access and increase equity in the college admission process are likely to be transformational for underserved student populations, especially those who are low-income, students of color, first generation, former foster youth, and from rural areas.

Reducing persistent inequalities in college access by income, race, and geography would benefit from systemic change in the policies and practices surrounding college admissions. Simplifying the college search by eliminating the need for students to apply to college altogether has the potential to be more effective and equitable than the traditional admissions system. Such a strategy could level the college admissions playing field and eliminate the need for students to have extensive financial, social, and cultural capital to access college. This holds great potential for reducing inequalities in college admissions and in subsequent educational attainment.

This chapter explores one promising policy that eliminates the need to apply for college: direct admissions (DA). DA sidesteps the typical college admissions process. Students are proactively guaranteed a place in college based on existing student-level data, which typically includes high school GPAs and standardized test scores. In this chapter, we consider both state- and institution-level DA systems. Typically, for state-level programs, all students in a state are admitted to all open-access institutions, and students who surpass a preidentified threshold based on high school academic performance (as measured by high school GPA, ACT/SAT, class rank, or a combination of measures) are also automatically admitted to selective institutions. Institution-level programs work similarly but tend to be more localized, with each institution setting their own academic performance threshold and students being admitted on a campus-by-campus basis. For both systems, students, parents, and high schools (principals, counselors, etc.) receive letters indicating a student has been automatically admitted to a set of institutions and outlining steps for how students can "claim their place" in college.

In 2015, Idaho developed the nation's first state-level DA program, admitting all high school graduates to its public postsecondary institutions. With its DA policy, Idaho reversed declining postsecondary enrollments and out-of-state migration. The state reported descriptive increases of 3.1 percent in overall enrollment and a 3-percentage-point decrease in the number of students leaving Idaho for college.[5] Given the high-yield, low-cost potential of DA, this practice has already begun to spread to new states and through new providers. With the high school class of 2018, South Dakota began their own DA system, which they call "proactive admissions."[6] Furthermore, the Illinois General Assembly passed a 2019 law that developed a pilot program to automatically admit high-performing high school graduates to targeted public institutions beginning in 2020–21; Connecticut's governor proposed an automatic admissions system for four of the state's public universities; and the Minnesota legislature has moved forward on similar legislation.[7]

PRINCIPLES OF DIRECT ADMISSIONS

While there is variance in the exact design of DA systems, there are seven important principles that, in combination, distinguish DA from other types of policy interventions targeted at reforming college admissions practices. Each of these principles in a DA system should reduce inequities in the college search process and increase college going.

1. **Proactive.** DA is proactive in not requiring students to search for colleges but instead pushes information to students at a time when they are considering post–high school opportunities. Functionally, DA draws upon behavioral economic principles to reduce search

costs and the amount of financial, social, and cultural capital needed to apply to college while also providing students with college-going signals.[8]

2. **Guaranteed.** DA systems provide guaranteed admission to students. This guarantee is more valuable than informational campaigns targeted at increasing college enrollment. It also reduces risks for students in the college search process.

3. **Universal.** DA systems provide a guaranteed admissions place for all students exiting high school. Having open-access institutions available does not appear to be enough to resolve all of the problems with high-school-to-college transitions or advance equity in admissions. A universal policy, combined with the other principles of a DA system, should increase access for all students, not only high-achieving students. All students benefit from being proactively sent information and guaranteed admissions offers to have certainty, in a personalized way, about which postsecondary options exist for them.

4. **Transparent.** DA offers clear information about admissibility at an institution by providing students with a guaranteed spot. No longer do students need to guess if their credentials will get them into a particular institution.

5. **Simple and personalized.** DA systems offer straightforward and clear communication about college admissions in a personalized way. For some students, DA systems will open more and higher quality postsecondary opportunities, which, on average, can result in attending institutions with higher per-student spending and graduation rates.

6. **Low-cost.** DA relies on existing data, so it is a low-cost policy option for states or institutions to increase college enrollment. Especially when compared to traditional institutional admissions practices of admissions office recruiting activities, high school visits, college fairs, labor intensive reading and evaluating applications, or tuition discounting, DA is low-cost. Likewise, when compared to other

interventions that seek to increase college access and equity (such as mentoring programs, traditional grant-aid programs, wrap-around services, etc.), DA is an exceptionally low-cost policy.

7. **Involves trusted adults.** DA notifications are sent to students, parents, and high schools. In this way, trusted adults both inside and outside the family also receive DA information.

Building upon these seven principles, DA holds potential to reduce equity gaps; alleviate potential access gaps for vulnerable (first generation, students of color, former foster youth, etc.), rural, and urban populations; and eliminate the need for extensive financial, social, and cultural capital to navigate the college application process. State-level DA systems only require an existing state longitudinal data system (SLDS) to connect students' K–12 records with colleges. Likewise, institution-level programs only need a data sharing agreement in place between K–12 partners and postsecondary institutions—or can use a national data source of student high school information, like the Common App, to operate a DA system.[9]

In all, DA is a promising reimagining of the college admissions process with the potential to improve access and equity for underserved student populations. In what follows, we describe the operation of DA in Idaho, South Dakota, and through the Common App, including additional details on each program's design and administration. Next, we discuss descriptive and causal impacts of our research on DA in Idaho, including outcomes for students, institutions, and states. We then provide key insights for policymakers and practitioners, including key design features to keep in mind when developing a DA system, as well as complementary policies that prior works have shown can also be used to increase college access and success. We conclude with a discussion of the potential for DA to reimagine the college application and admissions process, as well as its potential to improve equity across all points along the postsecondary education pipeline by proactively affording students—regardless of income, race, or location—with an opportunity to earn a college degree.

THE DETAILS: DIRECT ADMISSIONS IN PRACTICE

In this section, we discuss the details of the state-level DA systems in Idaho and South Dakota, as well as an institution-level pilot program run by the Common App. We also provide thoughts on how well each system meets the principles of DA as outlined above.

Idaho

In fall 2015, Idaho adopted the nation's first DA policy, whereby all high school graduates (beginning with the fall 2016 cohort) were admitted to a set of the state's public community colleges and universities derived from a predefined academic threshold based on a combination of a student's high school GPA and standardized test scores.[10] To achieve this aim, the DA system supports five primary objectives: (1) promote a college-going culture; (2) connect students, families, and K–12 schools with colleges early in the college-choice process; (3) ease the transition from high school to college; (4) signal postsecondary opportunities to high school students; and (5) reverse consistent enrollment declines at the state's public institutions.[11] While DA practices have been replicated elsewhere, the design of Idaho's system serves as a model program for other states.[12]

A number of key features of Idaho's public education sector facilitated the creation and operation of a DA system and made the state an ideal place for DA to develop. Idaho has a centralized governance structure, with the Office of the State Board of Education (OSBE) overseeing K–12 (Idaho Department of Education) and postsecondary operations, which includes four public community colleges and four universities. Two other important pre-existing structures facilitated Idaho's adoption of DA: universal SAT testing in high school and an SLDS. The state funds universal SAT testing for high school students as a graduation requirement. The state also operates a robust SLDS system called the Education Analytics System of Idaho (EASI). It spans the K–12 system, includes preschool and college records, and tracks individuals into the workforce by combining data from K–12 and postsecondary sectors, and the Idaho Department of Labor.[13] Because of Idaho's centralized education governance structure in OSBE, data sharing agreements between K–12 schools and postsecondary institutions were not required. One state agency held access to all of the elements of the predefined DA academic threshold (students' high school transcripts, ACT/SAT scores, and GPA), and had the authority to share that information with its own postsecondary arm to grant students admission to college. In addition, politically, it was important that the state's DA policy was championed by the President of the University of Idaho, the state's flagship and most selective institution.[14] All of these elements combined to allow for a seamless introduction of the DA policy.

Using data from EASI, DA proactively admits all high school graduates to in-state public community colleges or universities. In the design of its system, Idaho currently uses a common application, fee-free applications, and DA. Institutions agreed on a common threshold (based upon students' SAT/ACT score, unweighted GPA, and high school course credits at the end of their junior year), creating two groups of institutions where students can be admitted.[15] Students who surpass the threshold are guaranteed admission to all public institutions in the state. Other students are guaranteed admission to all open-access institutions in the state. Students are either admitted to all Group 8 institutions—the eight state institutions, including the selective Boise State University, Idaho State University, and University of Idaho—or to the remaining Group 6 institutions (College of Eastern Idaho, College of Southern Idaho, College of Western Idaho, Lewis-Clark State College, and North Idaho College, plus Idaho State University's College of Technology. Figure 11.1 exhibits this process and details admission by institutional group. Admission to an institution is contingent upon high school graduation (proof of graduation) and does not guarantee admission into a specific program or to competitive majors (e.g., nursing).

FIGURE 11.1 The Direct Admissions Process in Idaho

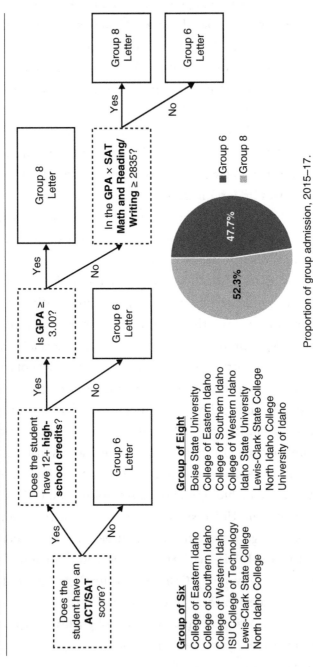

Proportion of group admission, 2015–17.

Group of Six
College of Eastern Idaho
College of Southern Idaho
College of Western Idaho
ISU College of Technology
Lewis–Clark State College
North Idaho College

Group of Eight
Boise State University
College of Eastern Idaho
College of Southern Idaho
College of Western Idaho
Idaho State University
Lewis–Clark State College
North Idaho College
University of Idaho

Idaho's DA system is proactive, transparent, simple, personalized, and involves trusted adults. In the fall of their senior year, students and parents receive a letter informing them of their admission, including information on how to apply and enroll in the college of their choice.[16] High schools also receive a list of all students who have been guaranteed admission through DA. Students applying after fall 2017 use Idaho's fee-free common application to apply to all in-state public institutions (plus two private, nonprofit institutions) via a single application called Apply Idaho.[17] This application is administrative in nature and allows students to select their institution and major but does not determine admission. Students must "claim their spot" as part of the DA system by June 30 of their senior year; failure to meet this deadline will revert students to the traditional admissions system.[18] Along with the admissions process, students are encouraged to apply for the Idaho Opportunity Scholarship and complete the Free Application for Federal Student Aid (FAFSA). Over 116,720 students in Idaho have been admitted through the DA system to six or more of the state's public colleges and universities since fall 2015.[19]

South Dakota

The DA system in South Dakota is called proactive admissions. Unlike the program in Idaho, the South Dakota program is not universal and only students above a predefined academic threshold are offered college admissions. Students falling below this threshold are not part of the program and must use traditional college admissions practices to apply to college. Each year, the South Dakota Department of Education proactively sends information to high school seniors who have met the criteria for guaranteed general acceptance. These students receive automatic eligibility for admission to any of the six public universities or four technical colleges in South Dakota. The admissions threshold is determined by the Smarter Balanced test (which is universally administered statewide in the eleventh grade) or ACT scores. Students who earn a Level 3 or 4 on the English language arts and math portions of the test or a score of 18 or higher on the ACT are offered guaranteed general acceptance. The South Dakota School of Mines & Technology requires an 18 in English and a 20 in math on the ACT. Once students are proactively admitted, they need to "claim their spot" by completing an application, paying an application fee, and submitting their high school transcripts by December 1 of their senior year of high school. Admission is only guaranteed to an institution since particular programs of study may have more stringent admissions requirements.[20] Proactive admissions was not available in South Dakota beginning in 2020–21 due to the COVID-19 pandemic.

Common App HBCU Pilot

During the 2020–21 academic year, the authors partnered with the Common App to conduct a three-state experiment (randomized controlled trial) on DA. In this pilot program, a consortium of Historically Black Colleges and Universities (HBCUs) in the mid-Atlantic region offered DA to students from their state. Institutions set their own thresholds for admissions using high school GPA and also selected the total number of students they were willing to accept through DA. In total, 3,300 high-achieving students (along with their high school counselors) received DA notifications through this program. All partner institutions provided application fee waivers as part of the DA program. Targeted students were those who, as of March 1, 2021, had a Common App profile but had not yet submitted an application to a college. In this way, the pilot program targeted students who were at risk of not making an immediate transition from high school to college. This pilot was not universal in that it only admitted students above the pre-identified GPA threshold to each institution. Ongoing research will estimate impacts of these proactive admissions offers on students' enrollment outcomes.

Among other innovations, DA is a technical solution for college admissions. With the spread of state longitudinal data systems, many states already have the data infrastructure to implement a DA system. At least

70 percent of states and territories reported having automated infrastructure to link K–12 student data to K–12 teacher data, postsecondary data, Perkins career and technical education data, and early childhood data. Half reported having automated links to workforce data.[21] Likewise, a number of states already have common application systems in place either statewide or for large systems of higher education.[22] Using these existing data systems to build a DA system is possible in many states at a low cost. In terms of informing students about their college admissions, the use of email notifications also reduces the costs of a DA system, making this strategy a low-cost solution for states and institutions.

While a direct admission system may seem like a large departure from the current college application and admissions process, it is important to note that existing practices largely remain in place—and that DA can be flexible to support student, institution, and state needs. With DA systems, any prospective student would still be able to apply to institutions using traditional admissions systems. In instances where a holistic admissions review would be warranted, such as when a student has a special skill or qualification not observed by the DA system (for example, athletic talent, musical gifts, a unique life experience, etc.), students are not precluded from applying to institutions, even those where they were not automatically admitted through DA. In addition, students continue to use traditional admissions avenues to apply to institutions that are not a part of the DA system such as nonprofit private, for-profit private, and out-of-state institutions. Likewise, institutions continue to use traditional admissions practices for students not part of the DA system such as international or out-of-state students. DA is set up to provide proactive, universal, transparent, simple, personalized information, and a guarantee of admissions to high school graduates as a way to *increase* college opportunity only—never to reduce it. DA systems can be modified and expanded in scope by including private K–12 schools, homeschooled students, private postsecondary institutions, or out-of-state institutions with tuition reciprocity agreements.

IMPACTS OF DIRECT ADMISSIONS

DA appears to be a viable, low-cost alternative to support college enroll-ment across racial, socioeconomic, and geographic contexts. DA eliminates many reasons why students do not apply, including onerous application forms, inconsistent admissions processes across institutions, application fees, and a lack of transparent information for students and families.[23] A proactive admissions system also provides important signals to students, parents, and K–12 schools that postsecondary enrollment is attainable, par-ticularly for low-income and racial minority students who do not apply to or enroll in higher education at the same rates as their higher-income and majority peers.[24] This policy also holds the potential for states to increase undergraduate enrollment, keep resident students in-state, and invigorate workforce development by educating a larger and more diverse populous.

Following the fall 2015 introduction of DA, Idaho reported substan-tial changes to students' college-going behaviors. These included an over-all increase in enrollment of 2,272 (3.1 percent) students from fall 2015 to 2016 and a 6.7 percent increase in the number of high school grad-uates who immediately enrolled in college, encompassing a 7.7 percent increase at four-year and a 4.8 percent increase at two-year institutions.[25] With the introduction of the common application, Apply Idaho, growth continued into fall 2017 with an 88 percent increase in applications com-pleted (up by 12,937), representing a cumulative enrollment increase of 6.7 percent (compared to a national increase of 2.2 percent) and a 3-percentage-point *decrease* (from 13 to 10 percent) in the number of stu-dents attending college out-of-state.[26] The proportion of college-going students who enrolled out-of-state fell from 29 percent in 2014, to 28 percent in 2015, and to 26 percent in 2016.[27] The proportion of high school graduates who enrolled in the fall immediately after graduation increased from 48 percent in 2015 to 49 percent in 2016.[28]

As a universal policy, DA should impact students across the ability spectrum and institutional types by increasing enrollments, altering stu-dents' college choice sets, and changing the composition of institutions' entering classes. When considering the impacts of DA, it is important to consider changes across individual students, institutional groups, and the state at large.

Direct Admissions' Impact for Students

In spring 2016, after students had committed to their college of choice through Idaho's DA system, OSBE conducted a survey with the first cohort of DA students.[29] Responses from 1,410 students were analyzed, and 58 percent reported DA had an impact on their decision to attend college, with 55 percent reporting an impact on their choice of which college to attend.[30] Researchers found DA had no effect on students who already planned to attend college, identifying no disadvantages for this group. However, the policy did encourage students who would not have otherwise attended college to apply and enroll.[31] Additionally, students whose parents had no postsecondary education (i.e., first-generation students) self-reported that DA had a larger effect than their peers whose parents had college degrees.[32] Finally, while only 27.4 percent of students indicated speaking with a college counselor, 79.4 percent of students reported discussing their college plans with parents.[33] The survey also found that the DA system influenced students who were planning to attend an out-of-state institution to remain in-state. Qualitatively, DA had a profound impact on students. Following are some of the open-ended responses from student survey and focus group participants:

- "The application process can be scary for teens, and rejection is not easy. So, it was nice to get a letter of preapproved acceptance for some colleges."
- "The letter really changed my perspective. It genuinely opened doors for me that I'd never thought possible. I knew after receiving it that my dream of being a college English professor could come true."
- "I had originally planned on an out-of-state school, but the ease of just going right into an in-state school convinced me to stay."
- "I was really surprised. I didn't think any college would accept me but I was wrong."[34]

Direct Admissions' Impact for Institutions and States

When considering the impact of DA for institutions, it is expected that the policy change will both increase enrollments overall and change institutional destinations for students, altering institutions' student enrollment profiles. In statewide DA systems, we predict that the introduction of a DA system will result in a net enrollment loss at for-profit institutions. By offering options for admission to public institutions to students, individuals should be more likely to choose low-cost public options than considerably more expensive for-profit offerings. We also expect that community colleges will see net enrollment gains. Importantly, some of these enrollment gains will come from students who were not previously planning on attending college. Furthermore, four-year nonselective institutions are expected to see net enrollment gains alongside four-year selective institutions. The ability of students to start and complete degrees at four-year institutions opens more possibilities for individuals to obtain four-year bachelor's degrees, which are vital to increasing workforce demands of states. In-state private nonprofit institutions only benefit from DA if they are involved in the system. Finally, out-of-state institutions are expected to see a net enrollment loss when a DA system is introduced. This is particularly important in states where net migration loss is a political issue. In all of these instances, it is assumed that there will be improved outcomes for states through the potential of producing a more highly educated workforce, keeping more students in-state for college, and supporting the state's postsecondary sector by increasing enrollments and subsequent net tuition revenues. For institution-level DA programs, the institutions involved in offering DA are expected to experience enrollment gains.

Findings from Our Current and Ongoing Research into Direct Admissions

In prior research, the authors have studied Idaho's DA system to estimate the causal impacts of the program on state and institutional enrollment outcomes.[35] While Idaho reported descriptive changes in enrollment and college-going behavior, some of these changes could have been due to larger year-over-year shifts in enrollment that would have occurred without direct admissions or were due to changing student preferences for college over time (i.e., as a response to tuition and fee rates or workforce trends). To overcome this concern, we applied a rigorous quasi-experimental strategy (generalized synthetic control method) to answer the research question: what changes in institutional enrollment levels in Idaho are attributable to the introduction of DA? In our early analysis of the program, Idaho's implementation of DA was associated with a statistically significant increase in first-time, degree-seeking undergraduate enrollments of nearly 104 students *per campus* (or roughly 8.1 percent) and increased the enrollment of in-state students by over 140 students per campus (or roughly 14.6 percent). These large enrollment increases reflect the descriptive changes in enrollments reported by Idaho (described earlier) plus the expected declines in enrollment given national decreases in student full-time equivalent (FTE) enrollments over the past decade.[36] Thus, with the introduction of direct admissions, the state and its institutions not only experienced a 3 percent increase in overall postsecondary enrollments from the previous year's levels, but, importantly, that increase placed overall enrollments at a level approximately 5 percentage points higher than it would have been without direct admissions. These enrollment increases are driven entirely by the increased enrollment of in-state students following the introduction of direct admissions.

Furthermore, we also hypothesized that DA would increase the enrollment of students who are Pell-eligible (i.e., low-income). However, our results to-date do not suggest DA directly influenced these outcomes other than in a descriptive way.[37] While we think that DA has the potential to reduce equity gaps, we do not find clear evidence of this in Idaho. This may be due to a homogenous population composition and indicates that low-income students need more than guaranteed admissions to be able to attend college. We suspect that more

evidence of DA working to reduce equity gaps may be found in states
with more diverse populations and that greater access may be achieved
for low-income students in DA programs that incorporate student
financial aid. In all, our research suggests DA may be a low-cost and
effective mechanism to increase institutional and statewide enrollment
in postsecondary education, particularly for in-state students, but more
research is needed to better understand these impacts across student
subgroups and institutional types.

MOVING FORWARD: INSIGHTS FOR PRACTITIONERS AND POLICYMAKERS

As policymakers and admissions practitioners consider the design and
operation of DA systems, including the impacts that such a policy innovation could have across students, institutions, and states, it is important
to note key design features when positioning a DA system, as well as to be
aware of complementary policies that prior works have shown can also be
used to increase college access and success.

Important Elements of Direct Admissions Systems

Based upon our work, we have identified two important additional design
elements of DA systems that influence their operation and effectiveness:
the use of a common application and admissions application fee waivers.

Strong evidence supports the effectiveness of the use of a common
application in DA.[38] A common application allows students to use a single application to apply to multiple institutions, simplifying the college
application process. Common applications, with emphasis on simplifying the process from a student's point of view, increase enrollments by
making it easier to apply to college and to match with institutions based
on academic credentials. Common applications encourage students to

apply to multiple institutions—reducing students self-selecting out of institutions that would be a good fit—offer important educational opportunities, grant better financial aid packages, and have lower net prices. A common application as part of a statewide DA system also encourages students to explore more postsecondary options in-state, thereby increasing the odds that students remain in-state for college. Ideally, a common application will enable students to "claim their place" in DA by reducing the intimidation of the application process, making applying to college easier, faster, and more straightforward. A clearinghouse website for multiple institution applications could also be helpful in supporting DA systems but will be less effective than the creation of a single application. Including in-state private institutions in DA could also increase options for students and improve the potential to retain residents in-state for college.

As part of statewide DA systems, students are admitted to multiple campuses. However, application fees for students to "claim their place" at the institution of their choice dampen potential policy impacts, especially for low-income or financially constrained students. While application fee waivers are currently available for low-income students at most institutions, the process of obtaining a waiver can be a cumbersome deterrent.[39] Prior experimental evidence has shown that college application fee waivers are an effective mechanism to encourage high-achieving, low-income students to increase the number of applications they submit and to apply to selective institutions. Hoxby and Turner found that students provided with a fee waiver not only experienced a 31 percent increase in admissions to selective institutions but also increased their enrollment at selective institutions.[40] Idaho successfully transitioned to a fee-free system in 2017.[41] Likewise, fees were waived for all of the DA campuses in the pilot program run by Common App. However, application fees are required in the South Dakota proactive admissions system. This highlights the importance of reflecting on how differences between systems may yield different outcomes for students.

Complementary Policies to Promote Student Access and Success

Not only do DA systems conceptually reduce or eliminate many barriers students face in the college application and admission process, but such systems can also be combined with complementary strategies to increase student, institutional, and state outcomes. We focus on the potential for DA systems to deliver two complementary strategies: integrating student financial aid and providing targeted college and academic major match information to assist students' college-going decisions.

DA has the potential to combine proactive, transparent, simple, personalized, and early information on admissions and student financial aid. The more detailed and personalized the financial aid information is, the more useful it will be for students in making postsecondary enrollment decisions. In statewide DA systems, it seems plausible to guarantee state need-based grant aid awards based on information contained in the SLDS (like free/reduced lunch status). With the universal applicability of DA to all students in a state, as well as the states' administrative operation of direct admission systems, states could integrate financial aid information into students' DA letter, providing students and families with information on college options as well as on expected prices and/or financial aid awards. Including financial aid as part of DA is particularly important for students who are qualified to attend selective institutions, but steer clear of name-brand institutions for fear of high prices, including high-achieving, low-income students and first-generation students.[42] Heller found signaling the availability of aid to students encouraged the early consideration of college opportunities and promoted engagement in college-preparation behaviors, and Liu et al. similarly observed that early commitment aid increased students' application behaviors and college-going rates—and that students across racial groups responded differently to similar aid packages, with the expectation of more financial aid increasing African American and Hispanic students' applications to college.[43] While no existing common application and DA systems have yet integrated personalized information on student aid, we expect including aid information as part of a DA letter would further reduce inequalities in college admissions, especially for low-income and at-risk students.

In addition to having the potential to change the type of institution that a student attends, DA has the potential to improve student-to-institution and student-to-major match. It is estimated that 41 percent of all students undermatch or attend an institution that is not a good fit, with higher propensities observed for students who are first-generation, from low-socioeconomic families, or live in rural communities.[44] Providing college information effectively increases applications and enrollment, and the certainty of college admissions encourages low-income students to enroll in more selective institutions.[45] Thus, better matching has the potential to direct students to more resource-rich environments and thereby increase academic outcomes. While some of this may happen naturally as students realize the full range of institutions where they have been offered admission, DA systems can also be used more specifically to encourage better matches for students. By augmenting a DA system to proactively provide information about unique characteristics of institutions, majors offered, graduation rates, and average starting salaries of graduates, for example, students can be more informed consumers regarding their institutional choice.

CONCLUSION

DA as a policy holds strong potential for states, institutions (or systems), and students to rethink the college admissions process. Developing a student-centered admissions process that is proactive, guaranteed, universal, transparent, simple, personalized, low-cost, and involves trusted adults has the potential to change the life trajectory of all students, not only high-achieving students. Importantly, DA also has the potential to improve equity across all points along the postsecondary education pipeline by proactively affording students—regardless of income, race, or location—with an opportunity to earn a college degree.

ACKNOWLEDGMENTS

This chapter draws upon work supported by the Joyce Foundation, Spencer Foundation, and the Institute of Education Sciences. The authors gratefully acknowledge financial support from the Joyce Foundation under grant #39923 to the University of Illinois and our program officer, Sameer Gadkaree, as well as the helpful comments and feedback from session participants at the 2020 Association for Education Finance and Policy virtual conference. This research was also supported in part through funding from the Spencer Foundation under grant #202100258 to the Board of Trustees of the University of Illinois and through funding from the Institute of Education Sciences under grant #R305B200035 to the University of Pennsylvania. Any views or opinions expressed are those of the authors alone and do not represent the views or opinions of the Joyce Foundation, Spencer Foundation, Institute of Education Sciences, or the US Department of Education.

Beyond Admissions: Advancing Equity and Success for High-Achieving, Low-Income Students Through an Institutional Promise Program

KELLY E. SLAY AND KRISTEN M. GLASENER

THE PROGRESS AMONG HIGHER EDUCATION INSTITUTIONS to increase the economic diversity of their student bodies and create a supportive climate for low-income students has been slow. This is especially true at our nation's most selective institutions, where more students from the top 1 percent of the income distribution are enrolled than are students from the bottom half of the income distribution.[1] With ample evidence that students from low-income backgrounds are less likely to apply to selective campuses, in part because of limited information and misconceptions about costs, free-tuition institutional promise programs like the Illinois Commitment at the University of Illinois and the Go Blue Guarantee at the University of Michigan among others have emerged as a promising enrollment management strategy and mechanism for increasing access to selective institutions.[2] Yet understanding tuition costs is only one piece of a larger, intricate puzzle that students must navigate on the road to college. A growing body of research suggests that complexities in the college application process deter low-income students from applying to and enrolling in selective colleges. Limited availability of college counseling, combined with a lack of "college knowledge" leads to difficulties in completing the necessary steps for college enrollment.[3] This lack of information and support is often exacerbated by an increasingly complex college admissions process.[4]

To successfully enroll in college, prospective students must now complete numerous intricate tasks—from taking the right courses in high school and participating in the right extracurricular activities to filling out college applications, writing essays and completing lengthy financial aid forms.[5] Selective colleges have discretion over which materials are required for admission, and they choose different screening mechanisms to manage their applicant pools. For instance, some institutions rely on the Common Application, whereas others have their own applications. Some institutions require personal statements or supplemental essays, whereas others do not. Additionally, some colleges insist that students complete both the Free Application for Federal Student Aid (FAFSA) and the College Scholarship Service (CSS) Profile when applying for financial aid. And in response to the COVID-19 global pandemic, many campuses have implemented test-optional policies while others opt for test-blind admissions or eliminate test requirements all together.[6] There are also numerous deadlines (e.g., early vs. regular decision) for submitting application materials. Although each of these tasks is seemingly small, they can have an outsize effect on students' application and enrollment behavior. We argue that the admissions process is an administrative burden that in many cases prevents low-income students from gaining access to the colleges for which they are qualified.

Students who successfully navigate these complexities face additional challenges once enrolled in college. Transitioning and adapting to the college environment can be particularly difficult for low-income students, who often feel invisible at institutions largely designed to serve their more privileged peers.[7] The culture shock many low-income students experience when entering elite colleges negatively affects their acclimation into campus life.[8] In this chapter, we present evidence of the multiple costs that low-income students incur when enrolling at one highly selective, public flagship university and highlight how an institutional promise program alleviated some of the burdens students faced in the college enrollment process. As institutional promise programs diffuse rapidly throughout higher education, our findings demonstrate the need for admissions offices to move away from strategies that simply aim to enroll more low-income students to approaches that support students from recruitment all the way to graduation.

THE PRESENT STUDY

We draw from a longitudinal, qualitative study that explores the experiences of low-income students recruited to the University of Michigan via a randomized controlled experiment. The University of Michigan (U-M) is a highly selective, research-intensive university that consistently recruits students from over one hundred countries and each of the fifty states. Yet, several factors have complicated efforts to attract students from low-income backgrounds: the implementation of a 2006 statewide ban on affirmative action which changed how the institution could recruit and admit students; the rising cost of attendance; and notably, the elite profile of the students whom the university admits.[9] The median family income of a student at the university is $154,000 and nearly 10 percent of U-M students come from families with an annual income of $630,000 or more.[10] Students whose families represent the bottom 20 percent of income earners comprise just 3.6 percent of the student body.

To address these challenges, in 2015 U-M launched the "HAIL (High Achieving Involved Leader) Scholarship"—a targeted outreach initiative aimed at enhancing access to the university and increasing the economic diversity of its undergraduate student body.[11] The HAIL intervention was designed to induce high-achieving, low-income students in Michigan high schools to apply and enroll in the university. The intervention consisted of sending a personalized "large, glossy, and brightly colored" packet to a randomly selected group of students.[12] The packet included a letter from the president of the university congratulating them for being chosen for the HAIL scholarship, listed specific steps necessary to complete their application, and made clear that students did not have to complete the FAFSA or CSS Profile. Parents also were mailed a letter about this offer, and school principals were notified by email. Most importantly, the mailing guaranteed students' four years of free tuition, conditional upon acceptance. The offer was valued at $60,000.[13]

HAIL has been highly effective in expanding access to many underserved students across the state by eliminating financial barriers to a selective college education.[14] However, qualitative data collected over four years from HAIL scholars suggests that this type of intervention is best coupled with comprehensive strategies that remove hurdles that disproportionately burden low-income students once they are enrolled in college. We suggest that admissions professionals and campus administrators must make a sustained effort to understand other costs beyond tuition that students experience while in college—what Harvard sociologist Anthony Abraham Jack describes as the "the stress and isolation that can define everyday college life for these more vulnerable students."[15] In developing and managing institutional promise initiatives like HAIL, failing to account for the "hidden costs" low-income students are likely to incur may actually undermine larger institutional goals that otherwise strengthen high school recruitment networks, enhance college affordability, and improve economic diversity.

CONCEPTUAL FRAMEWORK

We situate our chapter within a growing body of literature on administrative burdens, which have been described as an "individual's experience of policy implementation as onerous."[16] Take, for example, the multistep process of applying for US citizenship, which requires complex paperwork and involves application fees, English proficiency, and understanding of US history, among other requirements.[17] In essence, administrative burden is the cost associated with policy implementation, where costs may be experienced by the organization creating the policy, groups whom the policy targets, or an amalgam of the two.[18] Although no policy implementation is without costs, individuals from minoritized groups are more likely to bear the weight of administrative burden and even "seemingly small burdens" can have substantial impacts on access to benefits and resources.[19]

While this framework has most often been used to examine social policies involving the federal and local governments (e.g., food stamps, unemployment benefits, social security, etc.), colleges also represent critical sites for policy development and implementation (see Table 12.1). Recent studies in higher education have applied administrative burden to examine the implementation of excess semester credit hour policies in

TABLE 12.1 **Components of Administrative Burden**

Administrative Burden	Description	Examples from Admissions/Financial Aid
Learning Costs	Learning eligibility for program/policy, what forms are required, and/or how to apply	• Searching for information on college admissions requirements • Meeting with counselor • Learning about FAFSA
Compliance Costs	Tasks, time, and energy necessary to demonstrate or maintain eligibility for program/policy; completing forms, documenting identity; responding to bureaucratic instructions	• Applying for a fee waiver for application • Completing FAFSA and required tax documents • Submitting proof of identity and GPA for scholarship requirement
Psychological Costs	Stress, sense of stigma, frustrations, cognitive strain, or loss of autonomy experienced when attempting to follow a policy, participate in programs, or navigate bureaucratic structures	• Sense of stigma from working a perceived "low-status" campus job, such as custodial work, in exchange for financial aid • Frustrations resulting from difficulty accessing help

Source: To illustrate the types of costs students may encounter in the college admissions and enrollment process, we have adapted Donald P. Moynihan, Pamela Herd, and Hope Harvey, "Administrative Burden: Learning, Psychological, and Compliance Costs in Citizen-State Interactions," *Journal of Public Administration Research and Theory* 25, no. 1 (2015): 43–69.

public universities in Texas and potential barriers to access for statewide promise programs.[20] In this chapter, we advance this work by exploring the administrative burden that the HAIL scholarship places on award recipients. We use Moynihan, Herd, and Harvey's categorization of learning, compliance, and psychological costs to inform our analysis of the costs associated with communication about and implementation of the HAIL intervention.[21]

CONCEPTUALIZING COSTS

The costs associated with administrative burden are categorized into three areas: learning, compliance, and psychological.[22] Individuals incur learning costs as they seek information about a policy and determine eligibility. The implications of these costs are especially apparent in college access research, where studies reveal how low-income students are often overwhelmed and misinformed about the admissions process, including knowing how to apply for financial aid and the range of programs for which they are eligible.[23] As a result, they are more likely to avoid submitting applications to selective institutions that are actually more affordable because of uncertainty about the likelihood of admission and the perceived cost of attendance.[24] Strategies that increase awareness of financial aid programs, offer assistance with completing application materials, and provide clear information about net costs and college options can reduce learning costs and increase college enrollment.[25]

Of the three costs, scholars have most often studied compliance costs—the burden or tasks, time, and energy necessary to demonstrate or maintain eligibility for benefits provided by a policy. The college-going process is laden with compliance costs that high school students must navigate to gain access to college. For instance, they must meet certain curricular requirements, take standardized tests, and submit an application, among other tasks. Compliance costs are also present in the final stages of the admissions process and once enrolled, when students and their families must complete the overly complicated FAFSA in order to receive and maintain financial aid awards.[26] Research has highlighted the disproportionate impact that these complex processes have on low-income students.[27]

Psychological costs represent the stigma, stress, and cognitive strain that individuals experience when attempting to follow a policy, participate in programs, or navigate structures and processes required to receive the benefits they seek.[28] The consequences of stigma for minoritized groups have been well documented by scholars who note the implications of isolation, identity threats, and various types of stressors for student outcomes.[29] Yet psychological costs remain "largely unexamined" compared to learning and compliance costs and only recently have scholars started to explore the administrative burdens of financial aid policies.[30] For example, students from low-income backgrounds may be subjected to psychological strain when asked to share information about their socioeconomic status on forms needed to demonstrate eligibility for income-based programs and, in some cases, when in exchange for financial aid, they are assigned campus work assignments widely perceived as degrading or low-status.[31]

Despite their rapid expansion, only two studies to our knowledge explore the administrative burdens of college promise programs.[32] Rosinger and colleagues analyzed eighteen statewide promise programs and identified fifty-five unique design features of these programs that contributed to learning, compliance, and psychological costs.[33] Notably, their index indicates the burdens students are "likely to experience" and not what they *actually* experienced.[34] Bell and Smith's mixed methods analysis of the Oklahoma Promise initiative revealed how the limited capacity of partner high schools to advise students on completing the program application exacerbated learning and compliance costs, which then reduced access to the scholarship and postsecondary education.[35]

Using an organizational lens, these studies reveal that the design, implementation, and management structures of promise programs can create barriers that deter students who aspire to attend college. Our chapter addresses a critical but missing perspective on the role of administrative burden in enrollment management by: (1) centering the voices of students and (2) moving beyond admissions to examine the costs students bear *post-enrollment* as they access the scholarship benefits that they have been promised.

METHODS

The current chapter is part of a larger mixed methods longitudinal study examining the college transition and academic and social experiences of HAIL scholars. We focus on qualitative data collected from two cohorts over four years.

Sampling and Data Collection

We used a purposeful sampling strategy to generate a diverse sample of HAIL scholarship recipients that reflected variation across participants' precollege contexts and racial and gender identities.[36] We followed two cohorts throughout their enrollment at U-M, conducting four waves of focus groups. Figure 12.1 illustrates our data collection process for the 2016 and 2017 HAIL scholar cohorts.

Each of our focus group sessions lasted between seventy-five and ninety minutes and followed a semistructured interview protocol. We audio recorded and transcribed each of the interviews and generated reflective memos, which informed our analysis of data. Focus groups were ideal for uncovering aspects of participants' experiences that may have been masked if not for the group interaction.[37] However, this data collection strategy also limited our ability to probe into individual narratives.[38] It is also possible that we may have received different information had we individually interviewed students.

FIGURE 12.1 HAIL Scholars Focus Groups, 2016–20

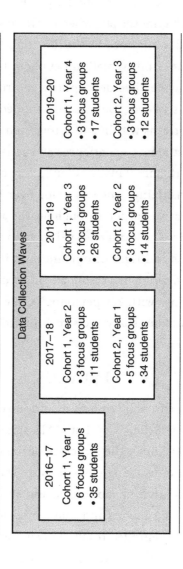

Data Collection Waves

2016–17

Cohort 1, Year 1
• 6 focus groups
• 35 students

2017–18

Cohort 1, Year 2
• 3 focus groups
• 11 students

Cohort 2, Year 1
• 5 focus groups
• 34 students

2018–19

Cohort 1, Year 3
• 3 focus groups
• 26 students

Cohort 2, Year 2
• 3 focus groups
• 14 students

2019–20

Cohort 1, Year 4
• 3 focus groups
• 17 students

Cohort 2, Year 3
• 3 focus groups
• 12 students

Data Analysis

We conducted our analyses in a series of iterative steps, using systematic coding and both inductive and deductive processes. First, we engaged in a focused review of the transcripts, whereby we constructed a preliminary codebook using codes informed by the literature, our research questions, and emergent themes from a small subset of our transcripts.[39] We refined these codes, creating detailed descriptions and rules that were added to a more comprehensive codebook that we applied to the corpus of data. We searched for patterns within and across each of our focus groups on various aspects of students' experiences and generated thematic memos to organize salient themes. Finally, we used Moynihan et al.'s categorization of costs as sensitizing concepts to uncover HAIL scholars' experiences of administrative burden throughout the admissions process and once they enrolled.[40] Our team engaged in various strategies to increase the trustworthiness and rigor of our findings, including interrogating our positionality, engaging in a systematic intercoding process, and sharing emergent findings with key personnel. Collectively, these strategies enhanced the rigor of our study and strengthened our interpretations.[41]

FINDINGS

Analyzing our data through the lens of administrative burden revealed a distinction between the costs that HAIL scholars incurred pre- and post-enrollment. Although the structure of the intervention was quite effective at reducing learning costs in early stages of the admissions process, which incentivized application and enrollment, the perceived absence of intentional supports and communication specific to the HAIL scholarship once they enrolled resulted in compliance costs and psychological burdens that affected students' academic and social adjustment and well-being. Still, study participants were largely agentic and found ways to navigate these unexpected challenges. In the sections that follow, we organize our findings according to Moynihan et al.'s conceptualization of costs, highlighting how students perceived and experienced different aspects of the HAIL program and the implications for their enrollment, transition, and success through college.

Learning Costs: Reducing Uncertainty Around Affordability and Admissions

Many of the barriers in admissions and financial aid processes that often deter applicants from low-income backgrounds were largely nonexistent for students targeted by the HAIL experiment. Key aspects of the intervention, including elimination of the FAFSA requirement, outreach to high school principals and parents, and step-by-step directions provided in the personalized mail packet, were particularly effective at reducing uncertainty and increasing simplicity in the admissions process. Our participants described the contents of the packet as "very helpful" and "beneficial," recalling that the detailed instructions and deadlines—which one student likened to a "treasure map"—simplified an otherwise daunting admissions process.

The elaborate, personalized materials along with the strategic framing of the intervention as a "scholarship" motivated students to reconsider their college options and gave them the "boost of confidence" needed to feel optimistic about their prospects of gaining admission. Reflecting on her application process, Vanessa shared, "Well the reason why I didn't think I wanted to apply [to U-M] was fear of rejection and the money, and so when I got the HAIL scholarship packet, I was like, 'Wow, I might actually be smart enough to go here.'" Several participants similarly expressed a shift in their perceptions of their academic readiness for U-M after receiving the scholarship packet. They were nervous but also felt empowered by the information they had received.

In addition to simplifying and demystifying the admissions process at U-M, the HAIL scholarship gave participants a sense of assurance that their tuition and fees would be covered. With news of the tuition promise, students felt they had clarity about how they were going to pay for college. Reducing the uncertainty around tuition costs removed a significant

information barrier—whether real or perceived—thereby reducing learning costs for many of our participants. HAIL scholars likened receipt of the
packet to a "weight" that had been lifted off their shoulders. Although students didn't have any concrete information on tuition costs at U-M prior to
receiving the materials, their preconceived notions about what they thought
it would cost to attend the university were compelling enough to keep
them from considering U-M a viable option altogether. In fact, without
the HAIL packet several students described attending U-M as "impossible"
and something that they could only "hope for" but never attain. As Laura
explained, "the financial burden would have been too much of a stress on
me and my family." However, the promise of tuition as it was spelled out
in recruitment materials assured her and other HAIL scholars of U-M's
affordability—although we soon learned that the vast majority of our participants had not, in practical terms, understood the scope and limitations
of the promise at the time they applied.

Ambiguity and the Absence of Compliance

From students' perspective, having been awarded a scholarship, it was
important to know exactly why they had been selected and what they
needed to do to maintain their scholarship. But communication about
HAIL seemingly sent mixed messages: on one hand, the personalized
packet and clear information conveyed to recipients that they were both
academically capable and "wanted" by U-M; on the other hand, once students made it through the admissions process and were on campus, they
had trouble finding information about the scholarship, which led them
to question whether they had truly earned their place at the university.
For example, with other deserving students at their high schools, HAIL
scholars wondered what they had done to earn the scholarship and why
other high-achieving peers did not receive the same offer. Absent concrete
information about criteria for the award, our participants questioned if,
despite initial impressions of HAIL as an academic scholarship, they had
only received the scholarship because of their financial circumstances. In

an effort to assure themselves and others that they were indeed deserving of the university's "investment," some students took on much more work than they could reasonably manage, which sometimes had negative implications for their academic outcomes and well-being. Rajita explained this sentiment, sharing, "I've ran [sic] student orgs . . . and worked four jobs at one point, all just to prove that I'm worthy of the scholarship, even though I don't really know if you have to do anything to qualify for the scholarship still." Without clear information about the selection criteria, HAIL scholars were left to speculate why they were chosen and if they had indeed "earned" the gift of free tuition or if, instead, it was a "handout" given to them by the university because of their low-income status.

This lack of transparency combined with limited information on minimum GPA or other compliance guidelines needed to maintain their scholarship contributed to feelings of frustration and anxiety. As one student shared, "Nobody knows what's going on. . . . I don't understand why we can't even get simple questions answered." Unlike traditional scholarships which may have ongoing requirements like GPA, service, or participation in activities, no such requirements were in place for HAIL. Although HAIL was framed as a "scholarship," in actuality, it was an informational intervention for students already eligible for need-based aid—that is, students that were part of the intervention received the same level of financial assistance they would have qualified for anyway given their family's economic status. Still, the enormity of receiving a four-year tuition "scholarship" to U-M led students to feel anxious—almost paranoid—of doing anything that could jeopardize their award, as illustrated by a third-year focus group participant:

> I was in the focus group my freshman year, and there has been no real clarity since then. I was confused about what is required of me. How can I lose this? What would have to happen for me to lose this scholarship? What does my grade point average have to be? I literally try to do searches like, what does your grade point . . . and I can't find anything so I'm sitting here, like is it good enough, is it not good enough?

Focus group participants consistently voiced their frustrations over unanswered questions and "very vague" responses they sometimes received about the GPA requirements and other aspects of the scholarship. There was no public web presence for the first three years of the HAIL intervention and with few exceptions, instructors, advisors, financial aid officers, and other university staff seemed to know very little or shared conflicting information, especially regarding the scope of the program (e.g., spring term, a fifth year in college, credit hours per semester, etc.). One student commented that he was "still trying to figure out what HAIL does and does not cover." As a consequence, not only was communication of clear and consistent compliance guidelines (i.e., GPA) a "huge stressor" for students who feared they weren't doing well enough academically, but also, the absence of information about the limits of the scholarship came at a cost to some scholars' academic progress. Some participants decided to forgo summer cocurricular opportunities and others, in an attempt to make certain they finished within four years, took on more than the recommended credit hours and struggled academically.

In short, while it is not uncommon for financial aid requirements to create undue burdens for students from minoritized backgrounds that impede their access and success in college, our participants *desired* and desperately needed clear compliance guidelines. Conflicting and hard-to-find information increased ambiguity around the award, leading some HAIL students to incur unexpected costs, including heightened insecurities about deservingness, the time spent looking for information, and the anxiety and stress that resulted from not being able to find it.

Psychological Costs: The Stigma and Stress of "Being Not Rich at U-M"

While the HAIL scholarship generously covered students' college tuition, several of our participants perceived an absence of support in other key areas, including managing unexpected expenditures and cultivating peer relationships. For example, a first-year HAIL scholar,

Brittany, lamented over the $30 fee she had to pay for a flu shot, which was required for nursing majors. Reflecting on her experience, she spoke to a broader frustration that students repeatedly voiced about the cost of being "poor" at U-M: "It's just things add up. . . . It is really difficult for me to survive here outside the [HAIL] Scholarship." With limited resources, some students would put off buying books or other materials like course packs for as long as they could despite fears of falling behind.

The collective weight of all the "small things," especially in their first few years, was compounded by more substantial expenses, such as off-campus housing and taxes. HAIL scholars often felt like they were caught between two undesirable options when it came to transitioning out of the dorms. On one hand, renting a "nice" house or apartment would require students to work more than twenty hours per week or take out additional loans. On the other hand, as we observed with a larger share of our participants, finding affordable housing often meant compromising on quality or living further away from campus. Even on the low end, housing costs were a significant expenditure for many HAIL students, as one of our participants explained:

> Rent and groceries are like my biggest concerns. My rent is like $880 a month, it's so ridiculous. And so much of the money I get from the university goes directly toward rent to the point where I will be working 24 to 32 hours a week and I'll probably have like $30 or $40 a month just for food.

A number of HAIL scholars, particularly those in their fourth year, were similarly frustrated that the tax implications of HAIL were not articulated and the scholarship was framed as a "free" opportunity. Some students appeared to be caught off guard by significant tax bills and were unable to find campus resources to resolve this challenge. We noted that a few of our participants had even resorted to securing student loans to pay taxes. Scott, a senior, who took out an additional $10,000 in loans over a three-year period elaborated on what he and others perceived as a limitation of the scholarship program:

> I think my absolute number one, top stressor outside of academics here comes straight from HAIL. Every year I've had to pay $3,500 to $5,000 in taxes because of the scholarship. My freshman year here, I got a huge, huge shock when I expected to get like $1,500 back. And I go on TurboTax and it tells me, I owed . . . like $3,100 freshman year. This year, it was $5,400.

Although the majority of participants shared that the tax implications of the scholarship were "surprising" and stressful to navigate, there were also students who expressed a more positive perspective about the costs they incurred. In the words of one fourth-year HAIL scholar, "What I ended up having to pay back on that tax return is essentially what I'm paying to go to college. I mean, it's definitely not a free education . . . but honestly, it's still better than the $26k I would have been paying." Still, these compounding sources of financial stress, which students believed should have been more clearly conveyed before they enrolled, often weighed heavily on them as they tried to balance work and school. Adding to the stress was the reality that students could not rely on their families for financial help. Reflecting on her situation, Stephanie shared, "I wonder what my mental state would be like if I wasn't worrying about the finances."

The work of managing "hidden" costs—expenses not covered by HAIL or plainly communicated to students—was often intensified by feelings of social isolation in a campus environment where HAIL scholars felt stigmatized because of their socioeconomic status. Several participants, even as they entered their third and fourth year, had difficulty finding friends who valued their cultural backgrounds and understood the limitations on time and resources imposed by their financial circumstances. Ellen, who was from a nearby suburb, shared, "I'm so lonely. I'm not that far away from home but I'm still not with people that I'm really comfortable with." In the same focus group, fighting through tears,

Hannah described a similar struggle: "My transition has been really hard for me just because . . . I'm just intimidated by the people around me." From students' perspective, a considerable drawback of the scholarship was that there was no formal structure or mechanism that tied recipients together. Citing the invisibility of their HAIL identities, scholars struggled to identify each other on campus—in classes and in their dorms—although nearly all of them desired opportunities to connect. When students met other HAIL scholars, it was described as "random," or an instance of "luck" for which they were incredibly grateful.

HAIL scholars who were a part of formal programs such as the Comprehensive Studies Program and Summer Bridge, both of which focus on supporting underrepresented students, had access to a ready-made community of peers who shared and validated their social identities, thereby lessening the psychological blow that a large share of our participants experienced day to day. Noting how "overwhelming" it was to feel as if they belonged, students who did not have access to these programs desperately desired structured, university-sanctioned opportunities to formally connect with HAIL scholars within and across cohorts. Several of our participants were confused and frustrated by what they perceived as a lack of support, especially when such mechanisms existed for other scholarship programs that targeted underrepresented students on campus. Yielding to the concerns expressed in early focus groups, campus administrators eventually implemented a welcome reception specifically for HAIL scholars. Still, we heard from students that the information-rich format did little to facilitate the kind of connections they believed they needed to cultivate a sense of belonging. Taking matters into their own hands, some students in our fourth-year focus groups recalled organizing meetings with campus leaders to advocate for more support and better communications about HAIL. A handful of other students helped develop an online crowdsourced guide for low-income students, "Being Not Rich at U-M," which garnered national attention and led to similar student-created guides at over thirty universities.[42] The guide emphasized "hidden" costs and provided strategies on everything from finding the best-paying jobs to buying clothes on a budget. Notably, topics such as "Making friends when you feel totally alienated on this campus," "De-stigmatize and emotional health," and "You deserve to have fun, too," centered students' perspectives and offered practical tips for thriving and not just surviving in college.

DISCUSSION AND IMPLICATIONS

Selective colleges and universities have tremendous power over the recruitment and selection of their students. They not only have discretion over which aspects of a student's application are given more or less weight, but they also adopt specific institutional policies and procedures that influence students' application and enrollment behavior.[43] In this chapter, we examine one institutional approach that reduced students' learning costs during the admissions process. However, our findings suggest that students targeted by the HAIL experiment desired more communication, access to support mechanisms, and compliance or administrative guidelines to provide them assurance that they would maintain their financial aid once enrolled. The absence of these supports exacerbated psychological costs for students that were part of this intervention. We suggest that there are important lessons to be learned from the HAIL intervention and discuss implications for college administrators hoping to adopt similar recruitment strategies.

Implications for Enrollment Management Professionals

The results of the HAIL experiment are encouraging. They demonstrate that a simple, low-cost, intervention that promises four years of free tuition and simplifies the financial aid process for academically qualified, low-income students can lead to significant changes in their application and enrollment behaviors. Our qualitative findings further illustrate why such a recruitment approach might be effective. The HAIL intervention alleviated many of the administrative burdens students face when applying to college. Specifically, we find that packaging need-based aid as a "scholarship" helped shift students' perceptions of their academic capabilities and encouraged them to reconsider their college options. By waiving the FAFSA requirement and removing the economic barriers to entry, the HAIL experiment removed many of the learning costs low-income students commonly face on the path to college, thus increasing access for underrepresented groups.

And yet, as our findings illustrate, financial aid does not cover all costs for low-income students, and there are many other factors that get in the way of full inclusion. Participants in our study experienced numerous challenges as they attempted to navigate complex structures and processes embedded in the college environment. HAIL recipients not only struggled to find clear, accurate, and timely information about how to maintain their financial aid award, but they were confused about "why they were chosen" for the scholarship. Transparent information that communicates to students both why they receive institutional aid and what they need to do to maintain that aid would help alleviate students' concerns.

Finally, although our chapter focuses on one institutional promise program, our findings suggest the importance of moving beyond admissions to consider other institutional supports that are critical in efforts to recruit, admit, and support low-income students. Students in our study emphasized that financial costs are not the only costs they must bear when enrolled at an elite institution. They also struggle to find their place on campus, especially when trying to juggle work and family obligations with their responsibilities of being a student. Colleges seeking to enroll a more socioeconomically diverse student body must also ensure that they align their student support structures to remove other administrative burdens commonly experienced by low-income students.

CONCLUSION

The college students we are educating today are more diverse than ever before. They come from various ethnic and racial identity groups and a myriad of socioeconomic backgrounds. If colleges care about educational equity, then they need to not only recruit more diverse students, but also ensure they thrive once enrolled. As Jack articulates it:

> Too often we think about those youth who make it out of distressed communities and into college—especially elite colleges—as having already won. These young people, we assume, hold a golden ticket . . . but graduation rates do not tell us of students' experiences in college, their trials or their triumphs. After all, it is one thing for students to graduate. It is another for them to do so whole and healthy, ready for whatever the next adventure begins. (189)

Enrollment management leaders, whose job it is to recruit, enroll, retain, and graduate a student body in accordance with their institution's mission, are uniquely positioned to bring multiple campus units together to create an institutional environment that will ensure success for all students regardless of their backgrounds. They have a responsibility to more intentionally align their diversity-related recruitment and financial aid policies with support structures for students. Doing so requires building connections with multiple units across the institutional environment that are often siloed. We advocate for institutions to thoughtfully engage in what organizational change scholar Adrianna Kezar describes as "the creation of a diverse student success infrastructure that supports long-term cultural change."[44] Drawing on studies from systems theory, Kezar suggests that colleges must assess whether their priorities, policies and practices align with their equity goals. Colleges frequently add programs and services "on the side" to address changes in their student body without engaging all campus units to support these efforts.[45] Recruitment of low-income students must be reinforced by practices that serve these students well once they are enrolled. Without undergoing efforts to change campus cultures and align policies, practices, and structures with the goals of diversity, equity, and inclusion, we suggest that innovative recruitment initiatives and financial aid policies like the HAIL intervention may inevitably be constrained as levers for creating more equitable and inclusive college campuses. Institutions must critically consider how they can become what McNair and colleagues refer to as "a student-ready college" that promotes student success holistically and strategically.[46]

Breaking through the Divide: Practitioners and Scholars Building Trust and Collaboration for Change

Nikki Kāhealani Chun, Shawn Felton, and OiYan A. Poon

"It's an amazing opportunity to be in this conversation through this book chapter. For me, as I balance a PhD program while transitioning into a new leadership role, I'm seeing how important it is to be both a practitioner and a scholar."
—Nikki Chun

"The work we do is about real people. Research is necessary to support our efforts and must be organic, relative, and timely, while being critical. We can't do our jobs without research; it forces us to examine ourselves, meaning, evidence, process and, ultimately, truth."
—Shawn Felton

"This book aims to bring together practice, leadership, and admissions with research in college admissions, to bring them into conversation with each other."
—OiYan Poon

THE STATED PURPOSE of this edited volume of research and analysis on admissions is to build bridges between research, practice, and policy. Each author and set of authors in this book offered insights into whether and how admissions practices contribute toward the reproduction of inequalities. They have also presented possibilities for change that moves admissions practice and work toward the advancement of more equitable outcomes in postsecondary education access.

In this chapter, we present a dynamic dialogue among two scholar-practitioners[1] (Nikki and Shawn) and a research scholar (OiYan) who are all immersed through their work and leadership in questions of equity and college admissions. Bridging research, practice, and policy requires responsive and ongoing dialogue. In December 2021, we recorded a 75-minute conversation—one of many discussions we have had over a year. Throughout our conversations, we discussed drafts of the chapters in this volume and collectively considered the values and pragmatics of developing, coconstructing, and sustaining relationships between researchers and practitioners. The conversation itself energized us about the possibilities for research-informed practice.

This was not our first conversation together. Nikki and OiYan first met in 2017, as PhD student, faculty advisor, and research team colleagues. Nikki and Shawn first met as emerging leaders attending a COFHE (Consortium on Financing Higher Education) conference in 2016, representing the California Institute of Technology (Caltech) and Cornell respectively. Currently, Nikki is vice provost of enrollment management at the University of Hawai'i at Mānoa and Shawn is executive director of undergraduate admissions and deputy chief admissions and enrollment officer at Cornell. In 2020, the three of us connected in conversation when OiYan invited seasoned practitioners in the field to offer feedback on initial findings from a research project.[2] In writing this chapter as a group, we explored our perspectives, experiences, and desires for developing stronger relationships, trust, and partnerships between practitioners and researchers interested in advancing equity in college admissions. Ever-present in our conversations was the question: how might we routinely engage in integrated and ongoing dialogues between researchers and practitioners who share interests in the admissions field?

Through our conversations, we identified time as a central barrier to bringing together research and practice. For admissions professionals, being asked to thoughtfully engage with and reflect on the latest research, on top of their demanding schedules, can be received as an overwhelming additional request. Yet, not being conversant and up to date on the latest research prevents admissions professionals from effectively leading for change in academic institutions, where research represents power.[3]

For research scholars on the tenure track, time also represents a challenge. Tenure and promotion clocks are relentless and refereed publication mechanisms often slow. Because the development of research-practice partnerships requires investments in time to cultivate reciprocal relationships that center mutual respect between parties, early-career scholars may receive guidance to steer away from public scholarship ethics and methodologies. Moreover, traditional and dominant post/positivist research norms can push scholars away from working too closely with people in the research setting of focus. Yet, scholars in education research often express desires to have their research lead to impacts and changes in practice, policy, and public discourse.[4]

If our conversations are indicative, both practitioners and scholars in the college admissions space share an interest to bridge the gap between research and organizational practices. The looming questions seem to be, "Okay, so now what? When? And, most important, how?"

CHAPTER OVERVIEW

If practitioners and researchers agree that research is important to informing practice, and that the conditions of practice must be understood by researchers for their inquiries to bear public and critical impact, then how do we collectively and more effectively bring practice and research together? In this chapter, we start by explaining how we coconstructed a collective conversation, as three people with different roles in the academy who share interests in equity. We then offer excerpts from a transcript of a recorded conversation we had in December 2021. In this discussion, we identified time, leadership, and trust as three key considerations for practitioners and researchers to "break through the divide" between admissions work norms and research on admissions practices and outcomes. We wrap up the chapter with a discussion on how to deepen bridge building between research and practice amid various challenges and limited time. We offer three ideas—facilitated dialogue series, researcher-in-residence programs, and research-practice partnerships (RPP)—as bridge-building opportunities. We contend that bringing together a diversity of perspectives between stakeholders in college admissions, grounded in research and evidenced analysis, can lead to more creativity in transformative leadership and change.

We humbly recognize that the gap between research and practice is vast and bigger than ourselves. This chapter is a mere pebble intentionally dropped into a chasm, rather than a large boulder meant to fill a canyon. A pebble may not seem like much today, but with enough pebbles over time, the chasm shrinks. In other words, if you—a scholar, leader, practitioner, researcher, or policy advocate—arrived at this chapter in search of *clear and proven solutions*, you will be disappointed. We offer this chapter to spark dialogue and encourage steps toward change, rather than to arrive at or offer solutions.

We invite you to engage with this chapter as *a conversation among colleagues*. We recognize that we raise as many questions as we offer steps towards change, and that is by design. We hope that you see yourself an integral part of this conversation by virtue of reading this chapter. As you read and engage, we encourage you to think about your role and the contributions you make, or would like to make, to the dialogue and collective work toward change and equity in college admissions.

COCONSTRUCTING THE CONVERSATION

In preparation for our scheduled conversation via Zoom, we settled on the following central guiding question: "how do we collectively and more effectively bring practice and research together?" Starting with the question of why we committed to writing this chapter, we allowed the conversation to flow naturally. Shawn joined in from New York. OiYan logged in from Chicago, and Nikki hopped on from Honolulu. As soon as we connected online, we immediately engaged in research-to-practice dialogue. We were so excited for our continuing conversation that we almost forgot to hit the record button!

Three themes emerged from our conversation. First, as discussed in the introduction, the practical and literal limitations of time are ever-present as a challenge to bridge building between practitioners and scholars. Second, we realized that leaders in admissions and enrollment management organizations can use their roles and agency to directly build bridges between research and practice. Finally, throughout our conversation, we continually returned to the role and importance of cultivating and sustaining trust in bridge building between practice and research. What follows are excerpts from a transcript of our conversation.[5] As you read them, we invite you to imagine you are the fourth person conversing with us. What questions emerge for you? What surprised or resonated for you about what the practitioners or researcher expressed in conversation?

What brings you to this book project?

OiYan: Just to get this conversation started, what brings you to this book project? And as a reminder, this book project's aim is to bring together practice and leadership and admissions with research in college admissions . . . bring them into conversation with each other.

Shawn: I know now from being in a leadership role, I need research to make salient what it is I'm trying to communicate and to justify directions, budget requests, resource needs, and the utilization of resources. You've got to have evidence and research comes down to having evidence to support the work you're trying to do.

Nikki: I was thinking about how leadership roles are filled by people that have researcher roots; they have their PhDs, they have their EdDs. So it's beneficial as a practitioner, especially one that is coming up through leadership roles, to understand both sides of their colleagues' work. Academia feels like a whole other language, and I'm not sure I would have been poised at all to have these conversations if I didn't have some kind of clue about the research side of it and the scholarship.

OiYan: So what I'm hearing from you is that in your positions, in admissions leadership at your respective institutions, you are having to manage a kind of power structure essentially within the university that is filled with academics, who are immersed in research. You have to manage and take direction, but also be able to push back given your own expertise, particularly in how admissions works. I'm hearing you talk about yourselves as organizational leaders who need to talk the [scholarly] language of the power structure in the academy.

Shawn: That's exactly right! Yes, as far as the organizational pyramid, the higher up you go, the more you need to speak in a different language that matters more to those who are in the highest levels and roles of authority.

Under the premise that this is a different language, how do we make time to teach and train staff in that language? How do we—quite literally—find or make time to fit the language of scholarship into our everyday work as practitioners?

Nikki: From a practical standpoint, how do we as practitioners integrate that language and integrate that into the work of our staff? Does it necessitate somebody pursuing a formal degree, or can we build this into the professional development of our staff so that they are able to function in the breadth of areas across colleagues? Shawn and I have pondered with each other, how do you literally fit that into your everyday work as practitioners, when our days can be pulled in so many other different directions? Do researchers account for the literal practicality of where your time is going day to day?

OiYan: Can I answer that? I know it was a hypothetical question, "Do researchers account for the daily workflow of the admissions practitioner?" As a researcher . . . yes, Shawn, I see you shaking your head now! How do you know what I'm going to say? I was going to say, "No, we as researchers are not thinking about the daily work norms and flows and demands of the practitioners." We are more likely to think, "Oh, I'm going to make such a difference with this research, and if only Shawn and Nikki would read it and then things would change!"

Shawn: One thing I wrote down here was that scholars tend not to be practitioners, and practitioners have little time to engage in scholarship. In my mind, if you don't get close to the work, you're not going to really know the work as well as you need to. So research becomes a little bit like journalism, and the last thing as a practitioner I want is a journalist who doesn't care, who doesn't know enough, and is just repeating what they heard, or rewriting what someone else told them. That's not going to help me, and I'm not going to trust it to help me be better, do better, get better, learn more, engage my staff, or talk to my higher-ups in their very specific and particular language and style.

Nikki: Right, and as a practitioner, I want to get better. For instance, I received this robust, data-rich report on advancing equitable approaches to financial aid, specifically prepared for the University of Hawai'i system. The report sits on my desk because I'm afraid that if it's not in my face, then I will forget this data. I know there is valuable data here, but I don't have time or space for it just yet. How do we integrate these reports into our everyday work? It's not practical to fill my desk with reports where I am waiting for it to become applicable or relevant. If someone like me doesn't push to weave this data in somewhere then the initial response to the report from most staff and practitioners is, "Well, then what do you expect me to do with this information, and when?"

I'm hearing on one hand, it's great to present this information to practitioners . . . but leadership matters. What if leadership is a third agent in this bridge building between practice and research?

OiYan: This question, "What do you expect me to do with this information?" makes me think, as a researcher, I'll write something like a forty-page article for a peer review journal, then I'll try to translate it into a short brief, present it at a NACAC (National Association for College Admission Counseling) conference, or host a presentation with practitioners. These are different modes of communication and ways to bring research forward. For me, my takeaway is, this raises a lot of research ethics questions for me. What are my ethical obligations and responsibility as a researcher and working with practitioners and leaders who share my values for equity? Is it my responsibility and obligation to continue in that conversation? I would think, yes. I'm just speaking for myself as one researcher, but I don't think that's true of most other researchers. Our reward systems as academics are very different, it's to get that research article published.

Nikki: OiYan, when you said "leadership matters," that made me think there might be a third agent in this, and that's leadership. Maybe it's a part of leadership ethics because leaders like me and Shawn care about bringing research into our roles. We have to bring it together. It benefits us to bring this together. It makes me think maybe there's a triangulation here, and maybe that's what this book helps us to get at—people like me and Shawn that care about practice and research have to keep our foot on the gas. But that's exhausting!

OiYan: So leadership is an interpretation of research. You're interpreting this work for the folks that you work with.

Shawn: Exactly. I become responsible for your research in terms of translating it or finding ways to apply it, if that's even possible. Maybe I disagree with it, but I do become responsible for being the carrier of that particular work, especially if it's something that finds its way onto the biggest screen possible. Honestly, I want to make sure we can include this, even if I disagree with it. I'm not afraid of research. I'm not afraid to be told, "You're doing it all wrong," and I don't want someone to write stuff to make me feel good. I would rather you know what you're talking about. I would rather you have done your homework, especially if you're going to make me look bad! Know what you're talking about; do your homework; tell the truth; and get out of the way. That's all I care about.

Nikki: So true, we can't have an ego in this role; in fact, empathy serves us better. When I translate research to the leaders and staff who have their boots on the ground, I bring empathy to the conversation. I communicate that putting recommendations from research into practice is not as easy as senior leaders make it out to be. Maybe the researchers themselves didn't know exactly the impact on practice when they made this recommendation to our senior-most leaders, who then maybe turned around and created expectations from those recommendations. In my role, I want to go back to those who have to operationalize this work with direction and support as we figure out "how" to make this real.

OiYan: Yeah, because as a researcher, I can't sit here and direct the practice. There are little interlocking practices, norms, systems, and structures in place that I don't have privy to know how that works. What are the mechanisms, rules, or mandates you're under? Even private institutions have trustee mandates they have to work through. So then it becomes a leadership creativity of facilitating a "let's think this all through and have a 'make it work' moment." Let's try things out. What do you think Shawn? I see you're ready to jump in there.

Shawn: Leadership has to engage research and practice equally. It's a requirement of this role, but I also see myself as an individual who's been doing this a long time. All the stuff that you said that isn't accessible, I actually think is accessible. It's just sometimes you have to do a little research . . . while you're doing your research. If somebody wants to know why we do something at Cornell, why not just ask me? I'll tell you what I can tell you, and what I can't tell you. But why not just ask me?

OiYan: I just ask what you can't tell me. I think researchers are wondering, "Can I trust you?"

Let's explore trust.

Shawn: I wrote down the word trust here as one of the things I thought we would be talking about because that's a real concern for me. It's because of this dichotomy, you're either doing the work, or you're watching the work happen and you're remarking on the work. The challenge is bringing those two things together within a frame, a time, a place that makes sense. Why is it that we can't do that in enrollment, but we can do that in economics?

OiYan: So why can't we do that in enrollment when we do it in economics? That's interesting.

Shawn: Yeah, or pick another discipline. We could do that in education, but we can't do that in enrollment. I don't know why, but in the case of enrollment, it feels like there is this very wide space between the practitioner and the researcher, and I don't know why we don't know how to navigate it better. It may be that enrollment management is new and research is so long in the tooth. . . . You've got two things that are trying to sort of find something in common.

OiYan: So with my researcher hat on, I am thinking about how I've been told so many times before by traditional positivist scientists, that my involvement with people who do the work I'm studying compromises the integrity of my research and my findings. I'm too involved, because the scientists are supposed to be removed, arm's distance, and told "Don't be involved." Trust is antithetical to that. What I'm hearing you say, Shawn, is an affirmation to me! If I really want to have my research matter, I have to really tend to trust relationship building with the people who live what I'm interested in researching, and who lead what I'm interested in studying.

Shawn: Something else that would be really fascinating to talk about—because that changes the relationships—the respect piece, the trust piece, what you have to prove, and what you don't have to prove. I know that I can't succeed if I'm only looking down. I need to look up and out. As a leader, I'm not going to succeed, and I'm not going to be able to help my staff move forward if I'm only paying attention to what I'm doing. If I think I have all the answers, and if I think that I can't grow and change anything, or hear anybody else, I'm not going to be successful.

Nikki: Hmm . . . OiYan, I think you created an environment of respect and trust when you hosted small group sessions of seasoned practitioners and shared your early research findings with us. As a member of your research team and a seasoned admissions practitioner, I developed a deeper appreciation for that different way you chose to communicate your research and engage us in shaping the recommendations you may choose to make. It was because you created an environment where I could listen to my colleagues in an entirely different context—it opened my world too. Otherwise, I don't know that I would've heard Shawn's thought process or questions. Maybe that's what we could be doing more of, is creating these shared moments, whether it's conference settings or part of other professional development programming.

OiYan: When I told some researchers that I completed fifty interviews of seasoned admissions practitioners for my study, I had people say, "Wow, that's a lot! How did you get people to trust you to spend that time with you?" And at the same time I'm nervous as a researcher. I know that when researchers present at NACAC, I've kind of seen a couple of them do these big research presentations, and a lot of people in the audience are like, this is the new thing, they're going to run off and do this thing. I get nervous about that because there are limitations to that research that need to be considered.

Shawn: We are working with people, and what you say matters every single minute of every single day. Practitioners know this. Researchers must be better about understanding this. Unfortunately, some research becomes more like journalism, and then more like politics, where I will consider how much I wish to engage based upon my time and interests and what I think the researcher's motivation and point of view is.

Time is limited, even for this conversation! What are some final thoughts you have as we wrap this up?

Nikki: I was thinking about Shawn's question, "How do we navigate this? Where is the map?" And I guess a working theory is that there is no map because our predecessors didn't leave one for us. I think about how we put our practitioner predecessors on pedestals. One of the observations from OiYan's research involving fifty seasoned admissions practitioners was that our profession is a family tree without branches, and that observation sticks with me. There's a culture in our practice of looking at our predecessors as if they knew everything and could do no wrong, but we—me and you, Shawn—are not our predecessors. To me, we represent a turning point in this profession because we are leaders who identify with backgrounds that have been historically silenced in higher education and in this profession. To that end, we have developed a humility about the work that is . . . different. I mean, it is a different experience for us, so there's not a whole lot of guidance as to how you carry this responsibility of building bridges between practice and research, while also carrying every other priority that comes our way.

Shawn: I was just thinking, "What if research integrated practitioners more so than it does now, and vice versa?" If you want to know about what I'm doing as a practitioner, if you—as a researcher—have questions, you can call me and ask me those questions. I'm going to answer your questions. If you are from the New York Times, I have to handle that differently because journalists use this information in a different way. But if you're just calling to talk to me with an academic interest, you're Dr. so-and-so PhD, and you have questions or you're writing a book . . . I can tell you the truth. Obviously, there might be some things I'm not able to share with anyone, but what if there was more integration of the two roles in an active, participatory, and intentional way?

Nikki: Ooh, I like the sound of that.

OiYan: There's research methodologies based on research-practice partnerships. I've been thinking a lot more about design-based research, which requires partnership. Let's try some things out with your office and see how it goes. There's a little tiny experiment for research and for practice to develop simultaneously together.

Shawn: Exactly. Yesterday, I was talking with my boss about this and we were both wondering aloud. "What's the problem and/or question here?" Practitioners and scholars are operating in parallel in many ways. It's just a matter of breaking through the divide a little bit more and not being afraid of truth and understanding. I don't fully know what the concern is. The data are what the data are. I'm more concerned about integration and explanation related to motivation. I understand there are realms where researchers are less engaged with subjects. And the idea of boundaries between researchers and subjects looks and sounds like this—"I can't know you, or understand you, or care about the impact of what I have to say or how I say it." That approach and positionality seems inauthentic, evasive, and problematic to me.

OiYan: If I care about you or get involved in what I'm studying, then the integrity of my research is questioned. That's old school, white colonial research, in my opinion. And it doesn't do anything to make it matter.

Nikki: I'm with Shawn. If someone is going to study what I do everyday, I want to know and trust them. It will motivate me to participate, and I know I'll learn something valuable along the way.

Shawn: Right. I feel the need to be part of the conversation, and I want to see researchers come to the table unafraid of getting to know me as a subject.

NOW WHAT?

After this conversation and the many others we've had, we are left thinking about remaining issues, takeaways, and where we go from here separately and collectively. We listened to each other. We challenged each other's work norms, shared common frustrations, and connected over shared values. We felt heard by each other. We found common ground for a greater collective understanding. We left the moment hopeful for additional conversation and the desire for collaborative actionable steps.

Perhaps part of the problem is that most researchers studying admissions and enrollment management have never been practitioners in undergraduate admissions, nor have they spent time observing the inner workings of an admissions office.[6] Moreover, we note how rare it is to have researchers attend and engage in admissions profession convenings (e.g., NACAC conferences), and for practitioners to attend scholarly research convenings. There is little to encourage this kind of cross-pollination of attendance, connection, and exchange of ideas at our respective annual conferences. However, our distinct professional convenings may not be the places for the development of collaborative work.

To be clear, we do not claim that quality research on admissions requires that scholars serve as current or past practitioners, or that practitioners must lead or be members of research teams. However, we do encourage more systemic investments in the cultivation of relationships between researchers and practitioners, their organizations, and networks, to bring a diversity of perspectives into conversation with each other. We assert that building communities for ongoing dialogues between diverse parties with interests in college admissions can lead to critically creative analyses that could propel innovative structural changes for equity.

Progress will require practitioners and researchers to intentionally build trust and respect with each other, through both dialogue and working together to experiment with ideas. To that end, we offer three suggestions for cultivating conversation and community building between practitioners and researchers to be more routine and commonplace. These three possibilities could catalyze a shift away from the divide between practice and research. They could induce collective dialogue and partnerships that serve as generative grounds for new innovations centering equity.

First, networks of practitioners and scholars could coconvene and cofacilitate regular virtual and in-person conversations between their respective constituencies. The COVID-19 pandemic has demonstrated that virtual convenings, though not ideal, can be instrumental. Could practitioner organizations like NACAC, ACCEPT (Admissions Community Cultivating Equity & Peace Today), or AACRAO (American Association of Collegiate Registrars and Admissions Officers) work with research centers, which focus on public scholarship, to collectively pilot a series of conversations? Perhaps intermediary organizations, like TICAS (the Institute for College Access & Success), Learning Policy Institute, Ed Trust, or IHEP (Institute for Higher Education Policy) could design and convene these dialogues. Whoever the organizer, they should work with various stakeholders to design each conversation and series of discussions for coconstructed learning, to generate further partnerships.

Second, we suggest the creation and design of a fellowship program to place research scholars in a postsecondary institution admissions office or temporarily on staff at an admissions professional association or organization. There are a few examples of such an idea. NACAC once had a scholar-in-residence type program, in which selected scholars worked closely with NACAC staff and organizational leaders on various projects. For instance, UCLA professor Patricia McDonough once served in this capacity, producing research to practice briefs for NACAC.[7] In another example, some researchers have independently gained the trust of individual college and university admissions offices and administrative spaces to allow them to observe admissions work.[8] This idea would require financial resources to support faculty leave or a postdoctoral fellowship, so scholars could allot the needed time and attention to their engagement and participation as a colleague in host organizations. During their time in residence, researchers could be asked to participate in daily organizational routines, such as simple administrative tasks, staff meetings, reading files, data analysis and internal report writing, and other work deemed helpful to the organization.

With researchers embedded in organizations, the organic conversations between colleagues would theoretically lead to new questions, ideas, and possibilities for inquiry and organizational change. For practitioners, a fellowship program like this could allow them the opportunity to be in regular conversation with a researcher, to consider research insights related to their work. Additionally, for scholars that spend some time in the shoes of practitioners, they might develop a firmer foundation, informed by organization norms and practices, for designing scholarly inquiry and presenting research that can bear more sustainable impacts on practice and policy. This idea recognizes that practitioners and researchers operate with different cultural norms and structural expectations.[9] Accordingly, the suggestion offers a mechanism for a sort of cultural exchange.

Finally, we encourage practitioners and researchers to consider the research-practice partnership (RPP) model and ethic of work between education scholars and practitioners. Since the start of the twenty-first century, RPPs have coalesced into somewhat of a movement, inclusive of the formation of the National Network of Education Research-Practice Partnerships (NNERP).[10] NNERP states that RPPs are "long-term mutually beneficial formalized collaborations between education researchers and practitioners . . . a promising strategy for producing more relevant research [that improves] the use of research evidence in decision-making, and engaging both researchers and practitioners to tackle problems of practice."[11] In RPPs, long-term partners collaboratively identify their working expectations, codesign and complete research projects together, mindful of power differentials and dynamics.

Collaborative researchers have documented the promises of RPPs for cultivating effective partnerships between various stakeholders—practitioners, researchers, community members, families and youth—to create systemic changes.[12] Relevant to the challenges to building partnerships we have presented in this chapter, a key benefit of RPPs is that they "create structures for ongoing communication and trust among all participants, including those whose knowledge has been devalued in the past."[13] RPPs are not short-term singular and discrete research projects. They are a bridge-building intervention that requires intentional investments of time and energy from all involved. We acknowledge that this does not solve the challenge of time noted at the top of this chapter. Such endeavors require a readiness among partners to engage in intentional and routine practices of relationship building and maintenance.

Relatedly, RPP scholars and NNERP have cautioned that "research-practice partnerships are challenging to create and difficult to maintain."[14] Anyone interested in initiating the development and cultivation of an RPP should be mindful that like any relationship, RPPs can present challenges that partners will need to navigate together. These challenges include differing work norms, languages, and cultures,[15] as well as power dynamics and inequities that must be explicitly discussed and disrupted through the RPP design.[16]

Related to inequalities in power, we want to note that in this chapter we have centered the discussion on partnerships and bridge building between admissions practitioners and researchers. We have yet to discuss the importance of building partnerships and collaborations with prospective and current college students, their families, schools, and other stakeholders. In experimenting with these three suggested ideas for building stronger trust and relationships for partnerships between practitioners and researchers, scholars and practitioners should also consider possibilities for including students, families, schools, school-based and community-based college access practitioners as equal partners with valuable contributions to offer. Future reflections and research should explore how these and other key stakeholders can be included in bridge-building work. For the scope of this chapter, we wanted to engage deeply with bridge-building possibilities between practitioners and researchers.

CONCLUSION

Breaking through divides does not happen overnight, but we must start somewhere. We invite our practitioner and scholar-practitioner colleagues and peers into this discussion to identify challenges and possible ways forward. We have offered three ideas for building bridges and partnerships between practitioners and researchers, to bring critical and collaborative systemic analysis to bear on practice and offer new systemic innovations for equity.

NOTES

PREFACE

1. Kirsten Hextrum, "Operation Varsity Blues: Disguising the Legal Capital Exchanges and White Property Interests in Athletic Admissions," *Higher Education Politics & Economics* 5, no. 1 (2019): 15–32.

2. Marie Bigham and OiYan Poon, "It's Time to Hack the Gates in College Admissions Systems," *Diverse Issues in Higher Education*, September 11, 2019, https://www.diverseeducation.com/students/article/15105411/its-time-to-hack-the-gates-in-college-admissions-systems.

3. For more on systems and practices in athletic admissions, see: Kirsten Hextrum. *Special Admission: How College Sports Recruitment Favors White Suburban Athletes* (New Brunswick, NJ: Rutgers University Press, 2021); Mitchell Stevens, *Creating a Class: College Admissions and the Education of Elites* (Cambridge, MA: Harvard University Press, 2007).

4. Mikhail Zinshteyn, "UC Officially Ditches Any Tests for Undergraduate Admissions," *CalMatters*, November 19, 2021, https://calmatters.org/education/higher-education/2021/11/uc-admissions-no-tests/.

5. Marie Bingham, OiYan A. Poon, and Douglas H. Lee, "Hack the Gates! How We Radically Reimagine College Admissions," *Spark: Elevating Scholarship on Social Issues*, July 30, 2020, https://medium.com/national-center-for-institutional-diversity/hack-the-gates-how-we-radically-reimagine-college-admissions-6ec1ab128cdb.

6. Estela M. Bensimon, "The Underestimated Significance of Practitioner Knowledge in the Scholarship on Student Success," *The Review of Higher Education* 30, no. 4 (2007): 441–69; Lori P. Davis, "2018 Keynote," ASHE 2018,

https://www.youtube.com/watch?v=B7zUFPKapzo&feature=youtu.be; Shaun Harper, "2017 Presidential Address," ASHE 2017, https://www.youtube.com/watch?v=17BVV1R7eUg&feature=youtu.be; J. F. Milem, "Considering Our Legacy: Doing Work That Really Matters," *The Review of Higher Education* 34, no. 2 (2011): 319–33; L. W. Perna, "Throwing Down the Gauntlet: Ten Ways to Ensure That Higher Education Research Continues to Matter," *The Review of Higher Education* 39, no. 3 (2016): 319–38; K. A. Renn, "Reimagining the Study of Higher Education: Generous Thinking, Chaos, and Order in a Low Consensus Field," The Review of Higher Education 43, no. 4 (202): 917–34.

CHAPTER 1

1. Liliana M. Garces, "Aligning Diversity, Quality, and Equity: The Implications of Legal and Public Policy Developments for Promoting Racial Diversity in Graduate Studies," *American Journal of Education* 120, no. 4 (2014): 457–80; Liliana M. Garces, "The False Notion of 'Race-Neutrality': How Legal Battles in Higher Education Undermine Racial Equity," *Change: The Magazine of Higher Learning* 52, no. 2 (2020): 51–55, https://doi.org/10.1080/00091383.2020.1732778.

2. Ben Backes, "Do Affirmative Action Bans Lower Minority College Enrollment and Attainment? Evidence from Statewide Bans," *Journal of Human Resources* 47, no. 2 (2012): 435–55, http://doi.org/10.1353/jhr.2012.0013; Liliana M. Garces, "Understanding the Impact of Affirmative Action Bans in Different Graduate Fields of Study," *American Educational Research Journal* 50, no. 2 (2013): 251–84; Peter Hinrichs, "The Effects of Affirmative Action Bans on College Enrollment, Educational Attainment, and the Demographic Composition of Universities," *Review of Economics and Statistics* 94, no. 3 (2012): 712–22, http://doi.org/10.1162/REST_a_00170; Huacong Liu, "How do Affirmative Action Bans Affect the Racial Composition of Postsecondary Students in Public Institutions?" *Educational Policy* (2020): 1–25, https://doi.org/10.1177/0895904820961007; Liliana M. Garces and David Mickey-Pabello, "Racial Diversity in the Medical Profession: The Impact of Affirmative Action Bans on Underrepresented Student of Color Matriculation in Medical Schools," *The Journal of Higher Education* 86, no. 2 (2015): 264–94.

3. Liliana M. Garces, "Lessons from Social Science for Kennedy's Doctrinal Inquiry in Fisher v. University of Texas II," *UCLA Law Review Discourse* 64 (2016): 17–39.

4. Paul Bowers, "Affirmative Action Comes to a Quiet End at College of Charleston," *The Post and Courier*, July 29, 2018, https://www.postandcourier.com/news/affirmative-action-comes-to-a-quiet-end-at-college-of-charleston/article_e89f0042-8b88-11e8-bbab-3f0dd42c81bb.html; Liliana M. Garces and Darkhan Bilyalov, "Navigating the Quicksand: How Postsecondary Administrators Understand the Influence of Affirmative Action Developments on Racial Diversity Work," *Teachers College Record* 121, no. 3 (2019): 1–40; Kristen

M. Glasener, Christian A. Martell, and Julie R. Posselt, "Framing Diversity: Examining the Place of Race in Institutional Policy and Practice Post-affirmative Action," *Journal of Diversity in Higher Education* 12, no. 1 (2019): 3–16; Pamela Barta Moreno, "The History of Affirmative Action Law and its Relation to College Admission," *Journal of College Admission* 179 (2003): 14–21.

5. Liliana M. Garces and Courtney D. Cogburn, "Beyond Declines in Student Body Diversity: How Campus-Level Administrators Understand a Prohibition on Race-conscious Postsecondary Admissions Policies," *American Educational Research Journal* 52, no. 5 (2015): 828–60, https://doi.org/10.3102/0002831215594878cghy.

6. Subini Ancy Annamma, Darrell D. Jackson, and Deb Morrison, "Conceptualizing Color-Evasiveness: Using Dis/ability Critical Race Theory to Expand a Color-Blind Racial Ideology in Education and Society," *Race Ethnicity and Education* 20, no. 2 (2017): 147–62.

7. Liliana M. Garces et al., "Repressive Legalism: How Postsecondary Administrators' Responses to On-campus Hate Speech Undermine a Focus on Inclusion," *American Educational Research Journal*, (2021), 1–28.

8. Lauren B. Edelman and Mark C. Suchman, "The Legal Environments of Organizations," *Annual Review of Sociology* 23 (1997): 479–515.

9. Garces et al., "Repressive Legalism," 5.

10. Garces et al., "Repressive Legalism," 28.

11. Garces et al., "Repressive Legalism," 5.

12. Neal H. Hutchens and Frank Fernandez, "Searching for Balance with Student Free Speech: Campus Speech Zones, Institutional Authority, and Legislative Prerogatives," *Belmont Law Review* 5 (2018): 103–28; Brandi Hephner LaBanc, Frank Fernandez, Neal Hutchens, and Kerry Brian Melear, *The Contested Campus: Aligning Professional Values, Social Justice, and Free Speech* (NASPA, Inc., 2020).

13. Garces et al., "Repressive Legalism," 31.

14. Sosanya Marie Jones, "Diversity Leadership under Race-Neutral Policies in Higher Education," *Equality, Diversity and Inclusion: An International Journal* 33, no. 8 (2014): 708–20.

15. Leslie D. Gonzales, Dana Kanhai, and Kayon Hall, "Reimagining Organizational Theory for the Critical Study of Higher Education," in *Higher Education: Handbook of Theory and Research*, vol. 33, ed. Michael B. Paulsen (Springer, 2018), 505–59.

16. Paul DiMaggio and Walter W. Powell, "The Iron Cage Revisited: Institutional Isomorphism and Collective Rationality in Organizational Fields," *American Sociological Review* 48, no. 2 (1983): 147–60.

17. Daniel N. Lipson, "Embracing Diversity: The Institutionalization of Affirmative Action as Diversity Management at UC-Berkeley, UT-Austin, and UW-Madison," *Law & Social Inquiry* 32, no. 4 (2007): 1020, https://doi.org/10.1111/j.1747-4469.2007.00085.x.

18. *Regents of the University of California v. Bakke*, 438 U.S. 265 (1978); Garces, "Aligning Diversity, Quality, and Equity," 457–80.

19. *Regents of the University of California v. Bakke*, 438 U.S. 265, 291 (1978).

20. *Gratz v. Bollinger*, 539 U.S. 244 (2003); *Grutter v. Bollinger*, 539 U.S. 306 (2003).

21. *Fisher v. University of Texas*, 570 U.S. 297 (2013). For a discussion of Texas' Top Ten Percent Plan, see Mark C. Long, Victor Saenz, and Marta Tienda, "Policy Transparency and College Enrollment: Did the Texas Top Ten Percent Law Broaden Access to the Public Flagships?" *The ANNALS of the American Academy of Political and Social Science* 627, no. 1 (2010): 82–105, https://doi.org/10.1177/0002716209348741.

22. *Fisher v. University of Texas*, 579 U.S. 365 (2016).

23. Bradley C. Canon and Charles A. Johnson, *Judicial Policies: Impact and Implementation*, 2nd ed. (Washington, DC: CQ Press, 1999), 16–23.

24. Glasener, Martell, and Posselt, "Framing Diversity," 3–16.

25. Moreno, "The History of Affirmative Action Law," 14–21.

26. Grady Newsource, "Georgia Daze Strives to Increase Black Student Applicants," University of Georgia, March 22, 2021, https://gradynewsource.uga.edu/georgia-daze-strives-to-increase-black-student-applicants/.

27. Bowers, "Affirmative Action Comes to a Quiet End."

28. Garces and Bilyalov, "Navigating the Quicksand," 1–40.

29. *Adams v. Richardson*, 356 F. Supp. 92 (D.D.C., 1973).

30. Garces and Bilyalov, "Navigating the Quicksand," 1–40, 22.

31. Garces and Bilyalov, "Navigating the Quicksand," 22.

32. Jones, "Diversity Leadership under Race-neutral Policies in Higher Education," 708–20; Joyce P. Perez, "Proposition 209: A Case Study on the Impact of Race-Based Legislation on Student Affairs at the University of California" (PhD diss., University of Southern California, 2009).

33. Neal H. Hutchens and Frank Fernandez, "Higher Education Governance," in *Contemporary Issues in Higher Education Law*, 4th ed., eds. Susan C. Bon, David H. Nguyen, and Jennifer A. Rippner (Education Law Association, 2019), 13–33.

34. Donna J. Nicol, "Activism for Profit: America's 'Anti-affirmative Action' Industry," *Al Jazeera*, February, 28, 2021, https://www.aljazeera.com/opinions/2021/2/28/activism-for-profit-americas-anti-affirmative-action-industry.

35. Garces, "Aligning Diversity, Quality, and Equity," 457–80; Carson McCullough, "Idaho Governor Signs Restrictions on Affirmative Action, Trans Athletes," *Courthouse News Service*, March 30, 2020, https://www.courthousenews.com/idaho-governor-approves-two-anti-transgender-bills/.

36. Backes, "Do Affirmative Action Bans Lower Minority College Enrollment," 435–55; Liliana M. Garces, "Racial Diversity, Legitimacy, and the Citizenry: The Impact of Affirmative Action Bans on Graduate School Enrollment,"

The Review of Higher Education 36, no. 1 (2012): 93–132; Hinrichs, "The Effects of Affirmative Action Bans on College Enrollment," 712–22; Garces and Mickey-Pabello, "Racial Diversity in the Medical Profession," 264–94; David Mickey-Pabello and Liliana M. Garces, "Addressing Racial Health Inequities: Understanding the Impact of Affirmative Action Bans on Applications and Admissions in Medical Schools," *American Journal of Education* 125, no. 1 (2018): 79–108.

37. Garces, "Understanding the Impact of Affirmative Action Bans," 251–84.

38. Eric Grodsky and Michal Kurlaender, "The Demography of Higher Education in the Wake of Affirmative Action," in *Equal Opportunity in Higher Education: The Past and Future of California's Proposition 209*, eds. Eric Grodsky and Michal Kurlaender (Harvard Education Press, 2010), 33–58; William C. Kidder and Patricia Gándara, "Two Decades after the Affirmative Action Ban: Evaluating the University of California's Race-neutral Efforts," UCLA: The Civil Rights Project / Proyecto Derechos Civiles, October 1, 2016, 1–54, https://escholarship.org/uc/item/55j5z74v.

39. Liu, "How do Affirmative Action Bans Affect the Racial Composition of Postsecondary Students," 18–19.

40. Liliana M. Garces and Uma M. Jayakumar, "Dynamic Diversity: Toward a Contextual Understanding of Critical Mass," *Educational Researcher* 43, no. 3 (2014): 115–24.

41. Sylvia Hurtado et al., "Predicting Transition and Adjustment to College: Biomedical and Behavioral Science Aspirants' and Minority Students' First Year of College," *Research in Higher Education* 48 (2007): 841–87; Angela M. Locks et al., "Extending Notions of Campus Climate and Diversity to Students' Transition to College," *The Review of Higher Education* 31, no. 3 (2008): 257–85, https://doi.org/10.1353/rhe.2008.0011; Berkeley Miller and Sutee Sujitparapitaya, "Campus Climate in the Twenty-First Century: Estimating Perceptions of Discrimination at a Racially Mixed Institution, 1994–2006," *New Directions for Institutional Research*, no. 145 (2010): 29–52.

42. Sylvia Hurtado et al., "A Model for Diverse Learning Environments: The Scholarship on Creating and Assessing Conditions for Student Success," in *Higher Education Handbook of Theory and Research*, vol. 27, eds. John C. Smart and Michael B. Paulsen (Springer, 2012), 41–122.

43. Garces and Cogburn, "Beyond Declines in Student Body Diversity," 828–60.

44. Garces and Cogburn, "Beyond Declines in Student Body Diversity," 841.

45. Camille G. Caldera and Sahar M. Mohammadzadeh, "Public Filings Reveal SFFA Mostly Funded by Conservative Trusts Searle Freedom Trust and DonorsTrust," *The Harvard Crimson*. February 7, 2019, https://www.thecrimson.com/article/2019/2/7/sffa-finance/.

46. Colleen Flaherty, "Legislating Against Critical Race Theory," *Inside Higher Ed*, June 9, 2021, https://www.insidehighered.com/news/2021/06/09/legislating-against-critical-race-theory-curricular-implications-some-states.

47. Amelia Davidson, "Students for Fair Admissions Sues Yale, Petitions to Escalate Harvard Case to Supreme Court," *Yale Daily News*, February 25, 2021, https://yaledailynews.com/blog/2021/02/25/students-for-fair-admissions-sues-yale-petitions-to-escalate-harvard-case-to-supreme-court/; Anemona Hartocollis, "Harvard Victory Pushes Admissions Case Toward a More Conservative Supreme Court," *The New York Times*, November 16, 2020, https://www.nytimes.com/2020/11/12/us/harvard-affirmative-action.html; Raga Justin, "UT-Austin Faces a Third Lawsuit Claiming that White Students were Unfairly Denied Admission under Affirmative Action," *The Texas Tribune*, July 22, 2020, https://www.texastribune.org/2020/07/22/ut-austin-affirmative-action-lawsuit-white/.

48. Joan Biskupic, "The Supreme Court Hasn't Been This Conservative Since the 1930s," CNN, September 26, 2020, https://www.cnn.com/2020/09/26/politics/supreme-court-conservative/index.html; Vincent Martin Bonventre, "Supreme Shift: What the 6-3 Conservative Majority Means Going Forward," *New York State Bar Association Journal* 93, no. 1 (2021): 9–14, https://nysba.org/app/uploads/2020/12/Journal_JanFeb_2021_web1.pdf; Bianca Quilantan, "Supreme Court will take up Harvard, UNC affirmative action challenge," *Politico*, January 24, 2022, https://www.politico.com/news/2022/01/24/supreme-court-affirmative-action-harvard-unc-00001236.

49. Garces, "The False Notion of Race Neutrality," 51–55.

50. Arguably, what is necessary to counter the sociopolitical forces that leverage the repressive force of the law on administrative action is a social movement for racial justice that resists the ongoing oppression of communities of color and helps transform our educational system to advance racial equity amidst the demographic changes of the twenty-first century. But such a focus is beyond the scope of this chapter.

51. Lani Guinier, "From Racial Liberalism to Racial Literacy: Brown v. Board of Education and the Interest-Divergence Dilemma," *The Journal of American History* (June 2004): 92–118. See also Liliana M. Garces and Cynthia Gordon da Cruz, "A Strategic Racial Equity Framework," *Peabody Journal of Education* 92, no. 3 (2017): 322–42.

52. Scott Jaschik, "Appeals Court Backs Harvard on Affirmative Action," *Inside Higher Ed*, November 16, 2021, https://www.insidehighered.com/admissions/article/2020/11/16/appeals-court-backs-harvard-affirmative-action; Melissa Korn, "University of North Carolina at Chapel Hill Wins in Admissions-Discrimination Suit," *The Wall Street Journal*, October 18, 2021, https://www.wsj.com/articles/university-of-north-carolina-at-chapel-hill-wins-in-admissions-discrimination-suit-11634593135.

CHAPTER 2

1. Craig S. Wilder, *Ebony and Ivy: Race, Slavery, and the Troubled History of America's Universities* (New York: Bloomsbury Press, 2013).

2. Calculated using National Postsecondary Student Aid Study: 2016 Undergraduates (NPSAS:UG) data on PowerStats with the following variables INCQUART, RACE, SELECTV3, and WTA000 weight.

3. Joshua Klugman, "The Advanced Placement Arms Race and the Reproduction of Educational Inequality," *Teachers College Record* 115, no. 5 (2013): 1–34, https://doi.org/10.1177/016146811311500506; Mitchell L. Stevens, *Creating a Class: College Admissions and the Education of Elites* (Cambridge, MA: Harvard University Press, 2007).

4. *Course, Counselor and Teacher Gaps: Addressing the College Readiness Challenge in High-Poverty High Schools* (Washington, DC: CLASP, 2015), https://www.clasp.org/sites/default/files/publications/2017/04/CollegeReadinessPaperFINALJune .pdf; James S. Coleman et al., *Equality of Educational Opportunity* (Washington, DC: US Government Printing Office, 1966), http://files.eric.ed.gov/fulltext/ED012275.pdf; *The Transformed Civil Rights Data Collection (CRDC): Revealing New Truths about Our Nation's School*, Office for Civil Rights (Washington, DC: US Department of Education, March 2012), https://www2.ed.gov/about/offices/list/ocr/docs/crdc-2012-data-summary.pdf.

5. Phillip M. Sadler, *AP: A Critical Examination of the Advanced Placement Program* (Cambridge, MA: Harvard Education Press, 2010).

6. *Character and the College Admission Process* (Arlington, VA: NACAC, n.d.), https://www.nacacnet.org/globalassets/documents/publications/research/character-brief/nacac_brief_character-0120_2.pdf.

7. See, for example, Suneal Kolluri, "Reconsidering Organizational Habitus in Schools: One Neighborhood, Two Distinct Approaches to Advanced Placement," *Harvard Educational Review* 89, no. 1 (2019): 109–31, https://doi.org/10.17763/1943-5045-89.1.109; Kayla Patrick, Allison Socol, and Ivy Morgan, *Inequities in Advanced Coursework: What's Driving Them and What Leaders Can Do* (Washington DC: Ed Trust, January 2020), https://edtrust.org/wp-content/uploads/2014/09/Inequities-in-Advanced-Coursework-Whats-Driving-Them-and-What-Leaders-Can-Do-January-2019.pdf.

8. National Center for Education Statistics, "Table 225.60: Number and Percentage of Public High School Graduates Taking Dual Credit, Advanced Placement (AP), and International Baccalaureate (IB) Courses in High School and Average Credits Earned, by Selected Student and School Characteristics: 2000, 2005, and 2009," *Digest of Education Statistics*, US Department of Education, Institute of Education Sciences, November 2012, https://nces.ed.gov/programs/digest/d19/tables/dt19_225.60.asp.

9. Jennifer D. Zinth, "Advanced Placement: Subsidies for Testing Fees," Education Commission of the States, last modified 2016, http://ecs.force.com/mbdata/MBQuestRT?Rep=AP0516; "Advanced Placement Incentive Program Grants," US Department of Education, last modified March 27, 2014, https://www2.ed.gov/programs/apincent/index.html.

10. Analysis of 18,473 regular and open high schools found in the Civil Rights Data Collection and Common Core of Data; low-income here is defined as FRL-eligible students. Comparisons of top and bottom FRL quintiles.

11. Michael N. Bastedo et al., "What Are We Talking about When We Talk about Holistic Review? Selective College Admissions and Its Effects on Low-SES Students," *The Journal of Higher Education* 89, no. 5 (2018): 782–805, https://doi.org/10.1080/00221546.2018.1442633.

12. *Best Practices for Developing a School Profile* (Arlington, VA: NACAC, 2020), https://www.nacacnet.org/globalassets/documents/knowledge-center/school-profiles/best-practices-school-profile.pdf; Tara P. Nicola, "Assessing Applicants in Context? School Profiles and Their Implications for Equity in the Selective College Admission Process," *Journal of Diversity in Higher Education* (Advance Online Publication 2021): https://doi.org/10.1037/dhe0000318.

13. Scott Jaschik, "If You Could Reform Admissions . . . ," *Inside Higher Ed*, March 8, 2021, https://www.insidehighered.com/admissions/article/2021/03/08/nacac-creates-commission-look-admissions-process-focus-race.

14. See, for example, Dania V. Francis, Angela C. M. de Oliveira, and Carey Dimmit, "Do School Counselors Exhibit Bias in Recommending Students for Advanced Coursework?," *The B.E. Journal of Economic Analysis & Policy* 194, no. 4 (2019), https://doi.org/10.1515/bejeap-2018-0189; Seth Gershenson, Stephen B. Holt, and Nicholas Papageorge, "Who Believes in Me? The Effect of Student–Teacher Demographic Match on Teacher Expectations," *Economics of Education Review* 52 (2016): 209–24, https://doi.org/10.17848/wp15–231; Adrian H. Huerta et al., "College Is . . . : Focusing on the College Knowledge of Gang-Associated Latino Young Men," *Urban Education* (2020): 1–30, https://doi.org/10.1177/0042085920934854; Tiffinie A. Irving, "Access to Academic Excellence: School Personnel's Perceptions and Practices of Student Participation in Advanced Placement Programs in a Predominately Minority High School" (PhD diss., Wichita State University, 2014), http://hdl.handle.net/10057/11366; Eugene Judson, Nicole L. Bowers, and Kristi Glassmeyer, "Recruiting and Encouraging Students to Complete Advanced Placement Science and Math Courses and Exams: Policies and Practices," *Journal for the Education for the Gifted* 42, no. 3 (2019): 243–65, https://doi.org/10.1177/0162353219855679; Kolluri, "Reconsidering Organizational Habitus"; Danny Lackey and Kendra Lowery, "Where Are the African American Males? Enrollment Criteria and the Placement of African American Males in Advanced Placement Courses," *Urban*

Education (2020): 1–30, https://doi.org/10.1177/0042085920959133; Amanda E. Lewis and John B. Diamond, *Despite the Best Intentions: How Racial Inequality Thrives in Good Schools* (New York: Oxford University Press, 2015); Patricia M. McDonough, *Choosing Colleges: How Social Class and Schools Structure Opportunity* (Albany: State University of New York Press, 1997); Jeannie Oakes and Gretchen Guiton, "Matchmaking: The Dynamics of High School Tracking Decisions," *American Educational Research Journal* 32, no. 1 (1995): 3–33, https://doi.org/ 10.3102/00028312032001003; Awilda Rodriguez and Esmeralda Hernandez-Hamed, "Understanding Unfulfilled AP Potential Across the Participation Pipeline by Race and Income," *Teachers College Record* 122, no. 9 (2020): 1–38, https://doi.org/10.1177/016146812012200909; Vanessa Witenko, Rebeca Mireles-Rios, and Victor M. Rios, "Networks of Encouragement: Who's Encouraging Latina/o Students and White Students to Enroll in Honors and Advanced-Placement (AP) Courses?" *Journal of Latinos and Education* 16, no. 3 (2017): 176–91, https://doi.org/10.1080/15348431.2016.1229612; Susan Yonezawa, Amy S. Wells, and Irene Serna, "Choosing Tracks: 'Freedom of Choice' in Detracking Schools," *American Educational Research Journal* 39, no. 1 (2002): 37–67, https://doi.org/10.3102/00028312039001037.

15. Francis, de Oliveira, and Dimmit, "Do School Counselors Exhibit Bias"; Rodriguez and Hernandez-Hamed, "Understanding Unfulfilled AP Potential."

16. *Helping to Ensure Equal Access to Education: Report to the President and Secretary of Education, Under Section 203(b)(1) of the Department of Education Organization Act, FY 2009–2012*, Office for Civil Rights (Washington, DC: US Department of Education, 2012), https://www2.ed.gov/about/reports/annual/ocr/report-to-president-2009-12.pdf.

17. Stevens, *Creating a Class*.

18. Ozan Jaquette, Bradley R. Curs, and Julie R. Posselt, "Tuition Rich, Mission Poor: Nonresident Enrollment Growth and the Socioeconomic and Racial Composition of Public Research Universities," *The Journal of Higher Education* 87, no. 5 (2016): 635–67, https://doi.org/10.1080/00221546.2016.11777417; Jerome A. Lucido, "How Admission Decisions Get Made," in *The Handbook of Strategic Enrollment Management*, ed. Don Hossler and Bob Bontrager (San Francisco: Jossey-Bass, 2014), 147–73.

19. Karina G. Salazar, "The Wealth and Color of Off-Campus Recruiting by Public Research Universities" (PhD diss., University of Arizona, 2019), http://hdl.handle.net/10150/634340; Karina G. Salazar, Ozan Jaquette, and Crystal Han, "Coming Soon to a Neighborhood near You? Off-Campus Recruiting by Public Research Universities," *American Educational Research Journal* 58, no. 6 (2021): 1–45, https://doi.org/10.3102/00028312211001810.

20. Salazar, Jaquette, and Han, "Off-Campus Recruiting"; Stevens, *Creating a Class*.

21. Michael N. Bastedo and Nicholas A. Bowman, "Improving Admission of Low-SES Students at Selective Colleges: Results from an Experimental Simulation," *Educational Researcher* 46, no. 2 (2017): 67–77, https://doi.org/10.3102/0013189X17699373.

22. Judy Phair, *Career Paths for Admissions Officers: A Survey Report* (Arlington, VA: National Association for College Admission Counseling, July 2014), https://www.nacacnet.org/globalassets/documents/publications/research/career-paths2014.pdf; *2019 Chief Admissions Officer: Summary of the AACRAO Career Profile Survey* (Washington, DC: AACRAO 2019), https://www.aacrao.org/docs/default-source/research-docs/career-profile/2019-chief-admissions-officer-report.pdf.

23. Nicholas A. Bowman and Michael N. Bastedo, "What Role May Admissions Office Diversity and Practices Play in Equitable Decisions?," *Research in Higher Education* 59 (2018): 430–47, https://doi.org/10.1007/s11162-017-9468-9.

24. Bowman and Bastedo, "Admissions Office Diversity and Practices."

25. Leah Hakkola, "'The Secret Knock': A Critical Discourse Analysis of How Recruiters Exercise Power and Privilege in Admissions," *Race and Ethnicity in Education* (2021): 1–18, https://doi.org/10.1080/13613324.2021.1924140.

26. Leah Hakkola, "Obstacles and Pathways: A Critical Discourse Analysis of Diversity in College Recruiting," *Journal of Diversity in Higher Education* 12, no. 4 (2019): 365–76, https://doi.org/10.1037/dhe0000111.

27. Hakkola, "'The Secret Knock.'"

CHAPTER 3

1. *Minoritized* refers to groups of people not necessarily in the numerical minority who have been assigned socially constructed characteristics of a minority; they are viewed and even treated by others as inferior, valueless, and subhuman to maintain control and power over them. We reject this socially constructed power structure. See Carolyn M. Shields, Russell Bishop, and Andre Elias Mazawi, *Pathologizing Practices: The Impact of Deficit Thinking on Education*, vol. 268 (Bern, Switzerland: Peter Lang, 2005).

2. *5-Year American Community Survey, 2014* (Washington, DC: US Census Bureau, 2014), http://factfinder.census.gov.

3. *Fingertip Facts on Education in California* (Sacramento: California Department of Education, 2021), https://www.cde.ca.gov/ds/ad/ceffingertipfacts.asp.

4. Frances Contreras, Thandeka Chapman, Eddie Comeaux, Gloria M. Rodriguez, Malo Hutson, and Eligio Martinez, *Investing in California's African American Students: College Choice, Diversity, and Exclusion* (Oakland: University of California Office of the President, 2015), http://iurd.berkeley.edu/research/EXCEL_Report_2016.pdf; Robert Teranishi, Walter Allen, and Daniel Solórzano, "Opportunity at the Crossroads: Racial Inequality, School Segregation, and Higher Education in California," *Teachers College Record* 106 (2004): 2224–45, http://dx.doi.org/10.1111/j.1467-9620.2004.00434.x.

5. University of California, *Annual Report on Undergraduate Admissions Requirements and Comprehensive Review* (Oakland: UC, 2021), https://senate.universityofcalifornia.edu/_files/committees/boars/documents/boars-2021-cr-report.pdf.

6. Contreras et al., *African American Students*; Tara Watford and Eddie Comeaux, "'Merit' Matters: Race, Myth and Admissions," *Bunche Research Report* 3, no. 3 (2006): 1–8.

7. *Undergraduate Admissions Summary* (Oakland: UC Office of the President, 2020), https://www.universityofcalifornia.edu/infocenter/admissions-residency-and-ethnicity; *ACS Housing and Demographic Data, 2019* (Washington, DC: US Census Bureau, 2021), https://www.census.gov/acs/www/data/data-tables-and-tools/data-profiles/2018/.

8. *Annual Report on Undergraduate Admissions Requirements and Comprehensive Review* (Oakland: University of California, 2013), https://senate.universityofcalifornia.edu/_files/committees/boars/BOARS2012-13AnnualReport.pdf.

9. "BOARS Report Says New Admissions Policy Working as Intended," *The Senate Source*, University of California Academic Senate, November 2013, https://senate.universityofcalifornia.edu/_files/news/source/BOARSreport.november2013.html.

10. *Annual Report on Undergraduate Admissions Requirements and Comprehensive Review* (Oakland: University of California, 2021), https://senate.universityofcalifornia.edu/_files/committees/boars/documents/boars-2021-cr-report.pdf.

11. *Annual Report on Undergraduate Admissions Requirements, 2021*.

12. Teresa Watanabe, "UC's Record-Smashing Applications Put Long-Held Diversity Goals Within Reach," *Los Angeles Times*, January 29, 2021, https://www.latimes.com/california/story/2021-01-29/uc-record-college-admission-applications-show-wide-diversity.

13. Robert Cooper and Daniel D. Liou, "The Structure and Culture of Information Pathways: Rethinking Opportunity to Learn in Urban High Schools During the Ninth Grade Transition," *The High School Journal* 91, no. 1 (2007): 43–56, https://doi.org/10.1353/hsj.2007.0020; Uma Jayakumar, Rican Vue, and Walter Allen, "Pathways to College for Young Black Scholars: A Community Cultural Wealth Perspective," *Harvard Educational Review* 83 (2013): 551–79, https://doi.org/10.17763/haer.83.4.4k1mq00162433128.

14. Jayakumar et al., "Pathways to College"; William E. Sedlacek, "Noncognitive Measures for Higher Education Admissions," *International Encyclopedia of Education* 3 (2010): 845–49, http://doi.org/10.1016/B978-0-08-044894-7.00177-9.

15. Contreras et al., *African American Students*; Eddie Comeaux and Tara Watford, "Admissions and Omissions: How 'the Numbers' Are Used to Exclude Deserving Students," *Bunche Research Report* 3, no. 2 (2006): 1–7.

16. Tara J. Yosso, "Whose Culture Has Capital? A Critical Race Theory Discussion of Community Cultural Wealth," *Race Ethnicity and Education* 8, no. 1 (2005): 69–91, https://doi.org/10.1080/1361332052000341006.

17. "Freshman Requirements," University of California: Admissions, 2021, https://admission.universityofcalifornia.edu/admission-requirements/freshman-requirements.

18. Annual Report on Undergraduate Admissions Requirements, 2021.

19. Annual Report on Undergraduate Admissions Requirements, 2021.

20. Yosso, "Whose Culture Has Capital."

21. Yosso, 77.

22. Yosso, 80.

23. Yosso, 78.

24. Yosso, 80.

25. Uma M. Jayakumar and Scott E, Page, "Cultural Capital and Opportunities for Exceptionalism: Bias in University Admissions," The Journal of Higher Education (2021): 1–31.

26. Contreras et al., African American Students; Jayakumar et al., "Pathways to College."

27. Miguel Ceja, "Understanding the Role of Parents and Siblings as Information Sources in the College Choice Process of Chicana Students," Journal of College Student Development 47, no. 1 (2006): 87–104, https://doi.org/10.1353/csd.2006.0003; Thandeka K. Chapman, Frances Contreras, and Eligio Martinez Jr., "African American Parents and Their High-Achieving Students: Issues of Race, Class, and Community in the College Choice Process, Journal of African American Studies 22, no. 1 (2018): 31–48, https://doi.org/10.1007/s12111-018-9392-x; Kassie Freeman, African Americans and College Choice: The Influence of Family and School (Albany: SUNY Press, 2005).

28. Cooper and Liou, "Structure and Culture"; Jayakumar et al., "Pathways to College"; Yosso, "Whose Culture Has Capital."

29. Jayakumar et al., "Pathways to College"; Christine M. Knaggs, Toni A. Sondergeld, and Becky Schardt, "Overcoming Barriers to College Enrollment, Persistence, and Perceptions for Urban High School Students in a College Preparatory Program," Journal of Mixed Methods Research 9, no. 1 (2015): 7–30, http://dx.doi.org/10.1177/1558689813497260; Irma Doris Mendiola, Karen M. Watt, and Jeffery Huerta, "The Impact of Advancement via Individual Determination (AVID) on Mexican American Students Enrolled in a 4-Year University," Journal of Hispanic Higher Education 9, no. 3 (2010): 209–20, https://doi.org/10.1177%2F1538192710368313.

30. Yosso, "Whose Culture Has Capital"; William E. Sedlacek, Beyond the Big Test: Noncognitive Assessment in Higher Education (Indianapolis: Jossey-Bass, 2004).

31. Yosso, "Whose Culture Has Capital."

32. Quinn Capers, Leon McDougle, and Daniel M. Clinchot, "Strategies for Achieving Diversity Through Medical School Admissions," Journal of Health Care for the Poor and Underserved 29, no. 1 (2018): 9–18.

33. Claartje J. Vinkenburg, "Engaging Gatekeepers, Optimizing Decision Making, and Mitigating Bias: Design Specifications for Systemic Diversity Interventions," The Journal of Applied Behavioral Science 53, no. 2 (2017): 212–34, https://doi.org/10.1177%2F0021886317703292.

34. William G. Bowen and Derek Bok, *The Shape of the River: Long-Term Consequences of Considering Race in College and University Admissions* (Princeton: Princeton University Press, 1998); Liang Zhang, "Gender and Racial Gaps in Earnings Among Recent College Graduates," *The Review of Higher Education* 32, no. 1 (2008): 51–72, https://doi.org/10.1353/rhe.0.0035.

35. Paul Bruno, *Getting Down to Facts II: District Dollars 2: California School District Finances, 2004–05 through 2016–17* (Stanford, CA: PACE, 2018), https://www.gettingdowntofacts.com/publications/ district-dollars-2-california-school-district-finances-2004-5-through-2016-17.

CHAPTER 4

1. *Altering the Course: Black Males in Medicine* (Washington, DC: Association of American Medical Colleges, 2015).

2. Gary L. Beck Dallaghan, Julie Story Byerley, Neva Howard, William C. Bennett, and Kurt O. Gilliland, "Medical School Resourcing of USMLE Step 1 Preparation: Questioning the Validity of Step 1," *Medical Science Educator* 29, no. 4 (2019): 1141–45; "JAMA 100 Years Ago," *Journal of the American Medical Association* 11 (1888): 276.

3. Arthur Dean Bevan, "Medical Education in the United States; The Need of a Uniform Standard," *Journal of the American Medical Association* 51, no. 7 (1908): 566–71; William G. Eggleston, "Reform of Medical Education," *Journal of the American Medical Association* 15, no. 1 (1890): 39-39.

4. Abraham Flexner, "Medical Education in the United States and Canada," *Science* 32, no. 810 (1910): 41–50.

5. American Medical Association, "How Far Can Legislation Aid in Maintaining a Proper Standard of Medical Education?" *Journal of the American Medical Association* 11 (1888b): 631–32.

6. "About FSMB," Federation of State Medical Boards, https://www.fsmb.org/about-fsmb.

7. "About NBME," NBME, https://www.nbme.org/about-nbme.

8. American Medical Association, "Competition, Supply and Demand, and Medical Education," *Journal of the American Medical Association* 11 (1888a): 382–83.

9. American Medical Association, "Medical Education and its Recognition by the Rich," *Journal of the American Medical Association* 37 (1901b): 32.

10. *Grutter v. Bollinger*, 539 U.S. 306 (2003).

11. Michael Bastedo, "Holistic Admissions as a Global Phenomenon," in *Higher Education in the Next Decade*, eds. Heather Eginns, Anna Smolentseva, and Hans de Wit (Boston: Brill, 2021), 91–114.

12. Amy N. Addams, Ruth Beer Bletzinger, Henry M. Sondheimer, S. Elizabeth White, and Lily May Johnson, *Roadmap to Diversity: Integrating Holistic Review Practices into Medical School Admission Processes* (Washington, DC: Association of American Medical Colleges, 2010), https://store.aamc.org/downloadable/download/sample/sample_id/195.

13. Douglas Grbic, Emory Morrison, Henry M. Sondheimer, Sarah S. Conrad, and Jeffrey F. Milem, "The Association Between a Holistic Review in Admissions Workshop and the Diversity of Accepted Applicants and Students Matriculating to Medical School," *Academic Medicine* 94, no. 3 (2019): 396–403.

14. Douglas Grbic, *The Socioeconomic Background of Medical School Applicants: A Preliminary Analysis* (Washington, DC: Association of American Medical Colleges, 2011); Douglas Grbic, Gwen Garrison, and Paul Jolly. "Diversity of U.S. Medical School Students by Parental Education," *Association of American Medical Colleges Analysis in Brief* 9 (2010): 2.

15. Sunny Nakae and Andrew M. Subica, "Academic Redlining in Medicine," *Journal of the National Medical Association* 113, no. 5 (2021): 587–94.

16. Robert A. Witzburg, and Henry M. Sondheimer, "Holistic Review—Shaping the Medical Profession One Applicant at a Time," *The New England Journal of Medicine* 368, no. 17 (2013): 1565.

17. Pierre Bourdieu, "Outline of the Theory of Practice: Structures and the Habitus," in *Practicing History: New Directions in Historical Writing after the Linguistic Turn*, ed. Gabrielle M. Spiegel (New York: Routledge, 2005): 179–98.

18. Greer Glazer, Jennifer C. Danek, Julia Michaels, K. Bankston, M. Fair, S. Johnson, and M. Nivet, *Holistic Admissions in the Health Professions: Findings from a National Survey* (Washington, DC: Urban Universities for HEALTH, 2014).

19. *Using MCAT® Data in 2022—Medical Student Selection* (Washington: DC, AAMC), https://www.aamc.org/media/18901/download.

20. Hanin Rashid, Kristen M. Coppola, and Robert Lebeau, "Three Decades Later: A Scoping Review of the Literature Related to the United States Medical Licensing Examination," *Academic Medicine* 95, no. 11S (2020): S114–21.

21. Gary L. Beck Dallaghan, Julie Story Byerley, Neva Howard, William C. Bennett, and Kurt O. Gilliland, "Medical School Resourcing of USMLE Step 1 Preparation: Questioning the Validity of Step 1," *Medical Science Educator* 29, no. 4 (2019), https://doi.org/10.1007/s40670-019-00822-1.

22. Danielle S. Walsh, "USMLE Step 1 Scoring System Change to Pass/Fail—Perspective of a Program Director," *JAMA Surgery* 155, no. 12 (2020): 1094–96.

23. Mark A. Albanese, Mikel H. Snow, Susan E. Skochelak, Kathryn N. Huggett, and Philip M. Farrell, "Assessing Personal Qualities in Medical School Admissions," *Academic Medicine* 78, no. 3 (2003): 313–21.

24. Clarence D. Kreiter, Ping Yin, Catherine Solow, and Robert L. Brennan, "Investigating the Reliability of the Medical School Admissions Interview," *Advances in Health Sciences Education* 9, no. 2 (2004): 147–59.

25. Kevin W. Eva, Jack Rosenfeld, Harold I. Reiter, and Geoffrey R. Norman, "An Admissions OSCE: The Multiple Mini-Interview," *Medical Education* 38, no. 3 (2004): 314–26.

26. Jean-François Lemay, Jocelyn M. Lockyer, V. Terri Collin, and A. Keith W. Brownell, "Assessment of Non-Cognitive Traits through the Admissions Multiple Mini-Interview," *Medical Education* 41, no. 6 (2007): 573–79.

27. Carol A. Terregino, Meghan McConnell, and Harold I. Reiter, "The Effect of Differential Weighting of Academics, Experiences, and Competencies Measured by Multiple Mini Interview (MMI) on Race and Ethnicity of Cohorts Accepted to One Medical School," *Academic Medicine* 90, no. 12 (2015): 1651–57; Anthony Jerant, Tonya Fancher, Mark C. Henderson, Erin J. Griffin, Theodore R. Hall, Carolyn J. Kelly, Ellena M. Peterson, and Peter Franks, "Associations of Postbaccalaureate Coursework with Underrepresented Race/Ethnicity, Academic Performance, and Primary Care Training among Matriculants at Five California Medical Schools," *Journal of Health Care for the Poor and Underserved* 32, no. 2 (2021): 971–86.

28. Steven E. Gay, Sally A. Santen, Rajesh S. Mangrulkar, Thomas H. Sisson, Paula T. Ross, and Nikki L. Bibler Zaidi, "The Influence of MCAT and GPA Preadmission Academic Metrics on Interview Scores," *Advances in Health Sciences Education* 23, no. 1 (2018): 151–58.

29. *AMCAS Applicant Guide* (Washington, DC: Association of American Medical Colleges, 2022), https://students-residents.aamc.org/media/11616/download.

30. Efrain Talamantes, Mark C. Henderson, Tonya L. Fancher, and Fitzhugh Mullan, "Closing the Gap—Making Medical School Admissions More Equitable," *New England Journal of Medicine* 380, no. 9 (2019): 803–5.

31. "The Thomas Haider Program at the UCR School of Medicine," University of California, Riverside School of Medicine, https://somsa.ucr.edu/haider-program.

32. "Georgetown Experimental Medical Studies Program (GEMS)," Georgetown University School of Medicine, https://som.georgetown.edu/diversityequityandinclusion/gems/; "MEDPREP," SIU School of Medicine, https://www.siumed.edu/medprep.

33. Jobe L. Payne, Christine M. Nowacki, Jorge A. Girotti, James Townsel, J. C. Plagge, and T. W. Beckham, "Increasing the Graduation Rates of Minority Medical Students," *Journal of Medical Education* 61, no. 5 (1986), https://doi.org/10.1097/00001888-198605000-00001; Jorge A. Girotti, "The Urban Health Program to Encourage Minority Enrollment at the University of Illinois at Chicago College of Medicine," *Academic Medicine: Journal of the Association of American Medical Colleges* 74, no. 4 (1999): 370–72.

34. Anthony Jerant, Tonya Fancher, Mark C. Henderson, Erin J. Griffin, Theodore R. Hall, Carolyn J. Kelly, Ellena M. Peterson, and Peter Franks, "Associations of Postbaccalaureate Coursework with Underrepresented Race/Ethnicity, Academic Performance, and Primary Care Training among Matriculants at Five California Medical Schools," *Journal of Health Care for the Poor and Underserved* 32, no. 2 (2021): 971–86; Kate Lupton, Chris Vercammen-Grandjean, James Forkin, Elisabeth Wilson, and Kevin Grumbach, "Specialty Choice and Practice Location of Physician Alumni of University of California Premedical Postbaccalaureate Programs," *Academic Medicine* 87, no. 1 (2012): 115–20.

35. Kevin Grumbach, "Commentary: Adopting Postbaccalaureate Premedical Programs to Enhance Physician Workforce Diversity," *Academic Medicine* 86, no. 2 (2011): 154–57.

36. Quinn Capers IV, Daniel Clinchot, Leon McDougle, and Anthony G. Greenwald, "Implicit Racial Bias in Medical School Admissions," *Academic Medicine* 92, no. 3 (2017): 365–69.

37. Quinn Capers, Leon McDougle, and Daniel M. Clinchot, "Strategies for Achieving Diversity through Medical School Admissions," *Journal of Health Care for the Poor and Underserved* 29, no. 1 (2018): 9–18.

38. Ann-Gel Palermo, personal communication, April 14, 2021.

39. Miguel A. Sorrel, Julio Olea, Francisco J. Abad, Jimmy de la Torre, David Aguado, and Filip Lievens, "Validity and Reliability of Situational Judgement Test Scores: A New Approach Based on Cognitive Diagnosis Models," *Organizational Research Methods* 19, no. 3 (2016): 506–32.

40. Fiona Patterson, Victoria Ashworth, Lara Zibarras, Philippa Coan, Maire Kerrin, and Paul O'Neill, "Evaluations of Situational Judgement Tests to Assess Non-Academic Attributes in Selection," *Medical Education* 46, no. 9 (2012): 850–68.

41. Kelly L. Dore, Harold I. Reiter, Sharyn Kreuger, and Geoffrey R. Norman, "CASPer, an Online Pre-interview Screen for Personal/Professional Characteristics: Prediction of National Licensure Scores," *Advances in Health Sciences Education* 22, no. 2 (2017): 327–36.

42. Dore, et al. "CASPer."

43. Barret Michalec, "MCAT Testing during the COVID-19 Pandemic," *Academic Medicine* 95, no. 9 (2020): 1292–1293.

44. Anthony Wong, "School of Medicine Makes MCAT Optional Amid COVID-19 Testing Disruptions," *The Stanford Daily*, July 15, 2020, https://www.stanforddaily.com/2020/07/15/school-of-medicine-makes-mcat-optional-amid-covid-19-testing-disruptions.

45. Amy N. Addams, Ruth Beer Bletzinger, Henry M. Sondheimer, S. Elizabeth White, and Lily May Johnson, *Roadmap to Diversity: Integrating Holistic Review Practices into Medical School Admission Processes* (Washington, DC: Association of American Medical Colleges, 2010), https://store.aamc.org/downloadable/download/sample/sample_id/195.

46. Sunny Nakae and Andrew M. Subica, "Academic Redlining in Medicine," *Journal of the National Medical Association* 113, no. 5 (2021): 587–94.

47. Clyde W. Yancy and Howard Bauchner, "Diversity in Medical Schools—Need for a New Bold Approach," *Journal of the American Medical Association*, 325, no. 1 (2021): 31–32.

48. José E. Rodríguez, Ivette A. López, Kendall M. Campbell, and Matthew Dutton, "The Role of Historically Black College and University Medical Schools in Academic Medicine," *Journal of Health Care for the Poor and Underserved* 28, no. 1 (2017): 266–78.

49. Valerie Montgomery Rice, "Diversity in medical schools: a much-needed new beginning," *Journal of the American Medical Association* 325, no. 1 (2021): 23–24.

CHAPTER 5

1. Julie J. Park, *Race on Campus: Debunking Myths with Data* (Cambridge, MA: Harvard Education Press, 2018).
2. Jay Caspian Kang, "Why SAT Prep Doesn't Help Who You Might Think It Helps," *The New York Times*, September 9, 2021, https://www.nytimes.com/2021/09/09/opinion/sat-standardized-tests-ucs.html.
3. Lois Weis, Kristin Cipollone, and Heather Jenkins, *Class Warfare: Class, Race, and College Admissions in Top-Tier Secondary Schools* (Chicago, IL: University of Chicago Press, 2014).
4. Patricia M. McDonough, *Choosing Colleges: How Social Class and Schools Structure Opportunity* (Albany, NY: SUNY Press, 1997).
5. Julie J. Park, "It Takes a Village (or an Ethnic Economy): The Varying Roles of Socioeconomic Status, Religion, and Social Capital in SAT Preparation for Chinese and Korean American Students," *American Educational Research Journal* 49, no. 4 (2012): 624–50. http://www.jstor.org/stable/23249215.
6. Min Zhou and Susan S. Kim, "Community Forces, Social Capital and Educational Achievement: The Case of Supplementary Education in the Chinese and Korean Immigrant Communities," *Harvard Educational Review* 76, no. 1 (2006): 1–2.
7. Park, "It Takes a Village."
8. Park, "It Takes a Village."
9. Christopher Avery, "Evaluation of the College Possible Program: Results from a Randomized Controlled Trial," NBER Working Paper No. w19562, October 25, 2013, https://ssrn.com/abstract=2345057.
10. Sigal Alon, "Racial Differences in Test Preparation Strategies: A Commentary on 'Shadow Education,' American Style: Test Preparation, the SAT and College Enrollment," *Social Forces* 89, no. 2 (2010): 463–74.
11. Soo-yong Byun and Hyunjoon Park, "The Academic Success of East Asian American Youth: The Role of Shadow Education," *Sociology of Education* 85, no. 1 (2012): 40–60, https://doi.org/10.1177/0038040711417009.
12. Lani Guinier, *The Tyranny of the Meritocracy: Democratizing Higher Education in America* (New York, NY: Penguin Random House, 2016).
13. Eliza Shapiro, "Only 8 Black Students Are Admitted to Stuyvesant High School," *The New York Times*, April 29, 2021, https://www.nytimes.com/2021/04/29/nyregion/stuyvesant-black-students.html.
14. Derek C. Briggs, "Preparation for College Admission Exams" (Discussion paper, National Association for College Admission Counseling, 2009).
15. Avery, "Evaluation of the College Possible Program."
16. Briggs, "Preparation for College Admission Exams."

17. Julie J. Park and Ann H. Becks, "Who Benefits from SAT Prep? An Examination of High School Context and Race/Ethnicity," *The Review of Higher Education* 39, no. 1 (2015): 1–23; Ben Domingue and Derek C. Briggs, "Using Linear Regression and Propensity Score Matching to Estimate the Effect of Coaching on the SAT," *Multiple Linear Regression Viewpoints* 35, no. 1 (2009): 12–29.

18. Paul Tough, *The Years That Matter Most: How College Makes or Breaks Us* (New York, NY: Mariner Books, 2019).

19. Briggs, "Preparation for College Admission Exams."

20. https://news.mit.edu/2022/stuart-schmill-sat-act-requirement-0328

21. Quoted in Tough, *The Years That Matter Most*, 91.

22. Tough, *The Years That Matter Most*, 92.

23. Byun and Park, "The Academic Success of East Asian American Youth."

24. Park, "It Takes a Village."

25. It is important to emphasize that high participation in SAT/ACT prep by Asian Americans is not simply a matter of "Asian culture stressing education," but a complex interplay between structural and cultural forces that have fostered infrastructure facilitating educational mobility (Louie, 2004; Zhou & Kim, 2006). Vivian S. Louie, *Compelled to Excel: Immigration, Education, and Opportunity Among Chinese Americans* (Redwood City, CA: Stanford University Press, 2004).

26. Park and Becks, "Who Benefits from SAT Prep?"

27. Byun and Park, "The Academic Success of East Asian American Youth."

28. Kang, "Why SAT Prep Doesn't Help Who You Might Think It Helps."

29. Park and Becks, "Who Benefits from SAT Prep?"

30. Regina Deil-Amen and Tenisha L. Tevis, "Circumscribed Agency: The Relevance of Standardized College Entrance Exams for Low-SES High School Students," *The Review of Higher Education* 33, no. 2 (2010): 141–75.

31. Jennifer Lee and Min Zhou, *The Asian American Achievement Paradox* (New York, NY: Russell Sage Foundation, 2015).

32. Gary Orfield, Jongyeon Ee, Erica Frankenberg, and Genevieve Siegel-Hawley, "Brown at 62: School Segregation by Race, Poverty and State," Civil Rights Project / Proyecto Derechos Civiles, UCLA, May 16, 2016, https://civilrightsproject.ucla.edu/research/k-12-education/integration-and-diversity/brown-at-62-school-segregation-by-race-poverty-and-state/Brown-at-62-final-corrected-2.pdf.

33. Dana Goldstein and Jugal K. Patel, "Need Extra Time on Tests? It Helps to Have Cash," *The New York Times*, July 30, 2019, https://www.nytimes.com/2019/07/30/us/extra-time-504-sat-act.html.

34. Tough, *The Years That Matter Most*.

CHAPTER 6

1. https://www.usatoday.com/story/news/nation/2020/06/15/systemic-racism-what-does-mean/5343549002/

2. Estela M. Bensimon, "Reclaiming Racial Justice in Equity," *Change: The Magazine of Higher Learning* 50 (2018): 95–98; Julie Posselt, Theresa E. Hernandez, Cynthia D. Villarreal, Aireale J. Rodgers, and Lauren N. Irwin, "Evaluation and Decision

Making in Higher Education: Toward Equitable Repertoires of Faculty Practice," *Higher Education: Handbook of Theory and Research* 35 (2020): 1–63.

3. Michael Omi and Howard Winant, "The Theory of Racial Formation," *Beyond Black and White: A Reader on Contemporary Race Relations* 15 (2015): 15-26.

4. Eduardo Bonilla-Silva, *Racism Without Racists: Color-Blind Racism and the Persistence of Racial Inequality in America*, Fifth edition (Washington, DC: Rowman & Littlefield, 2018).

5. Victor Ray, "A Theory of Racialized Organizations," *American Sociological Review* 84, no. 1 (2019): 26–53.

6. Jerome Karabel, *The Chosen: The Hidden History of Admission and Exclusion at Harvard, Yale, and Princeton* (Boston: Houghton Mifflin, 2005); Marcia G. Synott, *The Half-Opened Door: Discrimination and Admissions at Harvard, Yale, and Princeton* (Greenwood Press, 1979); Melissa E. Wooten and Lucius Couloute, "The Production of Racial Inequality Within and Among Organizations," *Sociology Compass* 11, no. 1 (2017): e12446.

7. Nicholas Lemann, *The Big Test: The Secret History of the American Meritocracy* (New York; Macmillan, 2000).

8. Ted Thornhill, "We Want Black Students, Just Not You: How White Admissions Counselors Screen Black Prospective Students," *Sociology of Race and Ethnicity* 5, no. 4 (2019): 456–70; Karina G. Salazar, Ozan Jaquette, and Crystal Han, "Coming Soon to a Neighborhood Near You? Off-Campus Recruiting by Public Research Universities," *American Educational Research Journal* 58, no. 6 (2021): 1270–1314.

9. Julie Posselt, *Equity in Science: Representation, Culture, and the Dynamics of Change in Graduate Education* (Stanford, CA: Stanford University Press, 2020), 2.

10. Lionel K. McPherson, "Righting Historical Injustice in Higher Education," in *The Aims of Higher Education: Problems of Morality and Justice*, eds. Harry Brighthouse and Michael McPherson (Chicago, IL: University of Chicago Press, 2015), 113–34; Gloria Ladson-Billings, "From the Achievement Gap to the Education Debt: Understanding Achievement in US Schools," *Educational Researcher* 35, no. 7 (2006): 3–12.

11. Bonilla-Silva, *Racism without Racists*; Ray, "A Theory of Racialized Organizations."

12. Estela Bensimon, "The Case for an Anti-Racist Stance Toward Paying off Higher Education's Racial Debt," *Change* 52, no. 2 (2020): 7–11.

13. P. J. Henry, "Institutional Bias," in *The SAGE Handbook of Prejudice, Stereotyping, and Discrimination*, eds. John Dovidio, Miles Hewstone, Pete Glick, and Victoria M. Esses (London: Sage, 2010), 435.

14. Nicholas Bowman and Michael Bastedo, "What Role May Admissions Office Diversity and Practices Play in Equitable Decisions?" *Research in Higher Education* 59, no. 4 (2018): 430–47.

15. Bowman and Bastedo, "What Role."

16. Quinn Capers IV, Daniel Clinchot, Leon McDougle, and Anthony G. Greenwald, "Implicit Racial Bias in Medical School Admissions," *Academic Medicine* 92, no. 3 (2017): 365–69.

17. Thornhill, "We Want Black Students, Just Not You."

18. Michelle Van Ryn, Rachel Hardeman, Sean M. Phelan, John F. Dovidio, Jeph Herrin, Sara E. Burke, David B. Nelson, Sylvia Perry, Mark Yeazel, and Julia M. Przedworski, "Medical School Experiences Associated with Change in Implicit Racial Bias among 3547 Students: A Medical Student CHANGES Study Report," *Journal of General Internal Medicine* 30, no. 12 (2015): 1748–56; Javeed Sukhera, Alexandra Milne, Pim W. Teunissen, Lorelei Lingard, and Chris Watling, "The Actual Versus Idealized Self: Exploring Responses to Feedback about Implicit Bias in Health Professionals," *Academic Medicine* 93, no. 4 (2018): 623–29; Sophie Lebrecht, Lara J. Pierce, Michael J. Tarr, and James W. Tanaka, "Perceptual Other-race Training Reduces Implicit Racial Bias," *PloS one* 4, no. 1 (2009): e4215; Adam D. Galinsky and Gordon B. Moskowitz, "Perspective-taking: Decreasing Stereotype Expression, Stereotype Accessibility, and In-group Favoritism," *Journal of Personality and Social Psychology* 78, no. 4 (2000): 708.

19. Nicolás E. Barceló, Sonya Shadravan, Christine R. Wells, Nichole Goodsmith, Brittany Tarrant, Trevor Shaddox, Yvonne Yang, Eraka Bath, and Katrina DeBonis, "Reimagining Merit and Representation: Promoting Equity and Reducing Bias in GME through Holistic Review," *Academic Psychiatry* 45, no. 1 (2021): 34–42; David M. Quinn, "Experimental Evidence on Teachers' Racial Bias in Student Evaluation: The Role of Grading Scales," *Educational Evaluation and Policy Analysis* 42, no. 3 (2020): 375–92.

20. Anthony Giddens, *The Constitution of Society: Outline of the Theory of Structuration* (Oakland, CA: University of California Press, 1984).

21. Thomas J. Espenshade, Lauren E. Hale, and Chang Y. Chung, "The Frog Pond Revisited: High School Academic Context, Class Rank, and Elite College Admission," *Sociology of Education* 78, no. 4 (2005): 269–93; Sigal Alon and Marta Tienda, "Diversity, Opportunity, and the Shifting Meritocracy in Higher Education," *American Sociological Review* 72 (2007): 487–511.

22. Julie R. Posselt, Ozan Jaquette, Rob Bielby, and Michael N. Bastedo, "Access without Equity: Longitudinal Analyses of Institutional Stratification by Race and Ethnicity, 1972–2004," *American Educational Research Journal* 49, no. 6 (2012): 1091.

23. Giulia McDonnell Nieto del Rio, "University of California Will No Longer Accept SAT and ACT Scores," *New York Times*, May 15, 2021, https://www.nytimes.com/2021/05/15/us/SAT-scores-uc-university-of-california.html.

24. Katie Langin, "Ph.D. Programs Drop Standardized Exam: Amid Concerns about Diversity and the Test's Utility, Many Are Moving away from the GRE," *Science Magazine* (American Association for the Advancement of Science) 364, no. 6443 (2019): 816; Casey Miller and Keivan Stassun, "A Test That Fails," *Nature* 510, no. 7504 (2014): 303–4.

25. Rachel Rubin, "Who Gets In and Why? An Examination of Admissions to America's Most Selective Colleges and Universities," *International Education Research* 2, no. 2 (2014): 1–18.

26. Mitchell L. Stevens, *Creating a Class* (Cambridge, MA: Harvard University Press, 2020); Uma Mazyck Jayakumar and Scott E. Page, "Cultural Capital and Opportunities for Exceptionalism: Bias in University Admissions," *The Journal of Higher Education* 92, no. 7 (2021): 1109–39.

27. Kelly Ochs Rosinger, Karly Sarita Ford, and Junghee Choi, "The Role of Selective College Admissions Criteria in Interrupting or Reproducing Racial and Economic Inequities," *The Journal of Higher Education* 92, no. 1 (2021): 31–55; Posselt et al., "Evaluation and Decision Making."

28. Salazar and Han, "Coming Soon to a Neighborhood Near You?"

29. Caroline Minter Hoxby and Christopher Avery, "The Missing 'One-offs'," *Brookings Papers on Economic Activity* (2013): 1–65; Jonathan Smith, Jessica Howell, and Michael Hurwitz, "The Impact of College Outreach on High Schoolers' College Choices—Results From Over 1,000 Natural Experiments," *Education Finance and Policy* (2020): 1–43.

30. Michael N. Bastedo and Nicholas A. Bowman, "Improving Admission of Low-SES Students at Selective Colleges: Results from an Experimental Simulation," *Educational Researcher* 46, no. 2 (2017): 67–77; Michael N. Bastedo, Nicholas A. Bowman, Kristen M. Glasener, and Jandi L. Kelly, "What Are We Talking About When We Talk About Holistic Review? Selective College Admissions and Its Effects on Low-SES Students," *The Journal of Higher Education* 89, no. 5 (2018): 782–805.

31. Kelly Ochs Rosinger, "External evaluation of the California Consortium for Inclusive Doctoral Education," 2021. Unpublished manuscript developed at Pennsylvania State University.

32. Andres S. Belasco, Kelly O. Rosinger, and James C. Hearn, "The Test-Optional Movement at America's Selective Liberal Arts Colleges: A Boon for Equity or Something Else?" *Educational Evaluation and Policy Analysis* 37, no. 2 (2015): 206–23; Christopher T. Bennett, "Untested Admissions: Examining Changes in Application Behaviors and Student Demographics Under Test-Optional Policies," *American Educational Research Journal* 59, no. 1 (2021): 00028312211003526; Rosinger et al., "The Role of Selective College Admissions Criteria."

33. *Regents of the University of California v. Bakke*, 438 US 265 (1978), 311–12.

34. Charles Ogletree, *All Deliberate Speed* (New York: Norton, 2004), 327.

35. Liliana M. Garces, "Aligning Diversity, Quality, and Equity: The Implications of Legal and Public Policy Developments for Promoting Racial Diversity in Graduate Studies," *American Journal of Education* 120, no. 4 (2014): 457–80.

36. Liliana M. Garces and Courtney D. Cogburn, "Beyond Declines in Student Body Diversity: How Campus-level Administrators Understand a Prohibition on Race-conscious Postsecondary Admissions Policies," *American Educational Research Journal* 52, no. 5 (2015): 828–60.

37. Garces and Cogburn, "Beyond Declines." para. 7.

38. "Executive Order 13985 of January 21, 2021, Advancing Racial Equity and Support for Underserved Communities Through the Federal Government," *Code of Federal Regulations* (2021): 7009–13, https://www.federalregister.gov/documents/2021/01/25/2021-01753/advancing-racial-equity-and-support-for-underserved-communities-through-the-federal-government.

39. Julie R. Posselt *Inside Graduate Admissions: Merit, Diversity, and Faculty Gatekeeping* (Cambridge, MA: Harvard University Press, 2016).

40. Ray, "A Theory of Racialized Organizations."

41. Posselt, *Equity in Science.*

42. Bastedo et al., "What Are We Talking About"; Posselt, *Inside Graduate Admissions*; Dian Squire, "The Neoliberal and Neoracist Potentialities of International Doctoral Student of Color Admissions in Graduate Education Programs," *Philosophy and Theory in Higher Education* 1, no. 2 (2019): 29–53.

43. Johnson, Lyndon B. "To Fulfill These Rights." Transcript of speech delivered at Howard University, June 4, 1965, https://www.presidency.ucsb.edu/documents/commencement-address-howard-university-fulfill-these-rights.

44. Eddie R. Cole, *The Campus Color Line: College Presidents and the Struggle for Black Freedom* (Princeton University Press, 2020); Karabel, *The Chosen.*

45. It is noteworthy that although Nixon signed the Executive Orders for affirmative action, his administration actively defied other policies to advance racial equity (e.g., redlining, halting assistance on housing and community development).

46. Megan M. Holland and Karly Sarita Ford, "Legitimating Prestige through Diversity: How Higher Education Institutions Represent Ethno-Racial Diversity across Levels of Selectivity," *The Journal of Higher Education* 92, no. 1 (2021): 1–30; Eric Grodsky and Demetra Kalogrides, "The Declining Significance of Race in College Admissions Decisions," *American Journal of Education* 115, no. 1 (2008): 1–33; Nana Osei-Kofi, Lisette E. Torres, and Joyce Lui, "Practices of Whiteness: Racialization in College Admissions Viewbooks," *Race Ethnicity and Education* 16, no. 3 (2013): 386–405.

47. Anthony P. Carnevale and Jeff Strohl, *Separate & Unequal: How Higher Education Reinforces the Intergenerational Reproduction of White Racial Privilege* (Washington, DC: Georgetown Center on Education and the Workforce, 2013).

48. Rachel Baker, Daniel Klasik and Sean F. Reardon, "Race and Stratification in College Enrollment over Time," *AERA Open* 4, no. 1 (2018): 1–28; Posselt et al., "Access Without Equity."

49. Hironao Okahana, E. Zhou, and J. Gao, *Graduate Enrollment and Degrees: 2009 to 2019* (Washington, DC: Council of Graduate Schools, 2020). Robert Teranishi and Tara Parker link these patterns in the University of California system to high school composition: only 15 percent of first-time freshman at UC Berkeley came from high schools where more than 50 percent of the student population was Black or Latinx, even though 60 percent of all Latinx and 48 percent of all Black students attended racially segregated schools ("Social Reproduction of Inequality: The Racial Composition of Feeder Schools to the University of California," *Teachers College Record* 112, no. 6 [2010]: 1575).

50. Selectivity and prestige go hand in hand. Racialized notions of institutional quality are best revealed by the fact that elite universities can maintain their elite status while continuing to systematically under-enroll the country's emerging Black and brown majority.

51. Alexis N. Smith, Arthur P. Brief, and Adrienne Colella, "Bias in Organizations," in *The SAGE Handbook of Prejudice, Stereotyping, and Discrimination*, eds. John Dovidio, Miles Hewstone, Pete Glick, and Victoria M. Esses (London: Sage, 2010), 441–56.

CHAPTER 7

1. Sarah K. S. Shannon et al., "The Growth, Scope, and Spatial Distribution of People with Felony Records in the United States, 1948–2010," *Demography* 54 (2017): 1–24; Jeremy Travis, Bruce Western, and National Research Council (U.S.), eds., *The Growth of Incarceration in the United States: Exploring Causes and Consequences* (Washington, DC: The National Academies Press, 2014); Christopher Uggen and Robert Stewart, "Piling On: Collateral Consequences and Community Supervision," *Minnesota Law Review* 99 (2015): 1871.

2. Uggen and Stewart, "Piling On."

3. Richard Arum and Michael Hout, "The Early Returns: The Transition from School to Work in the United States," in *From School to Work: A Comparative Study of Educational Qualifications and Occupational Destinations*, ed. Yossi Shavit and Walter Muller (New York: Clarendon Press, 1998), 471–510; Matthew J. Mayhew et al., *How College Affects Students: 21st Century Evidence That Higher Education Works*, vol. 3 (John Wiley & Sons, 2016); U.S. Bureau of Labor Statistics, "Employment Projections: Unemployment Rates and Earnings by Educational Attainment," October 24, 2017, https://www.bls.gov/emp/ep_chart_001.htm.

4. Gary S. Becker, *Human Capital: A Theoretical and Empirical Analysis, with Special Reference to Education*, 3rd ed. (Chicago, IL: The University of Chicago Press, 1994); John Boli, Francisco O. Ramirez, and John W. Meyer, "Explaining the Origins and Expansion of Mass Education," *Comparative Education Review* 29, no. 2 (1985): 145–70; David K. Brown, "The Social Sources of Educational Credentialism: Status Cultures, Labor Markets, and Organizations," *Sociology of Education* 74 (2001): 19–34.

5. Thomas G. Blomberg and George B. Pesta, "Education and Delinquency," in *The Encyclopedia of Juvenile Delinquency and Justice*, ed. Christopher J. Schreck (New York: Wiley-Blackwell, 2017), https://onlinelibrary.wiley.com/doi/abs/10.1002/9781118524275.ejdj0044; Jason A. Ford and Ryan D. Schroeder, "Higher Education and Criminal Offending over the Life Course," *Sociological Spectrum* 31, no. 1 (2010): 32–58; Lindsey Livingston Runell, "Identifying Desistance Pathways in a Higher Education Program for Formerly Incarcerated Individuals," *International Journal of Offender Therapy and Comparative Criminology* 61, no. 8 (June 1, 2017): 894–918, https://doi.org/10.1177/0306624X15608374.

6. Grant Duwe and Valerie Clark, "The Effects of Prison-Based Educational Programming on Recidivism and Employment," *The Prison Journal* 94, no. 4 (2014): 454–78; Susan Lockwood et al., "The Effect of Correctional Education on Postrelease Employment and Recidivism: A 5-Year Follow-Up Study in the State of Indiana," *Crime & Delinquency* 58, no. 3 (May 1, 2012): 380–96, https://doi.org/10.1177/0011128712441695; Matias E. Berthelon and Diana I. Kruger, "Risky Behavior among Youth: Incapacitation Effects of School on Adolescent Motherhood and Crime in Chile," *Journal of Public Economics* 95, no. 1 (February 1, 2011): 41–53, https://doi.org/10.1016/j.jpubeco.2010.09.004; D. Mark Anderson, "In School and Out of Trouble? The Minimum Dropout Age and Juvenile Crime," *The Review of Economics and Statistics* 96, no. 2 (April 2, 2013): 318–31, https://doi.org/10.1162/REST_a_00360; Lance Lochner and Enrico Moretti, "The Effect of Education on Crime: Evidence from Prison Inmates, Arrests, and Self-Reports," *American Economic Review* 94, no. 1 (2004): 155–89, https://doi.org/10.1257/000282804322970751.

7. Gary S. Becker, *Human Capital: A Theoretical and Empirical Analysis, with Special Reference to Education*, 3rd ed. (Chicago, IL: The University of Chicago Press, 1994); David K. Brown, "The Social Sources of Educational Credentialism: Status Cultures, Labor Markets, and Organizations," *Sociology of Education* 74 (2001): 19–34; Mart van Dinther, Filip Dochy, and Mien Segers, "Factors Affecting Students' Self-Efficacy in Higher Education," *Educational Research Review* 6, no. 2 (2011): 95–108; Ford and Scroeder, "Higher Education and Criminal Offending"; Rajani Naidoo, "Fields and Institutional Strategy: Bourdieu on the Relationship between Higher Education, Inequality and Society," *British Journal of Sociology of Education* 25, no. 4 (2004): 457–71.

8. Richard Arum and Michael Hout, "The Early Returns: The Transition from School to Work in the United States," in *From School to Work: A Comparative Study of Educational Qualifications and Occupational Destinations*, ed. Yossi Shavit and Walter Muller (New York: Clarendon Press, 1998), 471–510; Anthony P. Carnevale, Stephen J. Rose, and Ban Cheah, *The College Payoff: Education, Occupations, Lifetime Earnings* (Washington, DC: Georgetown University Center on Education and the Workforce, 2013), https://repository.library.georgetown.edu/bitstream/handle/10822/559300/collegepayoff-complete.pdf?sequence=1; Matthew J. Mayhew et al., *How College Affects Students: 21st Century Evidence That Higher Education Works*, vol. 3 (John Wiley & Sons, 2016); U.S. Bureau of Labor Statistics, "Employment Projections: Unemployment Rates and Earnings by Educational Attainment," October 24, 2017, https://www.bls.gov/emp/ep_chart_001.htm.

9. Bradley D. Custer, "Applying to University with Criminal Convictions: A Comparative Study of Admissions Policies in the United States and United Kingdom," *Journal of Higher Education Policy and Management* 40, no. 3 (2019):239-255. https://doi.org/10.1080/1360080X.2018.1462436; Matthew W. Pierce, Carol W. Runyan, and Shrikant I. Bangdiwala, "The Use of Criminal History

Information in College Admissions Decisions," *Journal of School Violence* 13, no. 4 (2014): 359–76; Alan Rosenthal et al., *Boxed Out: Criminal History Screening and College Application Attrition* (New York: Center for Community Alternatives, March 2015), http://www.communityalternatives.org/pdf/publications/BoxedOut_FullReport.pdf; Marsha Weissman et al., *The Use of Criminal History Records in College Admissions Reconsidered* (New York: Center for Community Alternatives, November 2010), http://www.communityalternatives.org/pdf/Reconsidered-criminal-hist-recs-in-college-admissions.pdf.

10. U. S. Census Bureau, "Annual Estimates of the Resident Population by Sex, Age, Race, and Hispanic Origin for the United States: April 1, 2010 to July 1, 2019 (NC-EST2019-ASR6H)," 2021, https://www2.census.gov/programs-surveys/popest/tables/2010-2019/national/asrh/nc-est2019-asr6h.xlsx; Cristobal de Brey et al., "Digest of Education Statistics 2019. NCES 2021-009," National Center for Education Statistics, 2021; E. Ann Carson, "Prisoners in 2019," Bureau of Justice Statistics (Washington, DC: U.S. Department of Justice, October 2020), https://bjs.ojp.gov/content/pub/pdf/p19.pdf.

11. Robert Brame et al., "Demographic Patterns of Cumulative Arrest Prevalence by Ages 18 and 23," *Crime & Delinquency* 60, no. 3 (2014): 471–86; Tomeka Davis and Bobette Otto, "Juxtaposing the Black and White Gender Gap: Race and Gender Differentiation in College Enrollment Predictors," *Social Science Quarterly* 97, no. 5 (2016): 1245–66; Danielle Kaeble and Lauren E. Glaze, "Correctional Populations in the United States, 2015," Correctional Populations in the United States Series (Washington, DC: Bureau of Justice Statistics, December 29, 2016), https://www.bjs.gov/index.cfm?ty=pbdetail&iid=5870.

12. Robert Stewart and Christopher Uggen, "Criminal Records and College Admissions: A Modified Experimental Audit," *Criminology* 58, no. 1 (2020): 156–88, https://doi.org/10.1111/1745-9125.12229; Robert Stewart, "Criminal Records and College Admissions" (Ph.D. Dissertation, University of Minnesota, 2020), University of Minnesota Digital Conservancy, https://hdl.handle.net/11299/216823.

13. Stewart, "Criminal Records and College Admissions."

14. Barron's College Division Staff, *Barron's Profiles of American Colleges*, 2016, 32nd ed. (Hauppauge, NY: Barron's Educational Series, Inc., 2015).

15. Lora Cohen-Vogel et al., "The 'Spread' of Merit-Based College Aid: Politics, Policy Consortia, and Interstate Competition," *Educational Policy* 22, no. 3 (May 1, 2008): 339–62, https://doi.org/10.1177/0895904807307059; Paul J. DiMaggio and Walter W. Powell, *The New Institutionalism in Organizational Analysis*, vol. 17 (Chicago: University of Chicago Press, 2004); Jerome Karabel, *The Chosen: The Hidden History of Admission and Exclusion at Yale, Harvard, and Princeton* (Boston: Houghton Mifflin Harcourt, 2005); Daniel N. Lipson, "The Resilience of Affirmative Action in the 1980s: Innovation, Isomorphism, and Institutionalization in University Admissions," *Political Research Quarterly* 64, no. 1 (2011): 132–44; Lisa M. Stulberg and Anthony S. Chen, "The Origins of Race-Conscious

Affirmative Action in Undergraduate Admissions: A Comparative Analysis of Institutional Change in Higher Education," *Sociology of Education* 87, no. 1 (January 1, 2014): 36–52, https://doi.org/10.1177/0038040713514063; Harold S. Wechsler, *The Qualified Student: A History of Selective College Admission in America* (Transaction Publishers, 2014).

16. Arik Lifschitz, Michael Sauder, and Mitchell L. Stevens, "Football as a Status System in U.S. Higher Education," *Sociology of Education* 87, no. 3 (July 1, 2014): 204–19, https://doi.org/10.1177/0038040714533353.

17. Pierce, Runyan, and Bangdiwala, "The Use of Criminal History Information."

18. Malgorzata JV Olszewska, "Undergraduate Admission Application as a Campus Crime Mitigation Measure: Disclosure of Applicants' Disciplinary Background Information and Its Relation to Campus Crime," East Carolina University, 2007; Pierce, Runyan, and Bangdiwala, "The Use of Criminal History Information"; Carol W. Runyan et al., "Can Student-Perpetrated College Crime Be Predicted Based on Precollege Misconduct?," *Injury Prevention* 19, no. 6 (2013): 405–11.

19. Pierce, Runyan, and Bangdiwala, "The Use of Criminal History Information"; Weissman et al., *The Use of Criminal History Records in College Admissions Reconsidered.*

20. Rosenthal et al., *Boxed Out.*

21. *Task Force on the Safety of the Campus Community: Final Report* (Chapel Hill, NC: The University of North Carolina Office of the President, 2004).

22. *Task Force on the Safety of the Campus Community: Final Report.*

23. Stephanie F. Hughes, Teressa L. Elliott, and Margaret Myers, "Measuring the Impact of Student Background Checks on Reducing Crime in Higher Education," *Public Administration Research* 3, no. 2 (2014): 121, https://doi.org/10.5539/par.v3n2p121.

24. Runyan et al., "Can Student-Perpetrated College Crime Be Predicted?"

25. Runyan et al., "Can Student-Perpetrated College Crime Be Predicted?," 408.

26. Darby Dickerson, "Background Checks in the University Admissions Process: An Overview of Legal and Policy Considerations," *Journal of College and University Law* 34 (2008): 419–506; Rebecca R. Ramaswany, "Bars to Education: The Use of Criminal History Information in College Admissions," *Columbia Journal of Race and Law* 5 (2015): 145–64.

27. Devah Pager, Bart Bonikowski, and Bruce Western, "Discrimination in a Low-Wage Labor Market: A Field Experiment," *American Sociological Review* 74, no. 5 (2009): 777–99; James R. Todd, "It's Not My Problem: How Workplace Violence and Potential Employer Liability Lead to Employment Discrimination of Ex-Convicts," *Arizona State Law Journal* 36 (2004): 725.

28. Michael N. Bastedo and Nicholas A. Bowman, "U.S. News & World Report College Rankings: Modeling Institutional Effects on Organizational Reputation," *American Journal of Education* 116, no. 2 (2010): 163–83, https://doi.org/10.1086/649437; Nicholas A. Bowman and Michael N. Bastedo, "Getting

on the Front Page: Organizational Reputation, Status Signals, and the Impact of 'U.S. News and World Report' on Student Decisions," *Research in Higher Education* 50, no. 5 (2009): 415–36; W. Bentley MacLeod et al., "The Big Sort: College Reputation and Labor Market Outcomes," *American Economic Journal: Applied Economics* 9, no. 3 (2017): 223–61; James Monks and Ronald G. Ehrenberg, "The Impact of US News and World Report College Rankings on Admission Outcomes and Pricing Decisions at Selective Private Institutions," NBER Working Paper 7227, 1999; Mitchell L. Stevens, *Creating a Class: College Admissions and the Education of Elites* (Cambridge, MA: Harvard University Press, 2009); Matthew Hartley and Christopher C. Morphew, "What's Being Sold and to What End? A Content Analysis of College Viewbooks," *The Journal of Higher Education* 79, no. 6 (2008): 671–91.

29. Steven M. Janosik, "Parents' Views on the Clery Act and Campus Safety," *Journal of College Student Development* 45, no. 1 (2004): 43–56.

30. Devah Pager, "The Mark of a Criminal Record," *American Journal of Sociology* 108, no. 5 (2003): 937–75, https://doi.org/10.1086/374403; Pager, Bonikowski, and Western, "Discrimination in a Low-Wage Labor Market"; Christopher Uggen, Mike Vuolo, Sarah Lageson, Ebony Ruhland, and Hilary K Whitham, "The Edge of Stigma: An Experimental Audit of the Effects of Low-Level Criminal Records on Employment," *Criminology* 52, no. 4 (2014): 627–54.

31. William G. Bowen and Derek Bok, *The Shape of the River: Long-Term Consequences of Considering Race in College and University Admissions* (Princeton University Press, 2016); Mitchell L. Stevens, *Creating a Class* (2009); Prabhdeep Singh Kehal, Daniel Hirschman, and Ellen Berrey, "When Affirmative Action Disappears: Unexpected Patterns in Student Enrollments at Selective U.S. Institutions, 1990–2016," *Sociology of Race and Ethnicity*, April 26, 2021, 23326492211008640, https://doi.org/10.1177/23326492211008640.

32. Grant H. Blume and Mark C. Long, "Changes in Levels of Affirmative Action in College Admissions in Response to Statewide Bans and Judicial Rulings," *Educational Evaluation and Policy Analysis*, no. 2 (2014): 228–52; Eric Grodsky and Demetra Kalogrides, "The Declining Significance of Race in College Admissions Decisions," *American Journal of Education* 115, no. 1 (2008): 1–33, https://doi.org/10.1086/590673.

33. S. Michael Gaddis, ed., *Audit Studies: Behind the Scenes with Theory, Method, and Nuance* (Springer International Publishing, 2018); Devah Pager, "The Use of Field Experiments for Studies of Employment Discrimination: Contributions, Critiques, and Directions for the Future," *The Annals of the American Academy of Political and Social Science* 609, no. 1 (2007): 104–33.

34. I also recruited a well-matched pair of female testers, but one member of the pair withdrew from the study just before I entered the field.

35. Barron's College Division Staff, *Barron's Profiles of American Colleges*, 2016.

36. For a more detailed methodological explanation, see Stewart and Uggen, "Criminal Records and College Admissions."

37. Annie Phoenix and Syrita Steib, "Ban the Box in Higher Education: Lessons From Louisiana on Changing Laws and Leading Movements," *Journal of Contemporary Criminal Justice* 37, no. 2 (2021): 293–301, https://doi.org/10.1177/1043986221999883; Royel M. Johnson, Rafael E. Alvarado, and Kelly Ochs Rosinger, "What's the 'Problem' of Considering Criminal History in College Admissions? A Critical Analysis of 'Ban the Box' Policies in Louisiana and Maryland," *The Journal of Higher Education* 92, no. 5 (2021): 704–734, https://doi.org/10.1080/00221546.2020.1870849.

38. *Beyond the Box: Increasing Access to Higher Education for Justice-Involved Individuals* (Washington, D.C.: US Department of Education, 2016), https://www.aacrao.org/docs/default-source/signature-initiative-docs/disciplinary-notations/ed-guidance.pdf?sfvrsn=61d160cc_4.

39. Scott Jaschik, "SUNY Bans the Box," *Inside Higher Ed*, September 15, 2016, https://www.insidehighered.com/news/2016/09/15/suny-removes-question-criminal-convictions-application.

40. Michael Dresser, "Maryland Senate Overrides Hogan Veto of Bill Barring College Admissions from Asking about Arrests," *The Baltimore Sun*, January 12, 2018, http://www.baltimoresun.com/news/maryland/politics/bs-md-college-admissions-20180112-story.html; Johnson, Alvarado, and Rosinger, "What's the 'Problem' of Considering Criminal History in College Admissions?"

41. Jen Davis, "Change to Criminal History Question for 2019–2020 Application Year," The Common Application, August 19, 2018, https://www.commonapp.org/whats-appening/application-updates/change-criminal-history-question-2019-2020-application-year.

42. Amanda Agan and Sonja Starr, "Ban the Box, Criminal Records, and Racial Discrimination: A Field Experiment," *The Quarterly Journal of Economics* 133, no. 1 (2018): 191–235, https://doi.org/10.1093/qje/qjx028; Mike Vuolo, Sarah Lageson, and Christopher Uggen, "Criminal Record Questions in the Era of 'Ban the Box,'" *Criminology & Public Policy* 16, no. 1 (February 1, 2017): 139–65, https://doi.org/10.1111/1745-9133.12250.

43. White House, "Fair Chance Higher Education Pledge," 2016, https://obamawhitehouse.archives.gov/sites/whitehouse.gov/files/documents/Fair%20Chance%20Education%20Pledge.pdf.

44. Sarah Esther Lageson, Mike Vuolo, and Christopher Uggen, "Legal Ambiguity in Managerial Assessments of Criminal Records," *Law & Social Inquiry* 40, no. 1 (2015): 175–204.

45. Lageson, Vuolo, and Uggen, "Legal Ambiguity"; Marsha Weissman et al., *The Use of Criminal History Records in College Admissions Reconsidered*.

46. Weissman et al., *The Use of Criminal History Records in College Admissions Reconsidered*; Rosenthal et al., *Boxed Out*.

CHAPTER 8

1. Anna Brown, "Most Americans Say Higher Ed Is Heading in Wrong Direction, But Partisans Disagree on Why," *Pew Research Center*, July 26, 2018, https://www.pewresearch.org/fact-tank/2018/07/26/most-americans-say-higher-ed-is-heading-in-wrong-direction-but-partisans-disagree-on-why/; Stephanie Marken, "Half in U.S. Now Consider College Education Very Important," *Gallup*, December 30, 2019, https://www.gallup.com/education/272228/half-consider-college-education-important.aspx.
2. Marken, "Half in U.S. Now Consider College Education Very Important."
3. Brown, "Most Americans Say Higher Ed Is Heading in Wrong Direction"; Stephanie Marken, "About a Quarter of U.S. Adults Consider Higher Ed Affordable," *Gallup*, January 7, 2020, https://www.gallup.com/education/272366/quarter-adults-consider-higher-affordable.aspx.
4. Devlin Barrett and Matt Zapotosky, "FBI Accuses Wealthy Parents, Including Celebrities, in College-Entrance Bribery Scheme," *Washington Post*, March 12, 2019, https://www.washingtonpost.com/world/national-security/fbi-accuses-wealthy-parents-including-celebrities-in-college-entrance-bribery-scheme/2019/03/12/d91c9942-44d1-11e9-8aab-95b8d80a1e4f_story.html.
5. Barrett and Zapotosky, "FBI Accuses Wealthy Parents," para five.
6. John F. Gaski, "The College Admissions Racket," *Society* 56, no. 4 (2019): 357–59; Daniel Golden, "'The Epitome of Sleaze': Colleges Have Portrayed Themselves as Helpless Victims of Rick Singer. In Reality, They Have No One to Blame but Themselves," *The Chronicle of Higher Education* 66, no. 9 (2019): B10; Joseph C. Hermanowicz, "The Degradation of Merit," *Society* 56, no. 4 (2019): 340–47.
7. Patt Morrison, "College Admissions Scandal Shows How Desperate the Privileged Are to Keep It That Way," *Los Angeles Times*, March 20, 2019, https://www.latimes.com/opinion/op-ed/la-ol-patt-morrison-jerome-karabel-college-cheating-20190320-htmlstory.html.
8. Morrison, "College Admissions Scandal," para 24.
9. Jerry Lucido, Julie Posselt, and Maria Claudia Soler, "On Scandal, Trust, and the Role of College Presidents in Times of Crisis," *Higher Education Today*, October 28, 2020, https://www.higheredtoday.org/2020/10/28/scandal-trust-role-college-presidents-times-crisis/, para five.
10. Lucido, Posselt, and Soler, "On Scandal," para six.
11. Marc M. Camille, "Ethics and Strategic Enrollment Management," in *Handbook of Strategic Enrollment Management*, eds. D. Hossler and B. Bontrager (San Francisco: Jossey-Bass, 2015); Don Hossler, "Putting Students First in College Admissions and Enrollment Management," in *Fostering Student Success in the Campus Community*, ed. Gary L. Kramer (San Francisco: Jossey-Bass, 2007) 565–84.

12. Camille, "Ethics and Strategic Enrollment Management"; Alice Cox, "Admission Recruiting and Selection: Some Ethical Concerns," in *Ethics and Higher Education*, ed. William W. May (New York: American Council on Education/Macmillan Publishing Company, 1990): 84–102.

13. Edward B. Fiske, "Ethical Issues in Recruiting Students," *New Directions for Higher Education* 33 (1981): 41–48; Bobby Johnson, "Student Recruitment: Have We Gone Too Far?" *Journal of College Admission* 125 (1989): 25–28; Jerrie J. Johnson and Richard W. Sline, "Ethics: Recruitment and Matriculation Techniques," *The National ACAC Journal* 17, no. 3 (1973): 6–7; Larry H. Litten, "Avoiding and Stemming Abuses in Academic Marketing," *College & University* 56, no. 2 (1981): 105–22; Christopher H. Lovelock and Michael L. Rothschild, *Marketing in College Admissions* (New York: College Entrance Examination Board, 1980); Maureen Mackey, "The Selling of the Sheepskin," *Change* 12, no. 3 (1980): 28–33.

14. Sandy Baum, "Balancing Act: Can Colleges Achieve Equal Access and Survive in a Competitive Market?" *College Board Review* 186 (1998): 12–17; Derek C. Bok, *Universities in the Marketplace: The Commercialization of Higher Education* (Princeton, NJ: Princeton University Press, 2003); Victoria J. Gallagher, "Ethical Considerations in College Admission Practices: A Proposal for Dialogic Involvement," *Journal of College Admission* 13 (1992): 8–12; Ben Gose, "Questions Loom for Applicants and Colleges," *The Chronicle of Higher Education* 51, no. 25 (Feb 25, 2005): B1–B4; Hossler, "Putting Students First"; James W. Jump, "The Ethics of Need-Blind Admission," *Journal of College Admission* 147 (1995): 12–15; Julie L. Nicklin, "Cultivating Parents: Colleges See Them as Potential Contributors; Critics Decry Some Tactics Used," *The Chronicle of Higher Education*, November, 30, 1994, https://chronicle.com/article/Cultivating-Parents/84603/; Andrew Roth, "Admission, Ethics and Financial Aid: Formulating and Applying an Ethical Framework to the Need-Blind Debate," in *The Journal of College Admission Ethics Series*, eds. Elaina C. Loveland and Joyce Raynor (Alexandria, VA: NACAC, 2000), 61–82; James C. Walters, "Introduction," in *The Journal of College Admission Ethics Series*, eds. Elaina C. Loveland and Joyce Raynor (Alexandria, VA: NACAC, 2000), 5–6.

15. Robert L. Hodum and Glenn W. James, "An Observation of Normative Structure for College Admission and Recruitment Officers," *The Journal of Higher Education* 81, no. 3 (2010): 317–38; Robert L. Hodum, "A Normative Code of Conduct for Admissions Officers," *New Directions for Higher Education* 160 (Winter 2012): 29–39.

16. Jennifer Adelstein and Stewart Clegg, "Code of Ethics: A Stratified Vehicle for Compliance," *Journal of Business Ethics* 138, no. 1 (2016): 53–66; Muel Kaptein, "Toward Effective Codes: Testing the Relationship with Unethical Behavior," *Journal of Business Ethics* 99, no. 2 (2011): 233–51; Jennifer J. Kish-Gephart, David A. Harrison, and Linda Klebe Treviño, "Bad Apples, Bad Cases, and

Bad Barrels: Meta-Analytic Evidence about Sources of Unethical Decisions at Work," *Journal of Applied Psychology* 95, no. 1 (2010): 1–31; Ann E. Tenbrunsel, Kristin Smith-Crowe, and Elizabeth E. Umphress, "Building Houses on Rocks: The Role of the Ethical Infrastructure in Organizations," *Social Justice Research* 16, no. 3 (2003): 285–307; Linda Klebe Treviño, Niki A. Den Nieuwenboer, and Jennifer J. Kish-Gephart. "(Un)ethical Behavior in Organizations," *Annual Review of Psychology* 65 (2014): 635–60.

17. Nathan D. Grawe, *Demographics and the Demand for Higher Education* (Baltimore: Johns Hopkins University Press, 2018); Nathan D. Grawe, *The Agile College: How Institutions Successfully Navigate Demographic Changes* (Baltimore: Johns Hopkins University Press, 2021); Eric Hoover, "'Welcome to the Wild West': The Competition for College Applicants Just Intensified," *Chronicle of Higher Education*, September 29, 2019, https://www.chronicle.com/article/welcome-to-the-wild-west-the-competition-for-college-applicants-just-intensified; Eric Kelderman, "2020 Has Been a Hard Year for Higher Ed. Could 2021 Be Worse?" *Chronicle of Higher Education*, October 8, 2020, https://www.chronicle.com/article/2020-has-been-a-hard-year-for-higher-ed-could-2021-be-worse; National Association of College and University Business Officers, *2020 NACUBO Tuition Discounting Study* (Washington, DC: NACUBO, 2021), https://www.nacubo.org/Research/2020/NACUBO-Tuition-Discounting-Study.

18. Hossler, "Putting Students First."

19. Grawe, *The Agile College*; Robery Zemsky, Susan Shaman, and Susan Campbell Baldridge, *The College Stress Test: Tracking Institutional Futures across a Crowded Market* (Baltimore: Johns Hopkins University Press, 2020).

20. Charlotte West, "Safeguarding Ethics in College Admissions," *Trusteeship* 28 no. 1 (January/February 2020), https://agb.org/trusteeship-article/safeguarding-ethics-in-college-admissions-article/, para 22.

21. Blake E. Ashforth, Dennis A. Gioia, Sandra L. Robinson, and Linda K. Trevino, "Re-Viewing Organizational Corruption," *Academy of Management Review* 33, no. 3 (2008): 671; Thomas H. Jones, "Ethical Decision Making by Individuals in Organizations: An Issue-Contingent Model," *Academy of Management Review* 16, no. 2 (1991): 366–97.

22. Hoover, "'Welcome to the Wild West.'"

23. Hoover, "'Welcome to the Wild West.'"

24. "Justice Department Files Antitrust Case and Simultaneous Settlement Requiring Elimination of Anticompetitive College Recruiting Restraints," United States Department of Justice Press Release 19-1,380, December 12, 2019, https://www.justice.gov/opa/pr/justice-department-files-antitrust-case-and-simultaneous-settlement-requiring-elimination.

25. Eric Hoover, "'Act Now!' Say Hello to the New Enrollment Playbook," *Chronicle of Higher Education*, February 11, 2020, https://www.chronicle.com/article/act-now-say-hello-to-the-new-enrollment-playbook/.

26. Hoover, "'Welcome to the Wild West,'" para 12.

27. Hoover, "'Welcome to the Wild West,'" para 14.

28. West, "Safeguarding Ethics."

29. Richard J. Riel, "From Gatekeeper to Marketing Consultant: The Admission Officer's Changing Role," *College and University* 3 (1982): 327–29.

30. Scott Jaschik and Doug Lederman, *The Inside Higher Ed Survey of College and University Admissions Directors* (Washington, DC: Inside Higher Ed, 2015); Jack Stripling and Eric Hoover, "In Admissions, the Powerful Weigh In," *Chronicle of Higher Education*, November 29, 2015, https://www.chronicle.com/article/ in-admissions-the-powerful-weigh-in/.

31. Eric Hoover, "For Admissions Officials, Texas Controversy Highlights Dangers of Clout, *Chronicle of Higher Education*, February 16, 2015, https://www .chronicle.com/article/for-admissions-officials-texas-controversy-high-lights-dangers-of-clout, para two.

32. State of Illinois Admissions Review Commission, *Commission Meeting – 9th Open Meeting*, July 27 2009, http://www2.illinois.gov/gov/admissionsreview/ Pages/meetings.aspx, 3:25:11.

33. Admissions Review Commission, *Report and Recommendations* (Springfield, IL: State of Illinois, 2009).

34. Admissions Review Commission, *Report and Recommendations*.

35. Admissions Review Commission, *Report and Recommendations*.

36. Admissions Review Commission, *Report and Recommendations*.

37. State of Illinois Admissions Review Commission, *Commission Meeting – 4th Open Meeting*, July 8, 2009. http://www2.illinois.gov/gov/admissionsreview/ Pages/meetings.aspx.

38. Admissions Review Commission, *Report and Recommendations*.

39. Admissions Review Commission, *Report and Recommendations*.

40. Admissions Review Commission, *Report and Recommendations*.

41. Admissions Review Commission. *Commission Meeting – 3rd Open Meeting*, July 6, 2009, http://www2.illinois.gov/gov/admissionsreview/Pages/meetings.aspx.

42. State of Illinois Admissions Review Commission, *Commission Meeting – 2nd Open Meeting*, June 29, 2009, http://www2.illinois.gov/gov/admissionsreview/ Pages/meetings.aspx.

43. *FY2010 Budget Request for Operating and Capital Funds* (Champaign, IL: University of Illinois, 2008), 6.

44. *FY2010 Budget Request for Operating and Capital Funds*, 6.

45. State of Illinois Admissions Review Commission, *Commission Meeting – 4th Open Meeting*.

46. State of Illinois Admissions Review Commission, *Commission Meeting – 9th Open Meeting*, 3:36:36.

47. State of Illinois Admissions Review Commission, *Commission Meeting – 9th Open Meeting*, 37:53.

48. State of Illinois Admissions Review Commission. *Commission Meeting – 2nd Open Meeting*, 2:24:26.

49. State of Illinois Admissions Review Commission. *Commission Meeting – 3rd Open Meeting*, 1:41.

50. Karen Bussey et al., *"The Most Important Door That Will Ever Open": Realizing the Mission of Higher Education through Equitable Recruitment, Admissions, and Enrollment Policies*, Institute of Higher Education Policy, June 2021, https://www .ihep.org/wp-content/uploads/2021/06/IHEP_JOYCE_full_rd3b-2.pdf; Ozan Jaquette, Bradley R. Curs, and Julie R. Posselt, "Tuition Rich, Mission Poor: Nonresident Enrollment Growth and the Socioeconomic and Racial Composition of Public Research Universities," *The Journal of Higher Education* 87, no. 5 (2016): 635–73.

51. John J. Cheslock and Rock Kroc, "Managing College Enrollments," in *The Handbook for Institutional Researchers*, eds. Richard D. Howard, Gerald W. McLaughlin, and William E. Knight, (San Francisco: Jossey-Bass, 2012), 221–36; Jennifer DeHaemers and Michele Sandlin, "Delivering Effective Admissions Operations," in *Handbook of Strategic Enrollment Management*, eds. Don Hossler and Bob Bontrager (San Francisco: Jossey-Bass, 2014), 377– 95; William R. Doyle, "Changes in Institutional Aid, 1992–2003: The Evolving Role of Merit Aid," *Research in Higher Education* 51, no. 8 (2010): 789–810; Robert L. Duniway, "Benchmarking and Enrollment Management," *New Directions for Institutional Research* no. 156 (2012): 25–36; Jaquette, Curs, and Posselt, "Tuition Rich, Mission Poor."

52. Bussey et al., *"The Most Important Door"*; James A. Dearden, James A., Suhui Li, Chad D. Meyerhoefer, and Muzhe Yang, "Demonstrated Interest: Signaling Behavior in College Admissions," *Contemporary Economic Policy* 35, no. 4 (2017): 630–57; Eric Hoover, "The Dynamics of Demonstrated Interest, *The Chronicle of Higher Education*, May 25, 2010, http://chronicle.com/blogs/headcount/ the-dynamics-of-demonstrated-interest/24288.

53. Melissa Clinedinst, *2019 State of College Admissions* (Arlington, VA: NACAC, 2019), https://www.nacacnet.org/globalassets/documents/publications/ research/2018_soca/soca2019_all.pdf; Dearden et al., "Demonstrated Interest."

54. Bussey et al., *"The Most Important Door,"* 22.

55. Bussey et al., *"The Most Important Door,"* 22.

56. Dearden et al., "Demonstrated Interest."

57. Clinedinst, *2019 State of College Admissions*; Jerome A. Lucido, "How Admission Decisions Get Made," in *Handbook of Strategic Enrollment Management*, eds. Don Hossler and Bob Bontrager (San Francisco: Jossey-Bass, 2015), 147–74.

58. Christopher Avery, Andrew Fairbanks, and Richard Zeckhauser, *The Early Admissions Game: Joining the Elite* (Cambridge, MA: Harvard University Press, 2004); Christopher Avery and Jonathan Levin, "Early Admissions at Selective Colleges," *American Economic Review* 100, no. 5 (2010): 2125–56.

59. Clinedinst, 2019 *State of College Admissions*.

60. Bussey et al., "The Most Important Door"; Jennifer Giancola and Richard D. Kahlenberg, *True Merit: Ensuring Our Brightest Students Have Access to Our Best Colleges and Universities* (Lansdowne, VA: Jack Kent Cooke Foundation, 2016).

61. Avery et al., *The Early Admissions Game*; Bussey et al., "The Most Important Door"; Giancola and Kahlenberg, *True Merit*.

62. Bussey et al., "The Most Important Door"; Dearden et al., "Demonstrated Interest"; DeHaemers and Sandlin, "Delivering Effective Admissions Operations."

63. Bussey et al., "The Most Important Door."

64. Avery et al., *The Early Admissions Game*; Bussey et al., "The Most Important Door"; Julie Park and M. Kevin Eagan, "Who Goes Early?: A Multi-Level Analysis of Enrolling via Early Action and Early Decision Admissions," *Teachers College Record* 113, no. 11 (2011): 2345–73.

65. Dearden et al., "Demonstrated Interest."

66. James R. Rest, *Moral Development: Advances in Research and Theory* (New York: Praeger, 1986); Scott J. Reynolds, "Moral Awareness and Ethical Predispositions: Investigating the Role of Individual Differences in the Recognition of Moral Issues," *Journal of Applied Psychology* 91, no. 1 (2006): 233–43; Linda K. Treviño, Gary R. Weaver, and Scott J. Reynolds, "Behavioral Ethics in Organizations: A Review," *Journal of Management* 32, no. 6 (2006): 951–90.

67. Tricia Bertram Gallant and Lester Goodchild, "Introduction," in *Creating the Ethical Academy. A Systems Approach to Understanding Misconduct and Empowering Change in Higher Education*, ed. Tricia Bertram Gallant (New York: Routledge, 2011), 3–11; John G. Bruhn, Gary Zajac, Ali A. Al-Kazemi, and Loren D. Prescott Jr., "Moral Positions and Academic Conduct: Parameters of Tolerance for Ethics Failure," *The Journal of Higher Education* 73, no. 4 (2002): 461–93; Nathan F. Harris and Michael N. Bastedo, "Corruption at the Top: Ethical Dilemmas in College and University Governance," in *Creating the Ethical Academy: A Systems Approach to Understanding Misconduct and Empowering Change in Higher Education*, ed. Tricia Bertram Gallant (New York: Routledge, 2011), 127–44; Jones, "Ethical Decision Making"; David C. Smith and Charles H. Reynolds, "Institutional Culture and Ethics," in *Ethics and Higher Education*, ed. William W. May (New York: American Council on Education/Macmillan Publishing Company, 1990), 21–31; Ann E. Tenbrunsel and Kristin Smith-Crowe, "Ethical Decision Making: Where We've Been and Where We're Going," *Academy of Management Annals* 2, no. 1 (2008): 545–607; Treviño et al., 2006.

68. Max H. Bazerman and Ovul Sezer, "Bounded Awareness: Implications for Ethical Decision Making," *Organizational Behavior and Human Decision Processes* 136 (2016): 95–105; Dolly Chugh and Max H. Bazerman, "Bounded Awareness: What You Fail to See Can Hurt You," *Mind & Society* 6, no. 1 (2007): 1–18; David De Cremer and Wim Vandekerckhove, "Managing Unethical Behavior in Organizations: The Need for a Behavioral Business Ethics Approach,"

Journal of Management & Organization 23, no. 3 (2017): 437–55; Henrich R. Greve, Donald Palmer, and Jo-Ellen Pozner, "Organizations Gone Wild: The Causes, Processes, and Consequences of Organizational Misconduct," *Academy of Management Annals* 4, no. 1 (2010): 53–107; Celia Moore and Francesca Gino, "Approach, Ability, Aftermath: A Psychological Process Framework of Unethical Behavior at Work," *Academy of Management Annals* 9, no. 1 (2015): 235–89.

69. Michael N. Bastedo, "Conflicts, Commitments, and Cliques in the University: Moral Seduction as a Threat to Trustee Independence," *American Educational Research Journal* 46, no. 2 (2009): 354–86; Max H. Bazerman, Don A. Moore, Philip E. Tetlock, and Lloyd Tanlu, "Reports of Solving the Conflicts of Interest in Auditing Are Highly Exaggerated," *Academy of Management Review* 31, no. 1 (2006): 43–49; Don A. Moore, Philip E. Tetlock, Lloyd Tanlu, and Max H. Bazerman, "Conflicts of Interest and the Case of Auditor Independence: Moral Seduction and Strategic Issue Cycling," *Academy of Management Review* 31, no. 1 (2006): 10–29.

70. R. McKenzie Rees, Ann E. Tenbrunsel, and Max H. Bazerman, "Bounded Ethicality and Ethical Fading in Negotiations: Understanding Unintended Unethical Behavior," *Academy of Management Perspectives* 33, no. 1 (2019): 26–42; Ann E. Tenbrunsel and David M. Messick, "Ethical Fading: The Role of Self-Deception in Unethical Behavior," *Social Justice Research* 17, no. 2 (2004): 223–36; Ann E. Tenbrunsel, McKenzie R. Rees, and Kristina A. Diekmann, "Sexual Harassment in Academia: Ethical Climates and Bounded Ethicality," *Annual Review of Psychology* 70 (2019): 245–70.

71. Rees, Tenbrunsel, and Bazerman, "Bounded Ethicality"; Tenbrunsel and Messick, "Ethical Fading."

72. Rees, Tenbrunsel, and Bazerman, "Bounded Ethicality"; Tenbrunsel and Messick, "Ethical Fading."

73. Tenbrunsel and Messick, "Ethical Fading."

74. Rees, Tenbrunsel, and Bazerman, "Bounded Ethicality"; Tenbrunsel, Rees, and Diekmann, "Sexual Harassment in Academia."

75. Tenbrunsel and Messick, "Ethical Fading."

76. Ann E. Tenbrunsel, Kristina A. Diekmann, Kimberly A. Wade-Benzoni, and Max H. Bazerman, "The Ethical Mirage: A Temporal Explanation as to Why We Are Not as Ethical as We Think We Are," *Research in Organizational Behavior* 30 (2010): 153–73; Tenbrunsel, Rees, and Diekmann, "Sexual Harassment in Academia."

77. Bazerman and Sezer, "Bounded Awareness"; Francesca Gino and Max H. Bazerman, "When Misconduct Goes Unnoticed: The Acceptability of Gradual Erosion in Others' Unethical Behavior," *Journal of Experimental Social Psychology* 45, no. 4 (2009): 708–19; Tenbrunsel, Rees, and Diekmann, "Sexual Harassment in Academia."

78. Bazerman and Sezer, "Bounded Awareness"; Francesca Gino, Don A. Moore, and Max H. Bazerman, *No Harm, No Foul: The Outcome Bias in Ethical Judgments* (Boston, MA: Harvard Business School, 2008); Celia Moore and Francesca Gino, "Ethically Adrift: How Others Pull Our Moral Compass from True North, and How We Can Fix It," *Research in Organizational Behavior* 33 (2013): 53–77; Ovul Sezer, Ting Zhang, Francesca Gino, and Max H. Bazerman, "Overcoming the Outcome Bias: Making Intentions Matter," *Organizational Behavior and Human Decision Processes* 137 (2016): 13–26.

79. State of Illinois Admissions Review Commission. *Commission Meeting – 3rd Open Meeting*, 20:12; State of Illinois Admissions Review Commission. *Commission Meeting –3rd Open Meeting*, 23:31.

80. Beth McMurtrie, "How Do You Create a Diversity Agenda? It Takes More Than Just a Plan on Paper," *The Chronicle of Higher Education*, May 15, 2016, https://www.chronicle.com/article/how-do-you-create-a-diversity-agenda/; Daryl G. Smith, *Diversity's Promise for Higher Education: Making it Work* (Baltimore: Johns Hopkins University Press, 2020); *Advancing Diversity and Inclusion in Higher Education*, Office of Planning, Evaluation and Policy Development and Office of the Under Secretary (Washington, D.C.: US Department of Education, 2016).

81. Jeffrey R. Young, "Show Them You Care," *Chronicle of Higher Education*, January 23, 2004, A35–36.

82. Bertram Gallant and Goodchild, "Introduction"; Robert Birnbaum, *How Colleges Work: The Cybernetics of Academic Organization and Leadership* (San Francisco: Jossey-Bass Publishers, 1988); Edgar H. Schein, *Organizational Culture and Leadership* (San Francisco: Jossey-Bass, 1985); Smith and Reynolds, "Institutional Culture and Ethics."

83. Henrich R. Greve, Donald Palmer, and Jo-Ellen Pozner, "Organizations Gone Wild: The Causes, Processes, and Consequences of Organizational Misconduct," *Academy of Management Annals* 4, no. 1 (2010): 53–107; Harris and Bastedo, "Corruption at the Top"; Terry Thomas, John R. Schermerhorn Jr, and John W. Dienhart, "Strategic Leadership of Ethical Behavior in Business," *Academy of Management Perspectives* 18, no. 2 (2004): 56–66.

84. Greve, Palmer, and Pozner, "Organizations Gone Wild"; Thomas, Schermerhorn, and Dienhart, "Strategic Leadership."

85. Blake E. Ashforth and Vikas Anand, "The Normalization of Corruption in Organizations," *Research in Organizational Behavior* 25 (2003): 1–52; Ronald R. Sims and Johannes Brinkmann, "Enron Ethics (or: Culture Matters More Than Codes)," *Journal of Business Ethics* 45, no. 3 (2003): 243–56.

86. "Summary of University of Illinois Admissions Firewall Practices," University of Illinois System, https://www.vpaa.uillinois.edu/cms/one.aspx?portalId=420456&pageId=782260.

87. Andrew Abbott, "Professional Ethics," *American Journal of Sociology* 88, no. 5 (1983): 855–85; Ashforth and Anand, "The Normalization of Corruption";

Paul J. DiMaggio and Walter W. Powell, "The Iron Cage Revisited: Institutional Isomorphism and Collective Rationality in Organizational Fields," *American Sociological Review* 48 no. 2 (1983): 147–60; Hodum, "A Normative Code."

88. *Guide to Ethical Practice in Admissions* (Arlington, VA: NACAC, 2020).

89. Camille, "Ethics and Strategic Enrollment Management"; Harris and Bastedo, "Corruption at the Top."

90. West, "Safeguarding Ethics," para 20.

91. Marya L. Besharov and Rakesh Khurana, "Leading Amidst Competing Technical and Institutional Demands: Revisiting Selznick's Conception of Leadership, in *Institutions and Ideals: Philip Selznick's Legacy for Organizational Studies*, ed., Matthew S. Kraatz (Bingley: Emerald Group Publishing, 2015), 53–88; Philip Selznick, *TVA and the Grass Roots* (Berkeley, CA: University of California Press, 1949); Philip Selznick, *Leadership in Administration* (New York: Harper and Row, 1957); Philip Selznick, "'Institutionalism' 'Old' and 'New,'" *Administrative Science Quarterly* 41, no. 2 (1996): 270–77.

92. Smith and Reynolds, "Institutional Culture and Ethics."

93. Besharov and Khurana, "Leading Amidst Competing Technical and Institutional Demands"; Selznick, "'Institutionalism' 'Old' and 'New.'"

CHAPTER 9

1. *Students for Fair Admissions, Inc. v. President & Fellows of Harvard College* (SFFA), 397 F. Supp. 3d 126, 203–04 (D. Mass. 2019) at 127.

2. Alex Posecznick, *Selling Hope and College: Merit, Markets, and Recruitment in an Unranked School* (Ithaca, NY: Cornell University Press, 2017); Mitchell Stevens, *Creating a Class: College Admissions and the Education of Elites* (Cambridge, MA: Harvard University Press, 2009).

3. A. J. Alvero, et al., "AI and Holistic Review: Informing Human Reading in College Admissions," AIES '20: *Proceedings of the AAAI/ACM Conference on AI, Ethics, and Society*, February 2020, 200–6, https://doi.org/10.1145/3375627.3375871; Michael N. Bastedo, et al., "What Are We Talking About When We Talk About Holistic Review? Selective College Admissions and Its Effects on Low-SES Students," *The Journal of Higher Education* 89, no. 5 (2018): 782–805; Michael N. Bastedo et al., "Admitting Students in Context: Field Experiments on Information Dashboards in College Admissions," *The Journal of Higher Education* (2021), https://doi.org/10.1080/00221546.2021.1971488; Don Hossler, et al., "A Study of the Use of Nonacademic Factors in Holistic Undergraduate Admissions Reviews," *The Journal of Higher Education* 90, no. 6 (2019): 833–59; Julie J. Park and M. Kevin Eagan, "Who Goes Early?: A Multi-level Analysis of Enrolling Via Early Action and Early Decision Admissions," *Teachers College Record* 113, no. 11 (2011): 2345–73.

4. Andrew S. Belasco et al., "The Test-Optional Movement at America's Selective Liberal Arts Colleges: A Boon for Equity or Something Else?" *Educational Evaluation and Policy Analysis* 37, no. 2 (June 2015): 206–23, https://doi.org/10.3102/0162373714537350; Christopher T. Bennett, "Untested Admissions: Examining Changes in Application Behaviors and Student Demographics Under Test-Optional Policies," *American Educational Research Journal* (2021), https://doi.org/10.3102/00028312211003526.

5. Karina G. Salazar et al., "Coming Soon to a Neighborhood Near You? Off-Campus Recruiting by Public Research Universities," *American Educational Research Journal* (2021), https://doi.org/10.3102/00028312211001810.

6. Daniel Hirschman and Ellen Berrey, "The Partial Deinstitutionalization of Affirmative Action in U.S. Higher Education, 1988 to 2014," *Sociological Science* 4 (2017): 449–68; Mike Hoa Nguyen et al., "Asian Americans, Admissions, and College Choice: An Empirical Test of Claims of Harm Used in Federal Investigations," *Educational Researcher* 49, no. 8 (2020): 579–94; OiYan A. Poon and Liliana M. Garces, "Asian Americans and Race-conscious Admissions: Understanding the Conservative Opposition's Strategy of Misinformation, Intimidation, and Racial Division," in *Civil Rights and Federal Higher Education* eds. By Nicholas Hillman and Gary Orfield (Cambridge, MA: Harvard Education Press, 2022), 53–74.

7. Nicholas A. Bowman and Michael N. Bastedo, "What Role May Admissions Office Diversity and Practices Play in Equitable Decisions?" *Research in Higher Education* 59, no. 4 (2018): 430–47, https://doi.org/10.1007/s11162-017-9468-9.

8. A. J. Alvero, et al., "AI and Holistic Review"; Julie Posselt, Theresa E. Hernandez, Cynthia D. Villarreal, Aireale J. Rodgers, Lauren N. Irwin, "Evaluation and Decision Making in Higher Education," in *Higher Education: Handbook of Theory and Research*, vol. 35, ed. Laura W. Perna (New York: Springer, 2020), https://doi.org/10.1007/978-3-030-11743-6_8-1.

9. This research was made possible (in part) by a grant from the Spencer Foundation (#201900049). The views expressed are those of the authors and do not necessarily reflect the views of the Spencer Foundation.

10. Rodney T. Ogawa et al., "CHAT-IT: Toward Conceptualizing Learning in the Context of Formal Organizations," *Educational Researcher* 37, no. 2 (March 2008): 83–95, https://doi.org/10.3102/0013189X08316207.

11. Ogawa et al., "CHAT-IT," 84.

12. Park and Eagan, "Who Goes Early?"

13. Hirschman and Berrey, "The Partial Deinstitutionalization of Affirmative Action."

14. Posselt et al., "Evaluation and Decision Making in Higher Education."

15. Adrianna Kezar, *How Colleges Change: Understanding, Leading, and Enacting Change* (New York: Routledge, 2018).

16. Posselt et al., "Evaluation and Decision Making in Higher Education."

CHAPTER 10

1. Anthony P. Carnevale and Stephen J. Rose, "Socioeconomic Status, Race/ Ethnicity, and Selective College Admissions," in *America's Untapped Resource: Low-income Students in Higher Education*, ed. Richard D. Kahlenberg (New York: The Century Foundation, 2003), 101–56.

2. We define *underrepresented* as those racial groups who have a smaller share of students enrolling in selective institutions than their share across the United States or within the state (for public institutions).

3. Amy Laitinen, Clare McCann, and Rachel Fishman, *Supporting Students of Color in Higher Education* (Washington, DC: New America, 2019).

4. Anya Kamenetz, "What If Elite Colleges Switched to a Lottery for Admissions?" *National Public Radio* (NPR), March 27, 2019, https://www.npr .org/2019/03/27/705477877/what-if-elite-colleges-switched-to-a-lottery-for-admissions.

5. Robert P. Wolff, "The College as Rat-Race: Admissions and Anxieties," *Dissent* 11 (1964): 13–20.

6. Wolff, "The College as Rat-Race."

7. Alexander W. Astin, "A Researcher's Proposal for Changes in Higher Education," *Educational Record* 51 (1970): 225.

8. Dalton Conley, "Enough Fretting Over College Admissions. It's Time for a Lottery," *The Washington Post*, August 13, 2018, https://www.washingtonpost .com/opinions/enough-fretting-over-college-admissions-its-time-for-a-lottery/2018/08/13/f65a072c-9a74-11e8-8d5e-c6c594024954_story.html.

9. Matt Feeney, "The Abiding Scandal of College Admissions," *The Chronicle of Higher Education*, April 16, 2021, https://www.chronicle.com/article/ the-abiding-scandal-of-college-admissions.

10. Fabio Rojas, "Should Harvard Randomize Admissions?" *Orgtheory.net*, September 2, 2020, https://orgtheory.wordpress.com/2020/09/02/should-harvard-randomize-admissions/.

11. Barry Schwartz, "Do College Admissions by Lottery," *Behavioral Scientist*, June 4, 2019, https://behavioralscientist.org/do-college-admissions-by-lottery/.

12. Natasha K. Warikoo, *The Diversity Bargain and Other Dilemmas of Race, Admissions, and Meritocracy at Elite Universities* (Chicago: University of Chicago Press, 2016).

13. Frederick Hess, "Why Pandemic Problems Should Get Colleges Like Harvard to Admit Students by Lottery Next Year," *Forbes*, April 7, 2020, https:// www.forbes.com/sites/frederickhess/2020/04/07/spotty-transcripts-no-test-scores-how-should-colleges-select-students-next-year/?sh= 309d6a123270.

14. Alia Wong, "Lotteries May Be the Fairest Way to Fix Elite-College Admissions," *The Atlantic*, August 1, 2018, https://www.theatlantic.com/education/ archive/2018/08/lottery-college-admissions/566492/.

15. Ginia Bellafante, "Should Ivy League Schools Randomly Select Students (At Least for a Little While)?," *The New York Times*, updated January 12, 2021, https://www.nytimes.com/2020/12/18/nyregion/ivy-league-admissions-lottery.html.

16. Lois Weis, Kristin Cipollone, and Heather Jenkins, *Class Warfare: Class, Race, and College Admissions in Top-Tier Secondary Schools* (Chicago: University of Chicago Press, 2014).

17. Astin, "A Researcher's Proposal."

18. Dalton Conley, "Harvard by Lottery," *The Chronicle of Higher Education*, April 1, 2012, https://www.chronicle.com/article/harvard-by-lottery/.

19. Schwartz, "Do College Admissions by Lottery."

20. Susan Sturm and Lani Guinier, "The Future of Affirmative Action: Reclaiming the Innovative Ideal," *California Law Review* 84 (1996): 953–1036.

21. Rebecca Zwick, *Who Gets In?* (Cambridge: Harvard University Press, 2017).

22. Zwick, *Who Gets In?*; see also Karen M. Stegers-Jager, "Lessons Learned From 15 Years of Non-Grades-Based Selection for Medical School," *Medical Education* 52 (2018): 86–95.

23. Carnevale and Rose, "Socioeconomic Status, Race/Ethnicity, and Selective College Admissions."

24. We use the language that the author used to describe this group of students.

25. Michael N. Bastedo, Nicholas A. Bowman, Kristen M. Glasener, and Jandi L. Kelly, "What Are We Talking About When We Talk About Holistic Review? Selective College Admissions and Its Effects on Low-SES Students," *The Journal of Higher Education* 89, no. 5 (2018): 782–805.

26. Zwick, *Who Gets In?*

27. Zwick, *Who Gets In?*

28. Dominique J. Baker and Michael N. Bastedo, "What If We Leave It Up to Chance? Admissions Lotteries and Equitable Access at Selective Colleges," *Educational Researcher* 51, no. 2 (2022), 134–45, published online 2 November 2021, https://doi.org/10.3102 percent2F0013189X211055494.

29. Richard V. Reeves and Dimitrios Halikias, "Race Gaps in SAT Scores Highlight Inequality and Hinder Upward Mobility," *The Brookings Institution*, February 1, 2017, https://www.brookings.edu/research/race-gaps-in-sat-scores-highlight-inequality-and-hinder-upward-mobility/; Ember Smith and Richard V. Reeves, "SAT Math Scores Mirror and Maintain Racial Inequity," *The Brookings Institution*, December 1, 2020, https://www.brookings.edu/blog/up-front/2020/12/01/sat-math-scores-mirror-and-maintain-racial-inequity/.

30. This is a special case of random selection. Typically, a researcher will draw a large number of random samples and see that the distribution of the characteristic of interest (in this example color of cards) centers on the share present in the population. It is still true that a single, random sample has no guarantee of replicating the demographics of the larger population.

31. Julie J. Park, Nida Denson, and Nicholas A. Bowman, "Does Socioeconomic Diversity Make a Difference? Examining the Effects of Racial and

Socioeconomic Diversity on the Campus Climate for Diversity," *American Educational Research Journal* 50, no. 3, (June 2013): 466–96; Sean F. Reardon, Rachel Baker, Matt Kasman, Daniel Klasik, and Joseph B. Townsend, "What Levels of Racial Diversity Can Be Achieved with Socioeconomic-Based Affirmative Action? Evidence from a Simulation Model," *Journal of Policy Analysis and Management* 37, no. 3 (2018): 630–57.

32. Caroline M. Hoxby and Christopher Avery, "The Missing 'One-Offs': The Hidden Supply of High-Achieving, Low Income Students" (NBER working paper no. w18586, 2012).

33. Donghun Cho, "The Role of High School Performance in Explaining Women's Rising College Enrollment," *Economics of Education Review* 26, no. 4 (2007): 450–62; Angela Lee Duckworth and Martin E. P. Seligman, "Self-Discipline Gives Girls the Edge: Gender in Self-Discipline, Grades, and Achievement Test Scores," *Journal of Educational Psychology* 98, no. 1 (2006): 198; Rose E. O'Dea, Malgorzata Lagisz, Michael D. Jennions, and Shinichi Nakagawa, "Gender Differences in Individual Variation in Academic Grades Fail to Fit Expected Patterns for STEM," *Nature Communications* 9, no. 1 (2018): 1–8.

34. Rob Bielby, Julie Renee Posselt, Ozan Jaquette, and Michael N. Bastedo, "Why Are Women Underrepresented in Elite Colleges and Universities? A Non-Linear Decomposition Analysis," *Research in Higher Education* 55, no. 8 (2014): 735–60.

35. Sandy Baum and Eban Goodstein, "Gender Imbalance in College Applications: Does It Lead to a Preference for Men in the Admissions Process?" *Economics of Education Review* 24, no. 6 (2005): 665–75.

CHAPTER 11

1. Samuel M. Kipp III, Derek V. Price, and Jill K. Wohlford, *Unequal Opportunity: Disparities in College Access Among the 50 States*, New Agenda Series, Vol. 4, no. 3 (Indianapolis, IN: Lumina Foundation for Education, 2002), https://eric.ed.gov/?id=ED459670.

2. Carolyn Hoxby and Sarah Turner, "Expanding College Opportunities for High-Achieving, Low-Income Students" (Working paper no. 12-014, Stanford Institute for Economic Policy Research, Stanford University, 2013).

3. Daniel Klasik, "The College Application Gauntlet: A Systematic Analysis of the Steps to Four-Year College Enrollment," *Research in Higher Education* 53, no. 5 (2012): 506–49.

4. Laura W. Perna, "Studying College Choice: A Proposed Conceptual Model," in *Higher Education: Handbook of Theory and Research*, vol. 21, ed. John C. Smart (New York: Springer, 2006), 99–157; Susan M. Dynarski, C. J. Libassi, Katherine Michelmore, and Stephanie Owen, "Closing the Gap: The Effect of Reducing Complexity and Uncertainty in College Pricing on the Choices of Low-Income Students," *The American Economic Review* 111, no. 6 (2021): 1721–56; Brian G. Knight and Nathan M. Schiff, "Reducing Frictions in College Admissions:

Evidence from the Common Application," *American Economic Journal: Economic Policy* (forthcoming).

5. Kasia Kovacs, "An Admissions Experiment Succeeds," *Inside Higher Ed*, November 23, 2016, https://www.insidehighered.com/news/2016/11/23/idaho-universities-see-enrollment-rise-after-killing-admissions-application.

6. Catherine Gewertz, "Good Common-Core Test Scores Get You Accepted to College in This State," *Education Week*, September 19, 2017, http://blogs.edweek.org/edweek/high_school_and_beyond/2017/09/south_dakota_guarantees_college_admission_for_good_smarter_balanced_scores.html.

7. "Governor Lamont Announces Legislation Focused on Increasing Postsecondary Enrollment and Success among Connecticut Students," Office of Governor Ned Lamont, February 4, 2021, https://portal.ct.gov/Office-of-the-Governor/News/Press-Releases/2021/02-2021/Governor-Lamont-Announces-Legislation-Focused-on-Increasing-Postsecondary-Enrollment; Michael T. Nietzel, "Minnesota Bill Authorizing Direct Admission to College Moves Forward," *Forbes*, April 27, 2021, https://www.forbes.com/sites/michaeltnietzel/2021/04/27/minnesota-bill-authorizing-direct-admission-to-college-moves-forward/?sh=7631db70279d.

8. David Laibson and John A. List, "Principles of (Behavioral) Economics," *The American Economic Review* 105, no. 5 (2015): 385–90.

9. Started in 1975, the Common App is a private non-profit organization comprised of 900 members that allows students to complete a single college application that can be submitted to multiple institutions. Student-reported data on the Common App system can be used to support DA among member institutions. CommonApp, "Your Future Starts Here," https://www.commonapp.org/.

10. For more information on DA in Idaho, see https://nextsteps.idaho.gov/resources/direct-admissions-initiative.

11. Carson Howell, "Direct Admissions at Work: The Idaho Experience" (presented at the Direct Admissions Conference at the Forum on the Future of Public Education, University of Illinois, December 6, 2019, https://forum.illinois.edu/2019-conference#moreinfo; Dana Kelly, "Expanding College Admissions to All Idaho Seniors" (presented at the American College Application Convening, American College Application Campaign & ACT Center for Equity in Learning, 2018), https://www.acenet.edu/news-room/Documents/Expanding percent20College percent20Admissions percent20to percent20All percent20Idaho percent20Seniors percent20- percent20Dana percent20Kelly.pdf.

12. Direct Enrollment: Key Principles & Promising Practices (Olympia, WA: Washington Student Achievement Council, 2021), https://wsac.wa.gov/sites/default/files/2021-03-11-0121-Direct percent20Enrollment percent20Brief.pdf.

13. Carson Howell, Andy Mehl, Jay Pennington, Jason Pontius, and Sara Kock, "Using SLDS Data to Support College Admissions" (presented at the

Institute of Education Sciences Statewide Longitudinal Data Systems Grant Program, December 14, 2017),https://boardofed.idaho.gov/wp-content/uploads/2019/01/Webinar_Using_Data_to_Support_College_Admissions.pdf.

14. Josh Logue, "You're In: A New Statewide Initiative Automatically Admits Graduating Seniors to College in Idaho," *Inside Higher Ed*, November 30, 2015, https://www.insidehighered.com/news/2015/11/30/idaho-direct-enrollment-program-automatically-admits-high-school-seniors-public.

15. Howell et al., "Using SLDS Data."

16. Carson Howell and Blake Youde, "Direct Admissions: An Initiative of the State of Idaho Board of Education" (presented to the Idaho School Counselor Association, 2015), www.idahoschoolcounselors.org/wwwroot/userfiles/files/direct_admissions.pptx.

17. The Apply Idaho common application can be viewed at: https://apply.next-steps.idaho.gov/. In prior years, students needed to complete a college application, pay an application fee (where applicable, though fee waivers were available for low-income students, and fees paid are re-applied as a credit toward students' first semester's bill), and submit an official final high school transcript; Howell and Youde, "Direct Admissions."

18. Kelly, "Expanding College Admissions to All Idaho Seniors"; "Direct Admissions," *Next Steps Idaho*, https://nextsteps.idaho.gov/resources/direct-admissions-initiative.

19. "Data Dashboard: Transition to Postsecondary," Office of the Idaho State Board of Education, 2019, https://boardofed.idaho.gov/data-research/data-dashboard/transition-to-postsecondary/.

20. More information on the South Dakota program is available at the SDMyLife website: https://sdmylife.com/prepping-for-college/proactive-admissions.

21. Statewide Longitudinal Data Systems (SLDS) Survey Analysis, National Center for Education Statists Publication Number 2020157 (Washington, DC: NCES, 2019), https://nces.ed.gov/pubsearch/pubsinfo.asp?pubid=2020157.

22. Lexi Anderson, "State Information Request: The Use of Common Applications by Public Institutions," Education Commission of the States, October 21, 2016, https://www.ecs.org/state-information-request-the-use-of-common-applications-by-public-institutions/.

23. Lindsay C. Page and Judith Scott-Clayton, "Improving College Access in the United States: Barriers and Policy Responses," *Economics of Education Review* 51 (2016): 4–22.

24. Andrea Venezia and Laura Jaeger, "Transitions from High School to College," *The Future of Children* 23, no. 1 (2013): 117–36; Florence A. Hamrick and Frances K Stage, "College Predisposition at High-Minority Enrollment, Low-Income Schools," *The Review of Higher Education* 27, no. 2 (2004): 151–68, https://doi.org/10.1353/rhe.2003.0058.

25. Kasia Kovacs, "An Admissions Experiment Succeeds," *Inside Higher Ed*, November 23, 2016, https://www.insidehighered.com/news/2016/11/23/idaho-universities-see-enrollment-rise-after-killing-admissions-application; Kelly, "Expanding College Admissions."

26. Howell et al., "Using SLDS Data."

27. "Data Dashboard: Transition to Postsecondary."

28. "Data Dashboard: Transition to Postsecondary."

29. Carson Howell, "Surprise! You are Accepted to College: An Analysis of Idaho's Direct Admissions Initiative" (Ph.D. dissertation, Boise State University, 2018), https://scholarworks.boisestate.edu/td/1478/

30. Howell, "Surprise!"

31. Howell, "Surprise!"

32. Howell, "Surprise!"

33. Howell, "Surprise!"

34. As quoted in Howell, "Surprise!"; Howell, "Direct Admissions at Work."

35. Taylor K. Odle and Jennifer A. Delaney, "You Are Admitted! Early Evidence on Enrollment from Idaho's Direct Admissions System," *Research in Higher Education* (forthcoming). Our other research and writing to-date on DA was presented at a 2019 conference hosted by the University of Illinois Urbana-Champaign's Forum on the Future of Public Education and through a policy brief released through a collaboration with ACCEPT and Hack the Gates (Direct Admission Conference 2019, from the Forum on the Future of Public Education, University of Illinois, https://forum.illinois.edu/2019-conference); Jennifer A. Delaney and Taylor K. Odle, *Reducing Red Tape through Simplification: How Idaho Radically Reimagined College Admissions* (Hack the Gates, 2020), https://hackthegates.org/wp-content/uploads/2020/08/DelaneyOdle_DirectAdmissions_HTGreport.pdf.

36. "Student Enrollment: How Many Students Enroll in Postsecondary Institutions Annually?" U.S. Department of Education, National Center for Education Statistics, Integrated Postsecondary Education Data System, https://nces.ed.gov/ipeds/TrendGenerator/app/answer/2/2.

37. Odle and Delaney, "You Are Admitted!"; Charlotte West, "Congratulations! You Got into College without Even Applying," *The Washington Post*, March 14, 2020, https://www.washingtonpost.com/local/education/congratulations-you-got-into-college-without-even-applying/2020/03/14/588dabec-63f0-11ea-845d-e35b0234b136_story.html.

38. Brian G. Knight and Nathan M. Schiff, "Reducing Frictions in College Admissions: Evidence from the Common Application," *American Economic Journal: Economic Policy* (forthcoming).

39. Hoxby and Turner, "Expanding College Opportunities."

40. Hoxby and Turner, "Expanding College Opportunities."

41. "Are You Ready to Apply for College?," Apply Idaho, Idaho State Board of Education, 2019, https://apply.nextsteps.idaho.gov/.

42. Mari Luna De La Rosa, "Is Opportunity Knocking?: Low-Income Students' Perceptions of College and Financial Aid," *American Behavioral Scientist* 49, no. 12 (2006): 1670–86, https://doi.org/10.1177/0002764206289139.

43. Donald E. Heller, "Early Commitment of Financial Aid Eligibility," *American Behavioral Scientist* 49, no. 12 (August 2006): 1719–38, https://doi.org/10.1177/0002764206289136; Chengfang Liu et al., "Early Commitment on Financial Aid and College Decision Making of Poor Students: Evidence from a Randomized Evaluation in Rural China," *Economics of Education Review* 30, no. 4 (2011): 627–40.

44. Jonathan Smith, Michael Hurwitz, and Jessica Howell, "Screening Mechanisms and Student Responses in the College Market," *Economics of Education Review* 44 (2015): 17–28.

45. Susan M. Dynarski, C. J. Libassi, Katherine Michelmore, and Stephanie Owen, "Closing the Gap: The Effect of Reducing Complexity and Uncertainty in College Pricing on the Choices of Low-Income Students," *The American Economic Review* 111, no. 6 (2021): 1721–56.

CHAPTER 12

1. Raj Chetty, John N. Friedman, Emmanuel Saez, Nicholas Turner, and Danny, Yagan, "Income Segregation and Intergenerational Mobility Across Colleges in the United States," *The Quarterly Journal of Economics* 135, no. 3 (2020): 1567–1633.

2. Eleanor W. Dillon and Jeffrey A. Smith, "Determinants of the Match Between Student Ability and College Quality," *Journal of Labor Economics* 35, no. 1 (2017): 45–66; Susan Dynarski, C. J. Libassi, Katherine Michelmore, and Stephanie Owen, "Closing the Gap: The Effect of Reducing Complexity and Uncertainty in College Pricing on the Choices of Low-Income Students," *American Economic Review* 111, no. 6 (2021): 1721–56; for information on Go Blue Guarantee see Zack Friedman, "Go Blue: U-Michigan Offers Free College Tuition," *Forbes Magazine*, June 19, 2017, https://www.forbes.com/sites/zackfriedman/2017/06/19/student-loans-michigan/?sh=3911b29f3d4a; Caroline M. Hoxby and Christopher Avery, "The Missing 'One-Offs': The Hidden Supply of High-Achieving, Low Income Students" (NBER Working Paper No. w18586, December 2012); the expansion of college promise programs is well documented in Laura W. Perna and Edward J. Smith, eds., *Improving Research-Based Knowledge of College Promise Programs* (American Educational Research Association, 2020); for information on Illinois Commitment see Daniel Tucker, "'Free Tuition' is Now a Reality for Many University of Illinois Students," NPR, July 10, 2019, https://www.npr.org/local/309/2019/07/10/739955375/free-tuition-is-now-a-reality-for-many-university-of-illinois-students.

3. Christopher Avery, Jessica S. Howell, and Lindsay Page, A Review of the Role of College Counseling, Coaching, and Mentoring on Students' Postsecondary Outcomes (New York: College Board, 2014); David T. Conley, "The Challenge of College Readiness," Educational Leadership 64, no. 7 (2007): 14; Daniel Klasik, "The College Application Gauntlet: A Systematic Analysis of the Steps to Four-Year College Enrollment," Research in Higher Education 53, no. 5 (2012): 506–49.

4. Jonathan Smith, Michael Hurwitz, and Jessica Howell, "Screening Mechanisms and Student Responses in the College Market," Economics of Education Review 44 (2014): 17–28.

5. Susan M. Dynarski and Judith E. Scott-Clayton, "Complexity and Targeting in Federal Student Aid: A Quantitative Analysis," Tax Policy and the Economy 22, no. 1 (2008): 109–50. Dynarski et al., "Closing the Gap," 1721; Doo Hwan Kim and Barbara Schneider, "Social Capital in Action: Alignment of Parental Support in Adolescents' Transition to Postsecondary Education," Social Forces 84, no. 2 (2005): 1181–1206; Barbara Schneider and David Stevenson, The Ambitious Generation: America's Teenagers, Motivated but Directionless (New Haven: Yale University Press, 1999).

6. Neil Vigdor and Johnny Diaz, "More Colleges are Waving SAT and ACT Requirements," New York Times, May 21, 2020, https://www.nytimes.com/article/sat-act-test-optional-colleges-coronavirus.html.

7. Elizabeth Aries and Maynard Seider, "The Interactive Relationship Between Class Identity and the College Experience: The Case of Lower Income Students," Qualitative Sociology 28, no. 4 (2005): 419–43; Marsha Riley Arzy, Timothy Gray Davies, and Clifford P. Harbour, "Low Income Students: Their Lived University Campus Experiences Pursuing Baccalaureate Degrees with Private Foundation Scholarship Assistance," College Student Journal 40, no. 4 (2006): 750–66; Anthony Abraham Jack, The Privileged Poor: How Elite Colleges Are Failing Disadvantaged Students (Cambridge, Harvard University Press, 2019); Deborah M. Warnock and Allison L. Hurst, "'The Poor Kids' Table': Organizing Around an Invisible and Stigmatized Identity in Flux," Journal of Diversity in Higher Education 9, no. 3 (2016): 261.

8. Jack, The Privileged Poor; Kimberly Torres, "'Culture Shock': Black Students Account for Their Distinctiveness at an Elite College," Ethnic and Racial Studies 32, no. 5 (2009): 883–905.

9. Robert Kelchen, "An Analysis of Student Fees: The Roles of States and Institutions," The Review of Higher Education 39, no. 4 (2016): 597–619; Monica L. Rose, "Proposal 2 and the Ban on Affirmative Action: An Uncertain Future for the University of Michigan in Its Quest for Diversity," Public Interest Law Journal 17 (2007): 309–37; Benjamin Wermund, "In Trump Country, a University Confronts its Skeptics," Politico, November 9, 2017, https://www.politico.com/story/2017/11/09/university-of- michigan-admissions-low-income-244420.

10. Chetty et al., "Income Segregation and Intergenerational Mobility"; Alex Harring and Sammy Sussman, "Being Poor on Rich UM Campus Still

a Struggle as School Broadens Reach," *Bridge Michigan*, August 1, 2020, https://www.bridgemi.com/talent-education/being-poor-rich-u-m-campus-still-struggle-school-broadens-reach.

11. "HAIL" also refers to the University of Michigan's fight song, "The Victors," which mentions the word several times. The word is commonly shared among members of the university community and is found on merchandise, informal, and formal communications. See Dynarski et al., "Closing the Gap" for a thorough description of the intervention. Dynarski developed the intervention in collaboration with administrators and staff in the University of Michigan Office of Enrollment Management.

12. Dynarski et al., "Closing the Gap," 1732.

13. Students in the treatment group were already eligible for institutional aid based on their income status. The HAIL intervention reframed the aid as a scholarship.

14. The likelihood of applying to the University of Michigan was 26 percent among controls and 68 percent among students in the treatment group. The percentage of students enrolling at a highly selective institution, almost exclusively the University of Michigan, was 13 percent for controls and 28 percent for students offered the treatment. For more information on these results and extensive details about the structure of the intervention see Dynarski et al., "Closing the Gap."

15. Anthony Abraham Jack, "I Was a Low-Income College Student. Classes Weren't the Hard Part," *New York Times*, September 10, 2019, https://www.nytimes.com/interactive/2019/09/10/magazine/college-inequality.html.

16. Barry C. Burden, David T. Cannon, Kenneth R. Mayer, and Donald P. Moynihan, "The Effect of Administrative Burden on Bureaucratic Perception of Policies: Evidence from Election Administration," *Public Administration Review* 72, no. 5 (2012): 741.

17. Carolyn J. Heinrich, "Presidential Address: 'A Thousand Petty Fortresses': Administrative Burden in US Immigration Policies and its Consequences," *Journal of Policy Analysis and Management* 37, no. 2 (2018): 211–39.

18. Dominique J. Baker, "How Much is Too Much?: Administrative Burden and Texas State Policy," *Mission Foods Texas-Mexico Center Research* (2020): 15.

19. Victor Ray, Pamela Herd, and Donald P. Moynihan, "Racialized Burdens: Applying Racialized Organization Theory to the Administrative State," *Journal of Public Administration Research and Theory* (2022): 1–14.

20. Baker, "How Much is Too Much?"; Elizabeth Bell and Kylie Smith, "Perspectives from the Front-line: Street-level Bureaucrats, Administrative Burden and Access to Oklahoma's Promise," *EasyChair Pre-Print* 1093 (2019); Kelly Rosinger, Katharine Meyer, and Jialing Wang, "Leveraging Insights from Behavioral Science and Administrative Burden in Free College Program Design: A Typology," *Journal of Behavioral Public Administration* 4, no. 2 (2021): 1–26.

21. Donald P. Moynihan, Pamela Herd, and Hope Harvey, "Administrative Burden: Learning, Psychological, and Compliance Costs in Citizen-State Interactions," *Journal of Public Administration Research and Theory* 25, no. 1 (2015): 43–69.

22. Moynihan et al., "Administrative Burden."

23. Dynarski and Scott-Clayton, " Complexity and Targeting."

24. Sarah R. Cohodes and Joshua S. Goodman, "Merit Aid, College Quality, and College Completion: Massachusetts' Adams Scholarship as an In-kind Subsidy," *American Economic Journal: Applied Economics* 6, no. 4 (2014): 251–85; Hoxby and Avery, "The Missing 'One-Offs.'"

25. Bell and Smith, "Perspectives from the Front-Line;" Eric P. Bettinger, Bridget Terry Long, Philip Oreopoulus, and Lisa Sanbonmatsu, "The Role of Application Assistance and Information in College Decisions: Results from the H&R Block FAFSA Experiment," *The Quarterly Journal of Economics* 127, no. 3 (2012): 1205–42; Amy Finkelstein and Matthew J. Notowidigdo, "Take-up and Targeting: Experimental Evidence from SNAP," *The Quarterly Journal of Economics* 134, no. 3 (2019): 1505–56; Caroline Hoxby and Sarah Turner, "Expanding College Opportunities for High-achieving, Low Income Students," *Stanford Institute for Economic Policy Research Discussion Paper* 12 (2013): 14.

26. Dynarski and Scott-Clayton, "Complexity and Targeting."

27. Casey George-Jackson and Melanie Jones Gast, "Addressing Information Gaps: Disparities in Financial Awareness and Preparedness on the Road to College," *Journal of Student Financial Aid* 44, no. 3 (2015): 3; Lindsay C. Page and Judith Scott-Clayton, "Improving College Access in the United States: Barriers and Policy Responses," *Economics of Education Review* 51 (2016): 4–22.

28. Moynihan et al., "Administrative Burden."

29. Aisha N. Lowe, "Identity Safety and Its Importance for Academic Success," in *Handbook on Promoting Social Justice in Education*, ed. Rosemary Papa (New York: Springer, 2020): 1849–81; Samuel D. Museus, Varaxy Yi, and Natasha Saelua, "How Culturally Engaging Campus Environments Influence Sense of Belonging in College: An Examination of Differences Between White Students and Students of Color," *Journal of Diversity in Higher Education* 11, no. 4 (2018): 467; Julie R. Posselt and Sarah Ketchen Lipson, "Competition, Anxiety, and Depression in the College Classroom: Variations by Student Identity and Field of Study," *Journal of College Student Development* 57, no. 8 (2016): 973–89.

30. Moynihan et al., "Administrative Burden," 50.

31. Jack, *The Privileged Poor*, 189; Rosinger et al., "Leveraging Insights."

32. For information on the rapid expansion of promise programs see Laura W. Perna, Elaine W. Leigh, and Stephanie Carroll, ""Free College': A New and Improved State Approach to Increasing Educational Attainment?" *American Behavioral Scientist* 61, no. 14 (2017): 1740–56.

33. Rosinger et al., "Leveraging Insights."

34. Rosinger et al., "Leveraging Insights," 5.

35. Bell and Smith, "Perspectives from the Front-Line."

36. Sharan B. Merriam and Elizabeth J. Tisdell, *Qualitative Research: A Guide to Design and Implementation* (New Jersey: John Wiley & Sons, 2015).

37. David L. Morgan, *Focus Groups as Qualitative Research*, vol. 16 (Thousand Oaks: Sage publications, 1996).

38. Kimberly Griffin et al., "'Respect Me for My Science': A Bourdieuian Analysis of Women Scientists' Interactions with Faculty and Socialization into Science," *Journal of Women and Minorities in Science and Engineering* 21, no. 2 (2015): 159–79.

39. John W. Creswell and Cheryl N. Poth, *Qualitative Inquiry and Research Design: Choosing Among Five Approaches* (Thousand Oaks: Sage Publications, 2016); Matthew B. A. Miles, Michael Huberman, and Johnny Saldana, *Qualitative Data Analysis: A Methods Sourcebook* (Thousand Oaks: Sage Publications, 2014).

40. Moynihan et al., "Administrative Burden."

41. Yvonna S. Lincoln, "Emerging Criteria for Quality in Qualitative and Interpretive Research," *Qualitative Inquiry* 1, no. 3 (1995): 275–89; H. Richard Milner IV, "Race, Culture, and Researcher Positionality: Working Through Dangers Seen, Unseen, and Unforeseen," *Educational Researcher* 36, no. 7 (2007): 388–400.

42. "Being Not Rich at U-M," https://docs.google.com/document/d/1Ou-Ael-CrAg6soUJVbiviKAGBGF276w-UBlw-eMigwOA/edit. For more information on the diffusion of "Being Not Rich" guides see Emma Kerr, "Guides to 'Not Being Rich' Are Springing Up at Elite Colleges. Should Administrators Adopt Them?" *The Chronicle of Higher Education*, April 26, 2018, https://www.chronicle.com/article/guides-to-being-not-rich-are-springing-up-at-elite-colleges-should-administrators-adopt-them/.

43. Rosinger et al., "Leveraging Insights."

44. Adrianna Kezar, *Creating a Diverse Student Success Infrastructure: The Key to Catalyzing Cultural Change for Today's Student* (Los Angeles: Pulias Center for Higher Education, University of Southern California, 2019).

45. Daryl G. Smith et al., *Diversity Works: The Emerging Picture of How Students Benefit* (Washington, D.C.: Association of American Colleges and Universities, 1997).

46. Tia Brown McNair, Susan Albertine, Michelle Asha Cooper, Nicole McDonald, and Thomas Major Jr., *Becoming a Student-Ready College: A New Culture of Leadership for Student Success* (San Francisco: Jossey-Bass, 2016).

CHAPTER 13

1. Throughout the chapter, we use the terms *scholar-practitioner* and *practitioner* interchangeably. We recognize that practitioners are engaged in practices of inquiry through their leadership and work. As such, we ask that readers also acknowledge practitioners' roles in inquiry and organizational leadership.

2. This research was made possible (in part) by a grant from the Spencer Foundation (#201900049). The views expressed are those of the authors and do not necessarily reflect the views of the Spencer Foundation.

3. Adrianna Kezar and Jaime Lester, *Enhancing Campus Capacity for Leadership: An Examination of Grassroots Leaders in Higher Education* (Stanford, CA: Stanford University Press, 2011).

4. Na'ilah S. Nasir, "President's Blog: What We Heard During Our Field Engagement," *Spencer Foundation*, November 30, 2018, https://www.spencer.org/news/a-message-from-our-president-what-we-heard-during-our-field-engagement.

5. The transcript and dialogic format of this chapter was inspired by David Kekaulike Sing, Alapa Hunter, and Manu Aluli Meyer's article, "Native Hawaiian Education: Talking Story with Three Hawaiian Educators," *Journal of American Indian Education* 39, no. 1 (1999): 4–13.

6. We acknowledge that many research faculty are involved in admissions activities for their respective graduate programs. However, the practices and norms in graduate admissions are different from undergraduate admissions. See Julie Posselt, *Inside Graduate Admissions: Merit, Diversity, and Faculty Gatekeeping* (Cambridge, MA: Harvard University Press, 2016).

7. Patricia McDonough, *Effective Counseling in Schools Increases College Access* (Arlington, VA: NACAC, 2006), https://www.careerladdersproject.org/wp-content/uploads/2013/02/Effective-Counseling.pdf.

8. Some examples: Mitchell Stevens, *Creating a Class: College Admissions and the Education of Elites* (Cambridge, MA: Harvard University Press, 2007); Posselt, *Inside Graduate Admissions*.

9. Marie Bigham, OiYan A. Poon, and Douglas H. Lee, "Hack the Gates! How We Radically Reimagine College Admissions," *Spark: Elevating Scholarship on Social Issues*, University of Michigan National Center for Institutional Diversity, https://medium.com/national-center-for-institutional-diversity/hack-the-gates-how-we-radically-reimagine-college-admissions-6ec1ab128cdb.

10. Cynthia E. Coburn, William R. Penuel, and Caitlin C. Farrell, "Fostering Educational Improvement with Research-Practice Partnerships," *Phi Delta Kappan* 102, no. 7 (April 2021): 14–19.

11. National Network of Education Research-Practice Partnerships, a program of the Kinder Institute for Urban Research at Rice University, https://nnerpp.rice.edu/.

12. Coburn, Penuel, and Farrell, "Fostering Educational Improvement"; Ann M. Ishimaru and Megan Bang, "Designing with Families for Just Futures," *Journal of Family Diversity in Education* 4, no. 2 (2021/2022): 130–40; Nicole Mirra, Antero Garcia, and Ernest Morrell, *Doing Youth Participatory Action Research: Transforming Inquiry with Researchers, Educators, and Students* (New York, NY: Routledge, 2016).

13. Coburn, Penuel, and Farrell, "Fostering Educational Improvement," 19.

14. National Network of Education Research-Practice Partnerships. https://nnerpp.rice.edu/

15. Cynthia E. Coburn and William R. Penuel, "Research-Practice Partnerships: Outcomes, Dynamics, and Open Questions," *Educational Researcher* 45, no. 1 (2016): 48–54.

16. Coburn, Penuel, and Farrell, "Fostering Educational Improvement."

ACKNOWLEDGMENTS

WE FIRST DISCUSSED the idea for this book during a symposium at the 2019 ASHE conference in Portland, Oregon, entitled "Problematizing and Reimagining College Access, Selective Admissions, and Enrollment Management Structures." Even though it was on the last day of the conference, which is typically the worst day for attendance, we found ourselves in a packed room with a "who's who" of admissions research. The conversation was exhilarating and really highlighted the desire for dialogues about admissions research. We thank all those packed into that room in 2019!

With both the pandemic and racial reckonings in 2020, we continued our conversations imagining new possibilities for bringing research, practice, and policy together to transform college access and admissions to be more equitable. So, we approached Jayne Fargnoli at Harvard Education Press, who was immediately enthusiastic about this book project.

Thank you so much to Jayne, Anne Noonan, and Brittany Mytnik, and the whole team at Harvard Education Press for your interest, encouragement, support, and expert guidance in making this book happen.

Of course, it goes without saying that this book would not have been possible without the brilliant chapters by the intergenerational group of contributors—both scholars and scholar-practitioners—featured in this book. We are thankful to be in community with each of you, and we are excited to see where this area of scholarship and leadership will continue taking the field and higher education.

Finally, some personal thanks:

OiYan would like to thank her partner for life—Todd—for always supporting her and keeping her grounded, and Té Té for being her inspiration for everything.

Mike would like to thank his husband—Corey—for his everlasting patience, and all of researchers and admissions professionals who share their thoughts, ideas, and passion for this work.

ABOUT THE EDITORS

OIYAN A. POON (she/her/hers) is currently a program officer at the Spencer Foundation, an associate professor affiliate at Colorado State University, and visiting faculty member at the University of Maryland, College Park. In her research, she focuses on the racial politics of college access and affirmative action, Asian Americans, and college admissions practices. She has received grants from the Gates Foundation, Joyce Foundation, and Spencer Foundation to support her research. She has also served as an undergraduate admissions reader at University of California–Davis and a scholarship application reviewer for the Gates Millennium Scholars Program. Dr. Poon is a lead co-author of *amicus* briefs defending diversity and race-conscious admissions, submitted to federal courts including the US Supreme Court in the SFFA v. *Harvard* case. She has also worked closely in partnership with practitioner-leaders in college admissions. In 2019–20, with practitioner-leaders from ACCEPT she co-led the Hack the Gates project, which convened researchers and practitioners in college admissions to begin reimagining college admissions systems. Journalists from national media outlets, such *The New York Times, The Washington Post, The Atlantic, The Chronicle of Higher Education,* and

The New Yorker, have reported on her work. She has also appeared on shows and podcasts such as MSNBC's *The Reid Out* and National Public Radio's *Code Switch*, *All Things Considered*, and *Marketplace*.

MICHAEL N. BASTEDO is a professor in the Center for the Study of Higher and Postsecondary Education at the University of Michigan, where he also serves as Associate Dean for Research and Graduate Affairs in the School of Education. His scholarly interests are in higher education decision-making, particularly college admissions, stratification, enrollment management, rankings, and governance. In 2013, he received the Early Career Award from the American Educational Research Association (AERA), and in 2021 he was named an AERA Fellow. His recent books are *American Higher Education in the 21ˢᵗ Century* and *The Organization of Higher Education: Managing Colleges for a New Era* (both Johns Hopkins University Press). His most recent research, funded by The National Science Foundation, has been reported by journalists at National Public Radio, *The New York Times*, *The New Yorker*, *The Washington Post*, *Slate*, and *The Chronicle of Higher Education*, among others.

ABOUT THE CONTRIBUTORS

AMANDA ADDISON is a doctoral student in the Department of Leadership, Policy, & Organizations at Vanderbilt University's Peabody College. Her research interests include college access, financial aid, and the experiences of minoritized students in higher education. Prior to Peabody, Addison spent six years working as a high school mathematics teacher and later served as an associate director for undergraduate admissions. She holds a bachelor's in African studies and a master's in urban education from the University of Pennsylvania.

DOMINIQUE J. BAKER is an associate professor of education policy at Southern Methodist University. Her research focuses on the way that education policy affects and shapes the access and success of minoritized students in higher education. Baker has published research in the *American Educational Research Journal*, *Educational Evaluation and Policy Analysis*, and *The Journal of Higher Education*, among others. Her expertise has been highlighted by several outlets, including *The New York Times*, *The Washington Post*, NPR, *The Chronicle of Higher Education*, and *Inside Higher Ed*. She served as an assistant dean of admissions prior to earning her PhD from Vanderbilt University.

BHAVANI BINDIGANAVILE earned her B.A. degrees in Anthropology and Ethnic Studies from the University of California, Berkeley. She holds an M.A. in Higher Education from the University of Michigan, Ann Arbor. She is passionate about education equity and college access. She currently works as a College Access Program Manager in San Jose.

NIKKI KĀHEALANI CHUN (she/her/hers/ʻo ia) is a doctoral student in the Higher Education Leadership program at Colorado State University and the inaugural Vice Provost for Enrollment Management at the University of Hawaiʻi at Mānoa. She identifies as a Native Hawaiian and Chinese, cisgender, able-bodied, hetero woman of size who was the first in her family to attend college. Her research interests are shaped by her identities and include Native Hawaiians in higher education, Kanaka ʻŌiwi Crit, as well as diversity and inclusion in college admissions policies.

EDDIE COMEAUX is a professor at the University of California, Riverside. His research focuses on racial equity and policy issues in higher education. Comeaux has authored numerous peer-reviewed journal articles, book chapters, and other academic publications and reports. He has also published several books, including his most recent book: *High Achieving African American Students and the College Choice Process: Applying Critical Race Theory* (Routledge, 2020). Formerly, Comeaux served as the chair of the Board of Admissions and Relations with Schools (BOARS), cochair of the UC Feasibility Study Work Group, and cochair of the UC Standardized Testing Task Force.

JENNIFER A. DELANEY is an associate professor of higher education at the University of Illinois Urbana-Champaign where she is also the director of the Forum on the Future of Public Education and director of the higher education program. In addition, she is a member of the Illinois Board of Higher Education. Dr. Delaney's research focuses on public policy and higher education. Previously, she worked for the Advisory Committee on Student Financial Assistance, the National Center for Public Policy and Higher Education, consulted with the Commission on the Future of Higher Education, and was an assistant professor at the University of Wisconsin-Madison. Dr. Delaney earned a PhD in higher education administration from Stanford University, an EdM from Harvard University, and a BA from the University of Michigan.

STEVE DESIR is a doctoral candidate in the educational leadership program at the USC Rossier School of Education. His research interests include racial equity in college admissions, organizational change, and the use of theory-based psychological interventions to facilitate the advancement of racial equity in higher education. Desir's professional experiences span K–12 and higher education. He has experience leading college success and outreach efforts for non profit organizations and school districts in Boston and Los Angeles and also as a student affairs administrator at various colleges and universities.

JOANNE SONG ENGLER (she/her/hers) is a doctoral student in the Higher Education Leadership program at Colorado State University and currently serves as the Associate Dean of Students Affairs/Director of Residential Life for Thurgood Marshall College at UC San Diego. A 1.5 generation Korean American, her research interests include Asian American identity development, Asian Americans in education, and the impact of standardized testing in college access.

SHAWN FELTON is Executive Director of Undergraduate Admissions at Cornell University. He oversees undergraduate admissions and serves as the university's Deputy Chief Admissions and Enrollment Officer. He is responsible for admissions policy and practice, as well as broader enrollment management work with the university's undergraduate colleges and schools. Shawn has been with Cornell for more than eighteen years; before Cornell, Shawn served as Assistant Dean of Admissions at the University of Virginia (UVA), his alma mater. Shawn has a BA and an MA in music, specializing in ethnomusicology and music composition.

FRANK FERNANDEZ is assistant professor of higher education administration and policy and affiliate faculty with the Center for Latin American Studies at University of Florida. He writes about educational policy and equity issues. His work can be found in journals such as *American Educational Research Journal, Educational Researcher, Research in Higher Education, Review of Higher Education, Higher Education,* and *Journal of College Student Development.* He has also written about legal issues for *The Oxford Handbook of U.S. Higher Education Law, Contemporary Issues in Higher Education Law,* and *Penn State Law Review.* He coauthored *The Contested Campus: Aligning Professional Values, Social Justice, and Free Speech.* His research has been cited by *Business Insider* and *Inside Higher Ed.* He earned a PhD from The Pennsylvania State University.

LILIANA M. GARCES is associate professor at the University of Texas at Austin and affiliate faculty at the University of Texas School of Law and Center for Mexican American Studies. Her scholarship centers on the intersection of law and educational policy on access, diversity, and equity in higher education. Combining her expertise in law and education, Dr. Garces has represented the education community in the filing of legal briefs in US Supreme Court cases that have played consequential roles in interpreting law around race-conscious policies in education, including an *amicus curiae* brief filed in *Fisher v. University of Texas* by 823 social scientists.

KRISTEN M. GLASENER (she/her) is the National Director of Organizational Learning and Strategy at the Kessler Scholars Collaborative, a multi-institutional scholarship and holistic support program for first-generation students. Dr. Glasener holds a PhD in higher education from the University of Michigan. Her research focusing on selective colleges admissions and enrollment management has been published in *Research in Higher Education, Journal of Higher Education,* and *Journal of Diversity in Higher Education,* among others. Prior to joining the Kessler Scholars Collaborative, Dr. Glasener worked in selective college admissions and as a college counselor to support underserved students in navigating the college-going process.

NATHAN F. HARRIS (he/his) is an assistant professor of higher education at the Warner Graduate School of Education & Human Development at the University of Rochester. His scholarship explores ethical misconduct in higher education, the leadership of academic deans, and senior leadership teams in higher education. His research has been featured in numerous outlets, including *New Directions for Higher Education*, *Planning for Higher Education*, and *The Chronicle of Higher Education*. Prior to earning his doctorate at the Center for the Study of Higher and Postsecondary Education at the University of Michigan, Dr. Harris worked at The Corporate Executive Board and the Harvard Graduate School of Education.

JESSICA M. HURTADO (she/her/ella) is a PhD student in the Higher Education Leadership Program at Colorado State University. Her scholarly research interests center on the professional development of admissions officers to create career pathways and social mobility to transform medical education. Jessica is the inaugural director of admissions at the Spencer Fox Eccles School of Medicine at the University of Utah. Before that, she served as the director of admissions at New Mexico Highlands University. She earned a BA and an MPA from the University of New Mexico, where she worked in admissions at the UNM School of Medicine Combined BA/MD Degree Program.

KATHERINE LEBIODA (she/her) is a doctoral candidate at the University of Michigan's Center for the Study of Higher and Postsecondary Education, where her research interests include examining how postsecondary policies and practices structure and perpetuate inequity, particularly for Black and brown students. She previously worked as a research and policy analyst for the American Association of State Colleges and Universities and also has experience working in both graduate and undergraduate admissions at The George Washington University and the University of Michigan, respectively.

DOUGLAS H. LEE (he/him) is a doctoral student in the Higher Education Leadership program at Colorado State University. He is currently a research fellow at the Campaign for College Opportunity. He has previously worked as the Associate Director for Student Involvement and Leadership at the University of Utah Asia Campus in Korea and the assistant director of the Asian American Center at Northeastern University.

SUNNY NAKAE (she/her) serves as Senior Associate Dean for Equity, Inclusion, Diversity, and Partnership at the California University of Science and Medicine where she is also an associate professor of medical education. Her scholarship and practice focuses on access, diversity, and equity in medical education and health care. Dr. Nakae has held medical education leadership roles in diversity, admissions, and student affairs at University of Utah, Northwestern, Loyola University Chicago, and University of California Riverside. She has served on the Advancing Holistic Review Initiative at the Association of American Medical Colleges since 2014, and as lead faculty on the Accreditation Council for Graduate Medical Education's Equity Matters program since 2021. She is the author of *Premed Prep: Advice from a Medical School Admissions Dean* from Rutgers Press.

TAYLOR K. ODLE is an assistant professor in educational policy studies at the University of Wisconsin-Madison. Dr. Odle's work studies policies aimed at reducing inequalities in students' transitions from high school to college, including through evaluations of advising interventions, admissions practices, and financial aid programs. These works have been published in *Educational Evaluation and Policy Analysis, The Journal of Higher Education, Research in Higher Education*, and other outlets and featured in *The Washington Post, Inside Higher Ed*, and *The Chronicle of Higher Education*.

JULIE J. PARK is associate professor of education at the University of Maryland, College Park. Her research addresses how race, religion, and social class affect diversity and equity in higher education. Her book *Race* on *Campus: Debunking Myths with Data* (Harvard Education Press) uses social science data to challenge assumptions around how race works in college admissions and campus life. She is also the author of *When Diversity Drops: Race, Religion, and Affirmative Action in Higher Education* (Rutgers University Press). She served as a consulting expert for President and Fellows of Harvard College (Harvard Corporation) ("Harvard") in connection with the matter of *Students for Fair Admissions, Inc. v. Harvard*, Civ. Act. No. 1:14-14176.

JULIE R. POSSELT is associate dean of the Graduate School and associate professor of higher education at the University of Southern California. Her scholarship uses research-practice partnerships to examine institutionalized inequities in higher education and advance organizational change toward racial equity and inclusion. Posselt is author of *Inside Graduate Admissions: Merit, Diversity, and Faculty Gatekeeping* (Harvard University Press, 2016) and *Equity in Science: Representation, Culture, and the Dynamics of Change in Graduate Education* (Stanford University Press, 2020). She received a PhD from the University of Michigan-Ann Arbor, and held a National Academy of Education/Spencer Foundation postdoctoral fellowship.

ALI RAZA (he/him) is a PhD student in the Higher Education Leadership program and the Assistant Director of Involvement at Colorado State University. His research interests include Desi South Asians in higher education, college access, civic engagement, and organizational leadership and culture. Ali earned his MS in higher education from Florida State University and a BA from the University of Texas at Austin.

AWILDA RODRIGUEZ is an associate professor in the Center for the Study of Higher and Postsecondary Education at the University of Michigan. Her research focuses on the representation of Black, Latino, low-income, and first-generation students in postsecondary education at the intersection of higher education policy, college access, and choice. Rodriguez's work has been published in *Research in Higher Education, The*

Review of Higher Education, The Journal of Higher Education, Diverse Issues in Higher Education, and *The Chronicle of Higher Education.*

JOSHUA SKILES (he/him) is a doctoral student at the University of Michigan's Center for the Study of Higher and Postsecondary Education. His research interests center the role of place and geography in creating inequitable access to postsecondary education, and how policies and institutional practices can perpetuate or disrupt those processes. He earned his undergraduate and graduate degree from the University of Virginia, where he then worked in administration and in student and career advising.

KELLY E. SLAY is an assistant professor of higher education and public policy at Vanderbilt University. Drawing from professional experiences working on test-optional admissions policies and college recruitment programs, Dr. Slay's work primarily focuses on two areas: policies and structures that shape college choice and completion for students from minoritized backgrounds, particularly Black students; and the equity implications of enrollment management practices in post–affirmative action contexts. Her scholarship is published in the *Review of Higher Education, Teachers College Record,* and *Educational Policy,* among other outlets. She earned a PhD in higher education from the University of Michigan.

ROBERT STEWART is an assistant professor of criminology and criminal justice at the University of Maryland, and in 2022 he was named Emerson Collective Democracy Fellow. His research is focused on two fundamental questions: how are lives and communities shaped by the enduring effects of criminal legal system involvement; and how does higher education policy and practice marginalize or exclude but also open pathways for mobility and social membership for criminal legal system–impacted students. His work has been published in various academic journals, including *Criminology, Social Service Review, Federal Sentencing Reporter,* and the *Minnesota Law Review,* and findings from his research have been featured in *The Chronicle of Higher Education, Inside Higher Ed, The Marshall Project* and *The Weeds Podcast.*

INDEX